STANDARD GUIDE TO
SMALL-SIZE
U.S. PAPER MONEY
1928 TO DATE

Second Edition

Dean Oakes • John Schwartz

D1212379

Published by

krause
publications

700 E. State Street • Iola, WI 54990-0001
Telephone: 715/445-2214

Library of Congress Catalog Number: 93-80100
ISBN: 0-87341-494-2
Printed in the United States of America

Contents

CONTRIBUTORS

Raymond W. Morrow, James V. Doiron, Martin E. Vink,
Douglas Campbell, Bruce R. Holecek, Leon H. Bookman,
Donald W. Atkin, Greg Bannon, Daryl Crotts, Frank Trask,
C. Keith Edison, Milton Stewart, Baxter Worth Paschal III,
Harlan Berk, David Rollick, Gene Hessler, Michael Miuccio,
Ted Dumetz, Jr., Frank Bennett, Robert F. Giamboi,
Jerry Oliver, R. E. Wallace, H. M. Wallace, R. Logan Talks,
Scott McClure, Chuck Hayes, Joe Sande, Andrew Woodruf,
R. H. Klein, David S. Schlingman, R. C. Beach,
George T. McDuffie, Norman Dishman, Mike Crabb,
Lawrence Cookson, Lawrence O'Neal, Patrick D. Barnes,
Dennis L. Huff, Wil Arnold, Donald Gilletti, Jr.,
Eugene R. Seger, Tom Denly.

INTRODUCTION

The first reduced size notes appeared on Jan. 10, 1929. Their origin is traced to Secretary of the Treasury MacVeagh, who served between 1909 and 1913 under President Taft. He appointed a committee that reported favorably on the advantages and savings from adoption of smaller size notes, identical in size to the Philippine currency which had proven highly successful. World War I and the fact that MacVeagh left office one week after accepting the committee recommendations apparently prevented adoption of the idea.

On August 20, 1925, Secretary of the Treasury Andrew W. Mellon appointed a committee to study the whole question of "currency design, printing operations, issuance, and related interests associated with replacing the large size currency with smaller notes." In May of 1927, Secretary Mellon accepted the recommendations of his committee and directed the Bureau of Engraving and Printing to implement the plan.

CLASSES OF SMALL SIZE ISSUES

UNITED STATES NOTES, also called Legal Tender notes, are the longest lived of U.S. currency. First authorized in the Act of Congress, May 3, 1878. The May 3, 1878, act required that an outstanding amount of $346,681,016 be maintained. Small LT notes have been issued in $1, $2, $5 and $100. Printed but not issued were the $10 and $20 denominations.

Only one issue of the small size LT $1 was printed, the Series of 1928. On Aug. 10, 1966, the Treasury announced no more $2 notes would be printed and later discontinued the printing of $5 United States notes. The $100 U.S. note was printed in Series of 1966 and 1966A with star notes printed for only the 1966 series. All small size U.S. notes have red seals.

SILVER CERTIFICATES were authorized by Acts of Congress on Feb. 28, 1878, and Aug. 4, 1886. The blue seal distinguishes this class of currency printed in denominations of $1, $5 and $10. The silver law of 1963, which was designed to free the Treasury stockpile of silver bullion (security backing up Silver Certificates) paved the way for obsolescence of this class of currency. The Treasury stopped the redemption of Silver Certificates in silver dollars in 1964 and discontinued bullion redemption on June 24, 1968, based on $1.29 per ounce.

GOLD CERTIFICATES first authorized by the Currency Act of Mar. 3, 1863, have beautiful yellow seals. Gold Certificates were issued in denominations of $10, $20, $50, $100, $500, $1,000, $5,000 and $10,000 for general circulation and in the $100,000 for inter-bank use. The $100,000 denomination with portrait of Woodrow Wilson was Series of 1934.

All the regularly issued Gold Certificates were Series of 1928. Gold Certificates were printed for Series of 1928A and Series of 1934 but were never released and have since been destroyed. On Dec. 28, 1933, the Secretary of the Treasury issued an order forbidding the holding of Gold Certificates, and unlike gold coin, made no provision for collectors to hold them. Banks were ordered to turn in all stocks of Gold Certificates. On April 24, 1964, Secretary Dillon removed restrictions against the holding of Gold Certificates.

FEDERAL RESERVE BANK NOTES, first authorized under Act of Dec. 23, 1913, bore an obligation by the issuing bank rather than the United States. The notes were secured by U.S. Bonds deposited by the issuing bank with the Treasurer of the United States.

All small size Federal Reserve Bank Notes are Series of 1929 and have a brown seal. Many of these notes are quite scarce, especially the star notes and are avidly collected. According to the Treasury records, a little less than two million dollars is still outstanding for this series.

FEDERAL RESERVE NOTES, authorized by an Act of Congress on Dec. 23, 1913, bear the familiar green seal. These notes are the mainstay of our contemporary currency. Federal Reserve Notes are obligations of the United States and are a first lien on the assets of the issuing Federal Reserve Bank. In addition they are secured by a pledge of collateral equal to the face value of the notes. The collateral must consist of the following assets, alone or in any combination: [1] gold certificates, [2] Special Drawing Right Certificates, [3] United States Government Securities, and [4] "eligible paper" as described by statute.

Federal Reserve Notes are issued by the Federal Reserve Banks in denominations of $1, $2, $5, $10, $20, $50 and $100. On July 14, 1969, the Department of the Treasury announced that the issuance of $500, $1,000, $5,000 and $10,000 Federal Reserve Notes would be discontinued immediately because of the lack of demand.

NATIONAL BANK NOTES. President Lincoln signed the National Bank Act into law on February 25, 1863. The purpose of this legislation was to provide for a system of National Bank Note currency that would circulate freely. The currency was secured by United States bonds which the issuing banks deposited with the U.S. Treasurer. Holders of the circulation were protected from loss because if the bank failed, the bonds held by the Treasurer could be sold, and the proceeds used to redeem the outstanding currency.

More than $2.8 billion in small size National Bank Notes were issued between 1929 and 1935, all in the Series of 1929 bearing the federal signatures E. E. Jones, Register of the Treasury, and W. O. Woods, Treasurer. These notes were issued in denominations of $5, $10, $20, $50 and $100 by the national banks and bear the title and location of the bank to the left of the portrait, and the charter number of the bank just inside the right and left margins of the face. There were more than 6,000 issuing banks in 1929, representing all 48 states plus the territories of Alaska and Hawaii. Additional banks were organized between 1929 and 1935 that also issued these notes, and others failed or otherwise went out of business and ceased issuing. The result is that collectors are assured of countless varieties and some extreme rarities within this interesting series. National Bank Note collections commonly center on location themes and National Bank Note collecting represents one of the most dynamic and competitive phases of small note collecting.

The basic back and face designs of National Bank Notes were printed in sheets of 12, then cut vertically and overprinted with the bank information, and brown seals and serial numbers. There are two types of Series of 1929 notes. The serial numbers on type 1 notes have both prefix and suffix letters whereas the type 2 notes have only a prefix number. In addition, the charter numbers are printed in brown next to the serial number on type 2 notes.

The serial numbers on type 1 notes are sheet numbers. Consequently, all six notes in type 1 sheets have the same number, the difference being that the prefix letter cycled from A to F down the sheet. These were printed between 1929 and 1933. The serial numbers on type 2 notes are note numbers, and appear incremented down the sheets similar to other notes of the same vintage. These were printed between 1933 and 1935.

Series of 1929 National Bank Notes are not catalogued in this edition because a thorough listing by bank is beyond the scope of this work. You are referred to one of the comprehensive catalogs that treat this fascinating specialty in great detail such as the Standard Catalog of U.S. National Bank Notes by John Hickman and Dean Oakes (published by Krause Publications) or National Bank Notes, A Guide With Prices by Don Kelly.

SIGNATURE COMBINATIONS

All signatures on small currency appear on the face of the note. All United States Notes, Silver and Gold certificates, and Federal Reserve Notes carry two signatures — the signature of the Treasurer of the United States at the lower left and the signature of the Secretary of the Treasury at the lower right.

National Bank Notes and Federal Reserve Bank Notes have four signatures-all have E.E. Jones, Register of the Treasury at the upper left and W.O. Woods, Treasurer, at the top right. In the lower left appears the signature of the cashier of the bank, and in the lower right, the signature of the president of the bank. Federal Reserve Bank Notes have the signature of the bank cashier in the lower left and the signature of the governor of the bank in the lower right, with the following exceptions: New York notes have the signature of the deputy governor in the lower left instead of the cashier; Chicago has the assistant deputy governor replacing the cashier's signature; and St. Louis has the signature of the controller replacing that of the cashier. See Appendix IV for a list of all signature combinations as they have appeared on small size paper money.

PRINTING PAPER CURRENCY

Through the years, from the earliest times people have used cut or scratched lines to decorate their most prized possessions. By the end of the Roman Empire, they had learned to fill little cut lines with a dark gummy substance, smoke the surface, then wipe off the plate, and transfer the image to paper.

By mid-15th century, this art had been most highly developed in both Italy and Germany-and one of the first to actually engrave in ferrous metal for printing was the German, Albrecht Durer. His fine work was printed from copper plates, first by hand rollers, then later on the copper plate printing press, which was invented about 1545.

Paper money of the finest quality was printed by copper plates in mid-17th century England. The first official paper money in America was issued by the Massachusetts Bay Colony in 1690 to pay soldiers. By mid-18th century, several colonies were issuing very attractive notes. However, no transfer process was available and all plates had to be recut or newly engraved by hand, it was impossible to make printing plates bearing two identical designs. Despite the very severe penalties for counterfeiting, it was fairly easy.

The end of the 18th century seems to be the beginning of the American banknote printing industry. Jacob Perkins of Massachusetts invented a method of punching lettering and designs into the walls of steel cylinders and crossing them with engraved intersecting lines. These were then rolled into copper plates, and multiple intaglio impressions of exact fidelity were produced.

In 1812, Asa Spencer of Connecticut patented an engine-turning device to ornament watches. A stationary point traced or cut an endless design of perfect regularity, and this was quickly recognized as an effective deterrent for foiling counterfeiters. Perkins purchased the patent rights to this machine in 1815 and introduced it to the banknote business.

The first paper money issued by the U.S. Government came into being by Act of Congress in 1861 and was the result of the need for financing the Civil War—a plan proposed by Secretary of the Treasury, Salmon P. Chase [under President Lincoln] as both a system of taxation and one of floating loans. The Bureau of Engraving and Printing was established on Aug. 29, 1862

Until recently, currency was produced from wet paper printed on intaglio plates. The wetting is required because of the extreme pressures necessary to force the paper down into the incised lines of the plates in order to pick up the ink deposited therein.

Intaglio means that the design is cut or incised into the plate as compared to the raised letters on the more familiar type of printing. Experiments as early as 1938 in methods of dry printing were conducted. Development of non-offset ink allowed the dry method to be used starting in 1952.

With the introduction of the small size currency in 1929, all plates were standardized at 12-subject size. This 12-subject plate was considered maximum size under the wet method of printing because of the shrinkage of the sheets during the alternate wetting and drying of the paper between the printing of the back and the printing of the face of the notes. It was also necessary during this period to place a tissue between each sheet of printed paper to prevent the offset of ink prior to drying.

The size of the plate was increased to 18 subjects following the development of non-offset green ink in 1950 and a black ink in 1952. The door then was opened for increasing the size of the plates. 18-subject plates were first used in August 1952, and by September 1953, all presses had been converted to 18-subjects. With the introduction of the dry paper method for printing, plate size was increased to the 32-subject plate currently used. Illustrations showing the numbering of the various plate layouts follow this narrative.

When a new note is to be issued, designs are submitted to the designers of the BEP, who prepare a final model. The final model must be approved by the Secretary of the Treasury. Photographic copies of the approved model are furnished to the engravers.

Engravers reproduce the currency designs in pieces of soft steel, known as dies, by working with steel cutting instruments, or gravers, and powerful magnifying glasses. Each separate design, such as the portrait, the vignette, the ornaments, and the lettering, is hand cut by an engraver who has been specially trained in that particular style. A geometric lathe is used to cut the intricate lacy ornaments and borders, and a ruling machine is used to cut the fine cross-hatched lines in the portraits. It is practically impossible for an engraver to exactly reproduce his own work or that of another engraver.

When the hand-engraved pieces of soft steel, or dies, have been completed, they are cleaned, and then hardened by being heated in sodium cyanide and quickly dipped into brine. The design of each die is then transferred to a roll or cylinder of soft steel by placing the die on the bed of a transfer press and, under tremendous pressure, forcing the face of the soft roll into the intaglio engraving on the hard die.

The result is an exact duplicate of the original design standing out in relief on the face of the roll. To make a master die by the transfer process, the rolls from these several dies are passed separately over the soft die steel under great pressure. Different portions of the engraving are thereby united on the die in their proper positions. The master die is then finished and hardened and a master roll is made with all the designs necessary to make one note. An engraved steel master plate can then be made from the master roll on the transfer press.

The electrolytic process is now used for making plates for the printing of paper currency. The engraved steel master plate is placed in a nickel-plating bath and by means of electro-deposition another plate is built thereon to a required thickness. This plate is referred to as an alto, and when it is removed from the master, the design stands out in relief on a flat surface. A duplicate plate of the original steel master is then reproduced in the nickel plating bath from this relief design. These duplicate plates, with the design in the intaglio or cut-in impression as on the original master, are then electrolytically plated with chromium and made ready for printing.

SERIAL NUMBERS

There are two different serial numbering systems on U.S. currency, one for Federal Reserve Notes, and another for all the other classes. On Federal Reserve Notes, the prefix letter is always the same as the bank letter. For example all notes issued by the Federal Reserve Bank of Boston have serials that begin with A. The suffix letters progressively cycle through the alphabet as notes are printed producing a stream of blocks that for Boston look like AA, AB, AC, AD etc.

On other classes of currency, numbering always begins with the AA block, but after the first 100 million notes the first letter to change is the prefix letter. As numbering progresses, the prefix letters cycle alphabetically until the ZA block is used up. At this time, the suffix letter is changed to B and the prefix letters begin another cycle at A again.

The letter O is not used in either the prefix or suffix positions on any U.S. currency.

When 12-subject sheets were serial numbered, the sheets were first cut in half vertically. Next the half sheets were fed into the numbering press and serial numbering progressed down the half sheet beginning with 00000001 on position A or G depending on which half of the sheet went first. 00000002 was on the B or H position, etc. The half sheet was then cut into individual notes, these were arranged in order mechanically, and the next half sheet was fed through.

Starting with the 18-subject sheets in 1952, the notes were numbered through the stack, that is consecutively from sheet to sheet. The notes on a sheet were numbered with skips equal to the number of sheets in the production unit. At that time, a standard production unit was 8000, so the numbers on the number one sheet progressed from 00000001, 00008001 through 00144001. The numbering within a production unit, then as now, actually went backwards so that the smallest numbers landed on the top of the completed stack. Once all the sheets were numbered, the notes were then separated.

The 32-subject notes are printed in four quadrants of eight notes. The upper left quadrant sheet position letters are A1 through H1, the lower left quadrant A2 through H2, the upper right quadrant is A3 through H3 and the lower right quadrant is A4 through H4. The numbering advances 20,000 numbers per position starting with position A1 through H4, then A2 through H2, A3 through H3 and finally A4 through H4. In 1981 the production unit was changed to 40,000 sheets so that now the numbering advances 40,000 numbers between positions.

STAR NOTES

On April 14, 1910, Director of the Bureau of Engraving and Printing wrote to Lee McClung, the Treasurer, suggesting "that the Bureau be authorized to prepare a stock of notes numbered in sequence, distinguished from all other notes by a special letter or character printed before/after the serial number . . . that these notes be substituted for defective specimens . . . with notation on the pages indicating the package contained such substitutes."

The green light to proceed was given. Approval must have been antici-
pated, because on April 17, 1910, a rush order was sent to the American
Numbering Company in Brooklyn, N.Y., specifying eight stars for use on
automatic numbering blocks. The Bureau finished the first package with
stars on June 20, 1910, and delivered them to Treasurer McClung on July
12, 1910. Thus the earliest possible star notes are those of 1910 with the
Vernon-McClung signature. The first pack of stars was numbered
★75612001A through ★75612100A and were Series of 1899 Silver Certificates.

It is inevitable that some misprints, smudged notes, or otherwise imperfect notes will be made during note production. At the time of examination, these imperfect notes are replaced by new notes that have a star on
one end of the serial number. The percentage of spoiled notes is very
small, hence the number of star notes is rather limited. In the early series
of our small size notes, the spoilage percentage has been accurately estimated at less than 1% of total notes. No attempt is made to replace any
defective note with the same serial number star note.

Star notes also are used to replace the 100 millionth note instead of a
note with serial 00 000 000 as printed. We know of at least one instance
where, through error, the note with serial A 00 000 000 A escaped
replacement in the Bureau and was shown at the ANA convention in Boston, Mass., in 1973 by John Morrissey.

BLOCKS

A block refers to the prefix-suffix letter or star combination appearing in
a serial number. For example, serial F12345678A is from the FA block.
Likewise serial ★87654321A is from the ★A block. One popular way to
collect Small Size Currency is to collect all the blocks.

GROUPS

A group is a consecutive run of serial numbered notes within a given
block that has some unique identity. For example, the $1 SC 1935A
Hawaii and North Africa printings were interspersed within the same serial
number sequence as regular blue seal notes. In the FC block, serial
F41952001C to F41964000C were North Africa's and serials
F41964001C through F41976000C were Hawaii's. Thus there are four
groups in the FC block, one each of North Africa and Hawaii, and a lead-
ing and trailing blue seal.

Another interesting $1 SC block with groups is the 1935F and G print-
ings in the BJ block. Serials B00000001J through B5400000J are 1935F,
B540000001J through B71640000J are 1935G, B71640001J through
B72000000J are 1935F again, and B72000001J through B99999999J
are 1935G.

With the introduction of the Fort Worth $1 FRNs in the Series of 1988A
a few new groups have been created. For example, in the KC block, the
first 93,600,000 were printed in Washington, DC. and the last 6,400,000
were printed in Fort Worth and contain the distinctive FW prefix for the
face plate letter.

Some types of group collecting have come and gone, their lost popularity being attributed to the variation being way too minor or the concept underlying the uniqueness of the group being too tedious. One example is the COPE/conventional craze that began with the introduction of Currency Overprinting and Processing Equipment (COPE) in the $1 Series of 1969B FRNs. The COPE serial numbers had a slightly different look than the serials printed from the same type face on conventional older equipment. The Bureau published totals printed, separating the COPE and conventional serials. The collector had to have the list of numbers to tell what to collect! Another type of group developed when the Bureau began producing star notes in the Federal Reserve series wherein numbering skips separated printed serials. For a very short time, some die-hard collectors tried to collect from each of the myriad of printed groups. This got a bit tedious.

It turns out that if groups are to catch on, the variety must be readily distinguishable.

PLATE POSITION LETTERS

The position of a note in a sheet is revealed by the check letter that appears on the upper left corner on the face of the note on the 12-subject and 18-subject sheets, and the letter and number that appears in the upper left corner on the face of the 32-subject sheets. See the photos of the respective sheets illustrating the lettering conversions.

PLATE NUMBER

The plate number appears in the margin of the sheet (similar to the plate number on a sheet of postage stamps) and is trimmed off during the cutting operation.

CHECK NUMBERS

The tiny number in the lower right of both the face and back is called the plate check number for the cross-reference to the plate number.

Some collectors find great enjoyment in trying to establish a consecutive run of these check numbers, however one must recognize that the Bureau does not use all numbers in a series. The face and back check numbers are not related to each other.

LABEL SETS

Notes produced at BEP are packaged in 40 packs of 100 notes each. This package, commonly called a brick, has wooden blocks placed at each end of the stack along with a label denoting contents. The brick is then bound with two steel straps. It is then wrapped in heavy Kraft paper and a duplicate label denoting contents affixed to one end of the brick with a label of the Treasury seal affixed to the other end. Until Series 1974 the label showed the number of notes (4,000), the series year, the denomination of the notes inside, and the serial number of the first and last note.

With the Series 1974, the label remained the same except that it showed only the serial number of the first note in the brick. In recent years many collectors attempted to obtain these labels, with the first and last note in the brick and the term label set was applied.

SERIES DATE

Prior to the Series of 1974, the series date on the face of each bill indicated the year in which the face design of the note was adopted. The capital letter following the series year indicates that a minor change was authorized in a particular series. Such a change occurred with a new Secretary of the Treasury or Treasurer of the United States. This policy was changed when William E. Simon became Secretary of the Treasury. He directed that the series year would be changed whenever there was a change in the Office of the Secretary of the Treasury. Now the series dates are advanced by one letter, or a new year is selected, the latter being more common recently. Consequently each new signature now results in a surprise for the collector.

IN GOD WE TRUST

"In God We Trust" owes its presence on United States coins and notes largely to the increased religious sentiment existing during the Civil War. Salmon P. Chase, then Secretary of the Treasury, received a number of appeals from devout persons throughout the country, urging that deity be recognized suitably on our coins in a manner similar to that commonly found on the coins of other nations.

On Nov. 20, 1861, Secretary Chase instructed the Director of the Mint at Philadelphia to prepare a motto "expressing-this national recognition." The Secretary wrote "No nation can be strong except in the strength of God, or safe except in His defense." The motto first made its appearance on the two-cent coin, authorized by Act of Congress dated April 22, 1864. First appearance of the motto on our paper money was on the silver dollars shown on the back of the $5 1886.

A law passed by the 84th Congress and approved by the President on July 11, 1955, provides that "In God We Trust" shall appear on all United States paper currency and coins. One-dollar bills bearing the inscription were first made available to the public at most of the country's banks on Oct. 1, 1957. As the Bureau of Engraving and Printing converted to the dry intaglio process of printing, the motto "In God We Trust" was included in the back design of all classes and denominations of paper currency.

Matthew H. Rothert, past President of the American Numismatic Association, presented the suggestion to Secretary of the Treasury George W. Humphrey in November 1953, and is credited with the ultimate adoption of the idea.

THE $ SIGN

There are many accounts of the origin of the $ sign. The most widely accepted explanation being that it is the result of evolution of the Mexican or Spanish "Ps" pieces of eight. The theory, derived from a study of old manuscripts, is that the "S" gradually came to be written over the "P" developing a close equivalent of the $ mark. It was widely used before the adoption of the United States dollar in 1785.

MULES

A mule is a note that has a micro size check number on one side and a macro size number on the other. Micro numbers measure 0.6mm high whereas the macro numbers are 1mm high.

Mules came about with the adoption of macro plate check numbers beginning in January 1938. Mules flowed from the Bureau of Engraving and Printing for the next 15 years. They ceased in 1953 when the last of the 12-subject $50 and $100 Federal Reserve micro back plates were finally retired with the phasing out of 12-subject plates.

The change to macro numbers was of sufficient importance to the Bureau of Engraving and Printing that they advanced the series designations on the new macro face plates by one letter. For example, the $5 Silver Certificates went from Series of 1934 to 1934A despite the fact that the treasury signatures remained Julian-Morganthau. The difference was entirely in the size of the plate check numbers.

During the transition to all macro plates, both micro and macro plates were in use, often side by side on the same press. This occurred because the Bureau had a policy of using up obsolete plates rather than scrapping them. Whenever micro faces were mated with macro backs, or macro faces were mated with micro backs, we had a mule.

As shown below, mules were created in every denomination from $1 to $10,000. In fact, high denomination notes were among the most commonly muled owing to large stocks of 12-subject high denomination micro back plates.

The first macro plate to go to press was the number 1 Series of 1935A $1 Silver Certificate face on January 6, 1938. The first $1 macro back, plate 930, did not go to press until January 28, 1938, consequently all the 1935A $1s printed between January 6 and January 27 were mules. Those sheets were competing with $5 1934A SCs for the distinction of being the first mules to be overprinted with serial numbers. It turns out that the first Series of 1934A $5 faces (macro) went to press on January 14, a week after the first $1s. All were mated with micro backs and these were the first $5 mules of any class.

The $5 SC sheets advanced to the serial numbering stage more quickly than the $1s. On January 25, the first mule to be serial numbered was a $5 SC bearing number **D50352001A**. The first $1 SC 1935A mule, **M07668991A**, was numbered the next day. Two days later on January 28, 1938, the first muled star note was printed, a $1 Series of 1935A with serial **★17076001A**. Macro plates for the other classes and denominations gradually came on line in succeeding months.

By far the most diverse mules involved the three $5 classes. Micro $5 face plates gradually wore out and the first to go were the SC Series of 1934 plates on August 18, 1938, next were the LT Series of 1928B plates on December 1, 1940, and finally the last Series of 1934 FRN (Richmond) on January 23, 1946. With the exception of two plates, the last of the micro $5 backs was retired on February 14, 1940. However, a stockpile of old preprinted micro backs continued to provide micro backs through about June of 1942.

Overlapping the depletion of $5 micro plates were the introductions of $5 macro plates in the following order: SC Series of 1934A faces on January 14, 1938, macro backs on March 16, 1938, LT Series of 1928C on May 31, 1939, and FRN Series of 1934A (New York) on July 31, 1941. The mix of these plates assured a highly varied $5 mule production for years.

A great added surprise came in 1944 when an unfinished, now ancient, $5 micro back plate bearing number 637 was discovered and completed on November 10, 1944. It first went to press on June 23, 1945 and was used rather continuously until June 16, 1949 when it was finally canceled. In the meantime a second ancient plate was discovered, plate 629, which was already completed but which had never been used. It too was sent to press, but for a very short period from November 17, 1947 through February 2, 1948. These extraordinary plates produced a plethora of our rarest and most eagerly sought mules.

Back 637 produced the following mules: SC 1934A, B, C; LT 1928D and FRN 1934A, B, C. In addition this plate undoubtedly appears unmuled with LT 1928C, E; and FRN 1934 faces although none have been reported. Plate 629 produced mules in the following series: SC 1934C, LT 1928E, and FRN 1934C. All 629 mules are prized rarities. Many 637 mules are major rarities, especially the Series of 1934A FRNs which rank as the most elusive of all mule rarities. Plates 629 and 637 are responsible for all the $5 mules produced after January 1946.

Complete list of mules by type.

Denom.	Class	Series	Face	Back
$1	SC	1935	micro	macro
		1935A	macro	micro
$2	LT	1928C	micro	macro
		1928D	macro	micro
$5	SC	1934	micro	macro
		1934A	macro	micro
		1934B	macro	micro
		1934C	macro	micro
	LT	1928B	micro	macro
		1928C	macro	micro
		1928D	macro	micro
		1928E	macro	micro
	FRN	1934 dark green seal	micro	macro
		1934 Hawaii	micro	macro
		1934A dark green seal	macro	micro
		1934B	macro	micro
		1934B NY 212*	intermediate	micro
		1934C	macro	micro
$10	SC	1934	micro	macro
		1934 North Africa	micro	macro
		1934A	macro	micro
	FRN	1934 light green seal	micro	macro
		1934 dark green seal	micro	macro
		1934A light green seal	macro	micro
		1934A dark green seal	macro	micro
$20	FRN	1934 dark green seal	micro	macro
		1934 Hawaii	micro	macro

		1934A light green seal**	macro	micro
		1934A dark green seal	macro	micro
		1934A Hawaii	macro	micro
$50	FRN	1934 dark green seal	micro	macro
		1934A dark green seal	macro	micro
		1934B	macro	micro
		1934C	macro	micro
		1934D	macro	micro
		1950	macro	micro
$100	FRN	1934 dark green seal	micro	macro
		1934A dark green seal	macro	micro
		1934B	macro	micro
		1934C	macro	micro
		1934D	macro	micro
		1950	macro	micro

$500, 1000, 5000, 10000, mules possible in all 1934 series.
Mule varieties involving late finished plates:

$10	SC	1934A 86, 87	macro	micro
		1934 204 dark green seal	micro	macro
$20	FRN	1934 204 Hawaii	micro	macro

*none reported
**may be possible from Chicago

LATE FINISHED PLATES

A small group of interesting but peculiar varieties came into being as a result of the conversion from micro to macro size plate check number, a conversion that began in January 1938. These are the notes printed from late finished plates. What happened was that the plates were assigned numbers and their manufacture was begun during the micro era. However, their completion was delayed until long after macro plate check letters were adopted. Consequently they carry macro check numbers but the numbers fall decidedly in the micro range.

The following is a list of these most unusual plates.

Plate	No.	Date Begun	Date Finished	Dates Used	Total Notes
$1 back	470	Sep 1, 1936	May 13, 1943	May 15, 1943-Jun 18, 1943	2,402,700
$5 SC 1934A	307	Apr 6, 1936	Jul 3, 1942	Jul 9, 1942-Jun 3, 1943	569,244
$10 SC 1934A	86	Jan 21, 1938	May 29, 1940	Jul 18, 1940-Jun 29, 1944	1,203,456
$10 SC 1934A	87	Feb 7, 1938	Sep 16, 1938	Dec 5, 1939-Jan 16, 1940	83,100
$20 back	204	Dec 21, 1934	Mar 18, 1944	Apr 4, 1944-Oct 2, 1946	3,328,728

You will see in the listings that these plates were responsible for a host of interesting and unusual varieties. By far the rarest are the $1 SC Series of 1935A notes from the 470 back. Notice that the $5 and $10 SC faces were completed as Series of 1934As which is consistent with their macro check numbers.

These varieties used to be called Trial Notes before the circumstances behind their manufacture became known.

EXPERIMENTAL NOTES

The most well known experimental notes are the $1 SC 1935A R and S (regular and special) paper tests. Several such paper tests have been conducted over the years. The most well documented include the $1 SC 1928A and 1928B XB, YB and ZB block notes, $1 SC 1935 AB, BB and CB block notes and recently the Natick paper test.

Approximately one million of the red R and S notes were placed in circulation in June 1944. Compilation of statistics was to be done as the notes were returned for redemption. However, the returns were so small that the volume never reached sufficient proportions for a valid analysis. The 1928A and 1928B experimentals, as well as the 1935 issue of experimentals were much better disguised. However, no test results seem to have been forthcoming.

New experiments conducted in 1981 on so-called Natick test paper resulted in the printing of $1 notes for Series 1977A (Richmond) serials **E** 76 800 001 **H** through **E** 80 640 000 **H**, a total of 3,849,000 notes; $1 Series 1977A (Philadelphia) serials C07 052 001★ through **C** 07 060 000★, a total of 256,000 notes with a gap of 12,000 serial numbers between positions; and $10 Series 1977A notes for Richmond in August 1981 with serials **E** 05 772 001★ through **E** 05 780 000★.

THE TREASURY SEAL

U.S. paper money of small size carries an imprint of the Treasury seal. It is the distinguishing mark which validates our currency, and in a manner of speaking is the authority, coupled with the expression of obligation and the two signatures that form a valid contract between the United States government and the holders of its currency. The color of the seal indicates the class of currency it adorns.

The Seal of the Treasury of North America is inscribed in Latin (Theasur. Amer. Septent Sigil) around the seal. A square for rectitude, a key for safety, and a set of scales for equality are distinguishable features. A modern version with inscription in English and removal of some of the heraldry was approved and first appeared on the $100 U.S. Note Series in 1966. Treasury Order No. 212 dated January 29, 1968 and signed by Henry H. Fowler officially approved the new Treasury seal.

OLD SEAL   **NEW SEAL**

The Treasury considers that the creator of its seal probably was Francis Hopkinson, who is known to have submitted bills to the Congress in 1780 authorizing design of departmental seals, including the Board of Treasury. Although it is not certain that Hopkinson was the designer, the seal is similar to others by him. Also obscured by the absence of historical proof is the reason for original wording that embraced all North America.

FEDERAL RESERVE SEAL COLOR VARIETIES

There are two distinct treasury seal colors on both 1928 and 1934 series Federal Reserve Notes. These will be treated in turn.

The treasury seals were changed from a dark green to a vivid lime green color sometime between 1930 and 1932. All the Series of 1928C and 1928D FRNs have the lime green seal. Many $5, $10 and $20 Series of 1928B and quite a few high denomination Series of 1928 and 1928A plates were in use after the change so lime green seals occur on notes from these plates as well. The change to the lime green color was progressive and collectors have been able to assemble sets of notes showing many gradations between the old green and newer lime green varieties.

The vivid lime green seals were continued into the 1934 series. The color was again changed around the fall of 1938, this time to a pale blue green color. As with the 1928 change, this change was gradational so several different intermediate hues have been observed, particularly, on the $10s and $20s. No $5 Series of 1934 lime green seal mules were printed because there were no $5 FRN printings between May 20, 1937 and July 10, 1941. This period spanned both the introduction of macro backs and the seal color change, so when $5 printings resumed, the Series of 1934 mules that rolled off the presses all got pale blue green seals.

These seal color varieties have caused serious cataloging problems since the inception of this catalog, and we are taking major steps to sort through these problems with this second edition. In doing so, we have gotten very precise with our definition of light (yellow) green seals. To be considered light the seal must be vivid yellow olive green only. All transitional intermediate seal colors have been categorized as dark. When in doubt, compare your note with a full vivid yellow olive green seal note, only. Do not compare backwards, i.e., with a dark seal to see if it is lighter. (They'll all come out light). Using this criteria, we hope that you will contribute serial number data to help us refine our sketchy data base.

SUBTLE DESIGN CHANGES ON FEDERAL RESERVE NOTES

The Federal Reserve Notes underwent substantial redesigns beginning with the following series: 1928, 1934, 1950 and 1963. The following is a list of important minor changes that have occurred over the years.

On 1928 series notes, the early issues have treasury seals which contain the number of the issuing bank. The number was changed to a letter beginning with the Series of 1928A $50 and $100 notes, and with the Series of 1928B $5, $10 and $20 notes. The number remained in the seal for the high denomination notes.

The word "The" was dropped from the Federal Reserve seals beginning with the Series of 1934B issues.

A new vignette was adopted for the backs of the $20's during the Series of 1934C printings wherein the balcony was added to the White House, the shrubbery grew considerably, and the word "the" was added to the line under the vignette. Both varieties appear on Series of 1934C notes.

IN GOD WE TRUST was added to the backs as follows: Series of 1963 $5, $10, $20, and Series of 1963A $50 and $100.

The new treasury seal was adopted on the Series of 1969 notes.

MAJOR REDESIGN ON FEDERAL RESERVE NOTES

With a primary goal to foil counterfeiters, the U.S. Treasury released the Series 1996 $100 Federal Reserve Note in early 1996, with a total redesign. Among the new significant features are the enlarged off-center portrait of Benjamin Franklin, the Franklin watermark, the use of color shifting inks, and a standard Federal Reserve Seal used for all districts with district designation of issuing bank indicated by a letter and number just below the upper left serial number. The additional letter preceding the serial number corresponds to the series, i.e., (A) represents Series 1996. Also found on the new designs are concentric fine line printing and micro-printing. The back of the note still shows Independence Hall, but has also undergone major redesign.

NORTH AFRICAN AND HAWAII SERIES

United States Silver Certificates printed with the Treasury seal in yellow, rather than the usual blue, were used in the initial stages of America's World War II military operations in North Africa and Sicily. The distinctive seal was adopted to facilitate isolation of the currency in event that military reverses caused substantial amounts to fall into enemy hands. Denominations issued were $1, $5 and $10. Circulation of the yellow seal currency was confined for some time to the military zones of operation, but subsequently restrictions against its circulation in the United States were removed. Except for the yellow seal, it is identical with other Silver Certificates of the same vintage.

A specially marked U.S. currency was introduced into Hawaii in July 1942, as an economic defense against a possible Japanese occupation. The notes were overprinted "HAWAII" horizontally on the back and vertically at each end on the face. Only the overprinted notes were allowed in Hawaii after Aug. 14, 1942, except in rare instances approved by the Governor of Hawaii. Notes utilized for this purpose were the $1 Silver Certificate Series 1935A and the San Francisco Federal Reserve notes of $5 Series 1934 and 1934A, the $10 Series 1934A and the $20 Series 1934 and 1934A. All of the Hawaii overprinted currency carried brown seals and serial numbers and the Julian-Morgenthau signatures. The prohibition of unmarked currency in Hawaii remained in effect until Oct. 21, 1944.

FANCY FACTS

Facts: Notes are 2.61 by 6.14 inches long. Laid end to end there would be approximately 11,900 notes per mile. Notes are .0043 inches thick, stacked there would be 233 notes per inch. 490 notes would weigh one pound, one million notes would be about a ton and would occupy about 42 cubic feet. The Bureau uses about 3,500 tons of paper and about 1,000 tons of ink each year.

HOW PAPER MONEY ENTERS CIRCULATION

The distribution of paper currency is made through the Federal Reserve banks and their branches. Member banks of the Federal Reserve System carry reserve accounts with the Federal Reserve bank of their district. When member banks need additional currency, they authorize the Federal Reserve bank to charge their reserve account and ship the currency. The Federal Reserve banks will ship needed currency on request. Non-member banks procure their currency through a correspondent member bank located in the same city with the Federal Reserve Bank.

DESTRUCTION OF UNFIT CURRENCY

When paper currency becomes worn and no longer fit for use, it is withdrawn from circulation, destroyed, and replaced by new notes. The worn notes are destroyed by incineration or pulverization. The destruction process is not complete until the notes have been reduced to an unidentifiable residue so that no recovery is possible.

Currency is verified as to genuineness, kind, value, and number of pieces before destruction. Dollar bills make up the bulk of the currency which is retired. One dollar bills normally last about 18 months, while higher-denomination bills last much longer.

Currencies in all denominations below $500 that are no longer fit for use are verified and destroyed at Federal Reserve banks and branches throughout the country, and by the United States Treasurer's Office, under procedures prescribed by the Department of the Treasury. Federal Reserve notes in denominations of $500 and above are canceled with distinctive perforations and cut in half lengthwise. The lower halves are shipped to the Department of the Treasury in Washington, D.C. where they are verified and destroyed. The upper halves are retained by the Federal Reserve banks and destroyed after the banks are notified by the Treasury that the lower halves have been verified.

EXCHANGE OF MUTILATED PAPER CURRENCY

Lawfully held paper money of the United States which has been mutilated will be exchanged at its face value if clearly more than one half of the original note remains. Fragments of such mutilated currency which are not clearly more than one half of the original note will be exchanged at face value only if the Treasurer of the United States is satisfied that the missing portions have been totally destroyed. Correspondence regarding mutilated currency should be addressed to the Office of the Treasurer of the United States, Room 1123, Main Treasury Bldg., Washington, D.C. 20220.

LEGAL TENDER

Public law 89-81, the Coinage Act of July 23, 1965, defines Legal Tender as follows:

"All coins and currencies of the United States (including Federal Reserve notes and circulating notes of Federal Reserve banks and national banking associations), regardless of when coined or issued, shall be legal tender for all debts, public and private, public charges, taxes, duties, and dues."

FANCY NUMBERS

Palindromes, or radar notes, are notes on which the serial number reads the same backwards or forwards, without regard to prefix or suffix letters. In addition to these, many collectors like ladders with serial numbers like 01 234 567 or down ladders such as 98 765 432 etc. Repeaters, such as 12 12 12 12 or 2222 3333 are very popular. Perhaps the most outstanding of the fancy numbers are those which have all eight digits the same, such as 11 111 111 or 44 444 444 etc.

LOW NUMBERS

Serial numbers under 9999 are generally considered low numbers, with serial number 00 000 001 of course being perfection. Today, most collectors are quite happy to find a note starting with four zeroes, and delighted to find one with even more zeroes. Naturally the notes rise in price with the number of zeroes at the beginning.

GRADING

We believe the following criteria will enable you to properly and accurately grade any note:

Crisp Uncirculated-A new bill, never used, clean and crisp. Keep in mind that some notes in certain series were not clean and crisp when printed. The 1935A $1 Silver Certificate is a good example of this-many of the 1935 have a dirty look to the paper, some are quite limp-and were so when originally issued. (CU)

Extremely Fine-About Uncirculated-Note is still crisp but may show minor wrinkles or few dirt specks. No heavy folds or creases. No stains or severe dirty spots. (EF-AU)

Very Fine-Shows some use, but still has some crispness. May have a few heavy folds but no creases that break the paper. Must have a uniformly nice appearance. (VF)

Very Good-Fine-Shows circulation, may have heavy folds or possibly a few creases that break the paper. May have minor stains. (VG-F)

Good-Entire note is there but may have minor tear. No crispness, may be dirty, stained, or have ink marking in field. Generally described as average circulated. (G)

Below these grades are fair and poor. Generally considered uncollectible except in the rarest notes.

WIDE AND NARROW MARGINS

$1 1935D Silver Certficates come wtih wide and narrow back designs. The green border below the large printed words ONE DOLLAR at the bottom of the back of the note is the identifying area. If this strip is thin, it is referred to as a "narrow" margin. If it is thick, it is called a wide margin.

The wide and narrow backs on $5 1928F US Notes, $5 1934D Silver Certificates and $5 1950 Federal Reserve Notes can be distinguished by the small circle on the lower right corner of the back of the bill. A careful examination of the photo reveals three double lines in the right half of the circle on the wide backs. The narrow back has only two double lines.

The wide and narrow backs on the $10 1934D Silver Certificates are distinguished by the ribbon through figure 10 in the bottom right corner of the back of the note. If there is an area of green between the end of the ribbon and the white margin at the edge of the note, it is a wide back. If this ribbon extends completely to the printed edge of the note, it is a narrow back.

Wide

Narrow

$5.00 Wide, Narrow, Wide II

$10.00 Narrow

$10.00 Wide

$1 Legal Tender   25

ONE DOLLAR NOTES

LEGAL TENDER

Red Seal

SERIES 1928

PLATE SERIALS: Face check #1 through #36 (exceptions #12, #31 and #33-35). NOTE: Check #12 has been seen despite Bureau records that it was not used.

SIGNATURES: Walter O. Woods, W.H. Woodin.

This series was printed in April and May 1933 but the majority were not released until the recession of 1948-49. These were then issued in Puerto Rico as an economy measure as follows:

Nov.1948	40,000	Jan. 1949	500,000	Feb. 1949	40,000
Mar. 1949	42,000	Apr. 1949	144,000		

Puerto Rico was chosen to keep the "odd one-time" issue from causing sorting problems in the Federal Reserve Banks on the mainland.

SERIAL NUMBERS	NOTES PRINTED	VG	Unc
A00 000 001A through A01 872 012A	1,872,012	$30.00	$150.00
★00 000 002A through ★00 007 892A		1000.00	3000.00

737.497
c.1

$1 SILVER CERTIFICATE
Blue Seal
SERIES 1928

Obligation-"This certifies that there has been deposited in the Treasury of the United States of America One Silver Dollar payable to the bearer on demand."

Legend, series 1928, 1928 A, 1928 B, 1928 C and 1928 D, "This certificate is receivable for all public dues and when so received may be reissued."

On series 1928 E, "This certificate is legal tender for all debts public and private."

PLATE SERIALS: Face check #2 through #1022 Back check numbers begin with #1.

SIGNATURES: H.T. Tate, A.W. Mellon.

Serial numbers on both regular and star notes begin with 000 000 001.

SERIAL NUMBERS	NOTES PRINTED	VG/F	CU
A-A – F-A	638,296,908	$8.00	$25.00
G-A		10.00	30.00
H-A		10.00	35.00
I-A		75.00	150.00
J-A		100.00	150.00
KA		125.00	200.00
L52 107 065A high observed		175.00	250.00
★00 000 039A – ★12 444 406A		25.00	150.00

SERIES **1928A**

PLATE SERIALS: Face check #5 through #1814

SIGNATURES: Walter O. Woods, A.W. Mellon.

SERIAL NUMBERS		NOTES PRINTED	VG/F	CU
D93 825 125**A**		2,267,809,500	$100.00	$500.00
E-A			50.00	200.00
FA			10.00	35.00
GA through **ZA**			6.00	22.50
BB, through,**FB**,			6.00	25.00
GB-HB			15.00	35.00
IB			100.00	200.00
J54 403 307**B**	high observed		50.00	100.00
★08 571 642**A**	through ★35 790 882**A**		15.00	150.00

Series **1928A** Experimentals

The first major experimental group of small notes was printed in November 1932 and delivered to the Treasury for release into circulation in January and February of 1933, during the period of the $1.00 Series 1928A and 1928B. The experimental set was to determine the effect of changing the relative amounts of linen and cotton paper fibers. The X--B and Y--B groups were each printed on paper of different proportions of the rag content with the Z--B group as the control, using the distinctive paper in regular use. The special numbers assigned to this experiment are given below.

The experimentals are randomly mixed between both series 1928A and 1928B because they were serially numbered from a single number register. An estimate of quantities printed within each is not yet possible.

SERIAL NUMBERS	NOTES PRINTED	VG/F	CU
X00 000 001**B** through **X**10 728 000**B**	10,728,000	$35.00	$250.00
Y00 000 001**B** through **Y**10 248 000**B**	10,248,000	30.00	125.00
Z00 000 001**B** through **Z**10 248 000**B**	10,248,000	35.00	175.00

Series **1928B** Experimentals

X00 000 001B through X10 728 000B	see	35.00	150.00
Y00 000 001B through Y10 248 000B	above	35.00	200.00
Z00 000 001B through Z10 248 000B		35.00	175.00

SERIES **1928B**

PLATE SERIALS: Face check #2 through #567.

SIGNATURES: Walter O. Woods, Ogden L. Mills.

SERIAL NUMBERS	NOTES PRINTED	VG/F	CU
V51 000 001A official low	674,597,808	$75.00	$200.00
WA		100.00	350.00
XA		50.00	100.00
YA		10.00	26.00
ZA		7.50	26.00
AB - JB		6.00	25.00
★27 276 950A through ★37 546 972A		50.00	450.00

SERIES **1928C**

PLATE SERIALS: Face check #1 through #9 (check numbers #5 and #10 were master plates and were not used).

SIGNATURES: Walter O. Woods, W.H. Woodin.

SERIAL NUMBERS	NOTES PRINTED	VG/F	CU
B29 448 001**B** official low	5,364,348	$150.00	$400.00
CB		250.00	750.00
DB - IB		150.00	400.00
J47 096 952**B** high observed		500.00	1000.00
★33 390 295**A** through ★36 697 318**A**		1500.00	5000.00

SERIES **1928D**

PLATE SERIALS: Face check #1 through #49.

SIGNATURES: W.A. Julian, W.H. Woodin

SERIAL NUMBERS	NOTES PRINTED	VG/F	CU
D82 596 001 through **IB**	14,451,372		
J54 890 954**B**		$35.00	$275.00
★35 006 672**A** through ★37 368 075**A**		1500.00	5000.00

SERIES **1928E**

PLATE SERIALS: Face checks #1 through #12. Check #5 and #6 were masters.

SIGNATURES: W.A. Julian, Henry Morgenthau, Jr.

SERIAL NUMBERS	NOTES PRINTED	VG/F	CU
F72 000 001B through J54 954 234B	3,519,324	$300.00	$1250.
★35 821 073A through ★37 560 000A		2500.00	7000.00

The highest serial numbers printed for all 1928 series are J55 796 000B and ★37 560 000A.

SERIES 1934

PLATE SERIALS: Face check #1 through #838. Back check numbers end at #3096
SIGNATURES: W.A. Julian, Henry Morgenthau, Jr.

SERIAL NUMBERS	NOTES PRINTED	VG/F	CU
A-A through G44 646 281A	682,176,000	$8.00	$40.00
★00 000 065A through ★07 660 451A	7,680,000	50.00	400.00

SERIES 1935

Experimental notes were printed in this series which are identifiable by block letters A--B, B--B and C--B.

PLATE SERIALS: Face check #1 through #1391

Back check #1 through #929

SIGNATURES: W.A. Julian, Henry Morgenthau, Jr.

SERIAL NUMBERS	NOTES PRINTED	VG/F	CU
A00 000 001**A-LA**	1,681,552,000	$5.00	$10.00
MA		7.50	15.00
NA		15.00	50.00
PA		25.00	75.00
QA		50.00	125.00
R81 552 000**A**		75.00	175.00
★00 039 001**A** through ★21 824 212**A**		25.00	150.00

SERIES 1935 MULE

These are Series 1935 notes with macro back check numbers (#930 or higher) and are actually Series 1935 faces printed on Series 1935A backs.

ALL SERIES 1935 MULES ARE SCARCE.

SERIAL NUMBERS	NOTES PRINTED	VG/F	CU
M81 121 635**A** low observed	see above	$250.00	$750.00
NA		50.00	100.00
PA		35.00	75.00
QA through **RA**		50.00	150.00
★21 825 275**A** through ★22 243 949**A**		100.00	300.00

SERIES 1935

Experimentals

A paper experiment patterned after the $1.00 Series 1928A and 1928B set was again tried during the $1.00 Series 1935. In this case the printing began on March 16, 1937 on the A—B block, utilizing the distinctive paper with a special finish. The printing of this group ended April 28, 1937. Printing started again on November 26, 1937 with the B—B block using special paper. On December 1, 1937, the C—B block was begun on regular paper as the control, and both terminated together on December 10th. These were all delivered within the year 1937. The special numbers assiged to this experiment are given below.

SERIAL NUMBERS	NOTES PRINTED	VG/F	CU
A00 000 001B through A06 180 000B	6,180,000	$15.00	$75.00
B00 000 001B through B03 300 000B	3,300,000	125.00	250.00
C00 000 001B through C03 300 000B	3,300,000	125.00	250.00

SERIES 1935A MULE

These are Series 1935A notes with the micro back check numbers (#929 or lower), and are actually Series 1935A faces printed on Series 1935 backs.

SERIAL NUMBERS	NOTES PRINTED	VG/F	CU
M07 668 001A official low Printed January 26,1938			
M07 777 770A low observed		$5.00	$35.00
NA - TA		6.00	30.00
UA - WA		8.00	35.00
XA - ZA		15.00	75.00
AB		25.00	100.00
BB		35.00	150.00
CB		25.00	75.00
DB		100.00	200.00
E96 998 982B high observed		300.00	500.00
★17 076 001A through ★37 095 331A		50.00	175.00

(Official low printed January 28,1938)

SERIES 1935A

Late Finished Plate

SERIAL NUMBERS: (reported) K20 895 155C and K20 895 156C
PLATE SERIAL: Back check number 470.
TOTAL QUANTITY PRINTED: 2,402,700 notes.
Only three known. One of these is damaged.

SERIES **1935A**

PLATE SERIALS: Face check numbers begin at #1, January 6, 1938. Back check numbers begin at #930, January 28,1938.

SIGNATURES: W.A. Julian, Henry Morgenthau, Jr.

SERIAL NUMBERS		NOTES PRINTED	VG/F	CU
MA	(only one note known)		$750.00	$2500.00
NA			100.00	250.00
PA			10.00	25.00
QA through **CD**			3.00	6.00
D45 624 000**D**	official high		5.00	10.00
★17 559 387**A**	low observed		5.00	10.00
★02 651 672**B**	high observed		75.00	150.00

HAWAII NOTES
SERIES **1935A**
Brown Seal

SERIAL NUMBERS	NOTES PRINTED	VG/F	CU
Y68 628 001**B** through **Y**71 628 000**B**	3,000,000	12.00	80.00
Z99 000 001**B** through **Z**99 999 999**B**	1,000,000	40.00	325.00
A99 000 001**C** through **A**99 999 999**C**	1,000,000	40.00	500.00
C000 000 001**C** through **C**07 000 000**C**	7,000,000	7.00	55.00
F41964 001**C** through **F**41 976 000**C**	12,000	50.00	400.00
L75 996 001**C** through **L**78 996 000**C**	3,000,000	10.00	55.00

P31 992 001C through P37 032 000C	5,040,000	7.00	55.00
S39 996 001C through S54 996 000C	15,000,000	7.00	50.00
★64 812 001A-★64 860 000A	48,000	100.00	850.00
★66 084 001A-★66 108 000A	24,000	100.00	850.00
★70 260 001A-★70 332 000A	72,000	75.00	750.00
★87 360001A-★87 408 000A	48,000	75.00	750.00
★91 128 001A-★91 140 000A	12,000	100.00	900.00
★64 812 607A-★91 139 361A observed			

NORTH AFRICA NOTES
SERIES 1935A
Yellow Seal

SERIAL NUMBERS	NOTES PRINTED	VG/F	CU
B30 000 001C through B31 000 000C	1,000,000	$12.00	$95.00
B51 624 001C through B52 624 000C	1,000,000	10.00	95.00
B99 000 001C through B99 999 999C	1,000,000	10.00	95.00
C60 000 001C through C62 000 000C	2,000,000	8.00	70.00
C78 000 001C through C79 904 000C	1,904,000	8.00	70.00
F41 952 001C through F41 964 000C	12,000	50.00	300.00
I30 000 001C through I40 000 000C	10,000,000	8.00	60.00
R90 000 001C through R99 999 999C	10,000,000	8.00	60.00
★68 364 001A through ★68 388 000A	24,000	100.00	750.00
★70 956 001A through ★71 004 000A	48,000	100.00	750.00
★79 560 001A through ★79 632 000A	72,000	100.00	750.00
★68 364 496A through ★79 627 768A observed range			

"R & S" NOTES
SERIES 1935A
Experimental R and S

The best known of the experimental printings were the "R" and "S" overprint issues in the S-C block of Series 1935A. In this case, the red "R" was overprinted on the regular distinctive paper and the red "S" on a special paper. They were delivered June 20, 1944 and issued into circulation to test their comparative durabilities. No conclusive results were determined from the trial issue. (Bureau of Printing and Engraving records show that 12,000 star notes of each "R" and "S" were printed.)
The special numbers assigned to this experiment are given below.

SERIAL NUMBERS	NOTES PRINTED	VG/F	CU
"R" Notes			
S70 884 001**C** through **S**72 068 000**C**	1,184,000	$20.00	$175.00
★91 176 001**A** through ★91 188 000**A**	12,000	500.00	2,500.00
★91 177 120**A** through ★91 186 149**A**			

SERIAL NUMBERS	NOTES PRINTED	VG/F	CU
"S" Notes			
S73 884 001**C** through **S**75 068 000**C**	1,184,000	15.00	150.00
★91 188 001**A**★91 200 000**A**	12,000	500.00	2350.00
★91 188 035**A**★91 192 619**A**			

SERIES 1935B

SIGNATURES: W.A. Julian, Fred M. Vinson

SERIAL NUMBERS	NOTES PRINTED	VG/F	CU
C93 384 001**D**	806,612,000	$35.00	$75.00
DD - KD		3.00	7.50
LD		5.00	15.00
M00 648 000**D**		250.00	500.00
★02 749 841**B** through ★12 668 468**B**		12.50	65.00

SERIES **1935C**

SIGNATURES: W.A. Julian, John W. Snyder

SERIAL NUMBERS		NOTES PRINTED	VG/F	CU
K99 996 001**D**	official low	3,088,108,000	$25.00	$60.00
LD - SE			2.50	5.50
TE			4.00	7.00
U86 153 076**E**			5.00	25.00
★12 972 850**B** through ★49 474 913B			5.00	35.00
★12961938B				

WIDE

SERIES **1935D WIDE**
From 12 Subject Sheets

PLATE SERIALS: Back check number: wide: #5015 or lower
SIGNATURES: Georgia Neese Clark, John W. Snyder

SERIAL NUMBERS	NOTES PRINTED	VG/F	CU
R88 104 001E	4,656,968,000✱	$35.00	$75.00
SE through FG		2.00	6.00
HG through IG		5.00	10.00
JG		10.00	20.00
KG		20.00	40.00
LG		50.00	100.00
M74 613 838G		75.00	150.00
★49 624 428B Low observed		3.50	20.00
★06 038 641C High observed		100.00	250.00

✱Includes all 1935D notes: 146,944,000 in sheets of 18; balance in sheets of 12.

SERIES **1935D NARROW**
From 12 Subject Sheets

PLATE SERIALS: Back check numbers: Narrow #5017 or higher.

SERIAL NUMBERS	NOTES PRINTED	VG/F	CU
U54 720 688E Low observed	see above	$750.00	$2500.00
VE		25.00	60.00
WE		20.00	40.00
XE		10.00	20.00
YE and ZE		5.00	10.00
AF through M98 128 000G		2.00	5.50
★55 213 765B low observed		3.50	15.50
★07 044 000C official high		7.50	35.00

NARROW

SERIES **1935D NARROW**

From 18 Subject Sheets

PLATE SERIALS: Face plate numbers 7463 or higher (with some alternating back to 12 subject sheets).

Back plate numbers 5689 or higher (with some alternating back to 12 subject sheets)

SERIAL NUMBERS	NOTES PRINTED	VG/F	CU
G00 000 001G / G99 999 999G	99,999,999	$4.00	$8.00
N00 000 001G / N46 944 000G	46,944,000	4.00	10.00
★00 000 001D			
through ★05 023 672D High observed		20.00	75.00

SERIES **1935E**

SIGNATURES: Ivy Baker Priest, George M. Humphrey

SERIAL NUMBERS	NOTES PRINTED	VG/F	CU
N46 944 001G / P81 000 000I	5,134,056,000		$5.00
★05 054 838D Low observed			7.50
★E			7.50
★56 708 222F High observed			7.50

SERIES **1935F**

SIGNATURES: Ivy Baker Priest, Robert B. Anderson

SERIAL NUMBERS	NOTES PRINTED	VG/F	CU
P81 000 01**I** through **B**54 000 000**J**	1,173,360,000		$5.00
B71 640 001**J** through **B**72 000 000**J**		$150.00	750.00
★57 367 573**F** low observed		6.00	
★10 542 728**G** high observed	53,200,000		7.50

SERIES **1935G NO MOTTO**

PLATE SERIALS: Back check #6786 or lower

SIGNATURES: Elizabeth Rudel Smith, C. Douglas Dillon

SERIAL NUMBERS	NOTES PRINTED	VG/F	CU
B54 000 001**J** through **D**48 960 000**J**	194,600,000		$5.00
★10 455 957**G** low observed			
★18 981147**G** high observed	8,640,000		9.00

SERIES **1935G MOTTO**

PLATE SERIALS: Back Check #6787 or higher

SIGNATURES: Same as 1935G without motto. *"In God We Trust"*

SERIAL NUMBERS	NOTES PRINTED	CU
D48 960 001**J** through **D**80 280 000**J**	31,320,000	$15.00
★19 126 644**G** low observed		
★20 149 712**G** high observed	1,080,000	35.00

SERIES **1935H**

PLATE SERIALS: Face check #8648 or lower.

Back check #6876 or lower, (Last plate used for 18 subject sheets)

SIGNATURES: Kathryn O'Hay Granahan, C. Douglas Dillon

SERIAL NUMBERS	NOTES PRINTED	CU
D80 280 001**J** through **E**10 800 000**J**	30,520,000	$5.00
★20 160 854**G** low observed		
★21 596 000**G** official high	1,436,000	10.00

SERIES **1957**
First of the 32-Subject Sheet

PLATE SERIALS: Face and back numbers begin at #1 with 32 subject sheets.

SERIAL NUMBERS: Both regular and star numbers begin at 00 000 001A.

SIGNATURES: Ivy Baker Priest, Robert B. Anderson

SERIAL NUMBERS	NOTES PRINTED	CU
A-A through **Z-A** and **A–B**	2,609,600,000	$4.50
B09 600 001**B** official high		35.00
★**A**, ★**B**, ★**C**	307,040,000	4.50
★07 640 000**D** official high		15.00

SERIES **1957A**

SIGNATURES: Elizabeth Rudel Smith, C. Douglas Dillon

SERIAL NUMBERS	NOTES PRINTED	CU
A00 000 001**A** through **Q**94 080 000**A**	1,594,000,000	$4.50
★00 000 001**A** through ★94 720 000**A**	94,720,000	5.50

SERIES **1957B**

PLATE SERIALS: Face check #789 was the official high. Back check #447 is highest known.

SIGNATURES: Kathryn O'Hay Granahan, C. Douglas Dillon

SERIAL NUMBERS	NOTES PRINTED	CU
Q94 080 001**A** Official low		$10.00
R-A through **Y**12 480 000**A** Off. high	718,400,000	4.50
★94 880 001**B** Official low		10.00
★44 160 000**B** Official High	4,928,000	5.50

In March 1964, Secretary of the Treasury Dillon halted the redemption of Silver Certificates in silver dollars and on June 24, 1968, redemption in silver bullion was discontinued.

Federal Reserve Notes
Green Seal
32 Subject Sheet
SERIES 1963

PLATE SERIALS: Face check numbers begin at #1. Back check numbers continued from silver certificates.

SIGNATURES: Kathryn O'Hay Granahan, C. Douglas Dillon

SERIAL NUMBERS	NOTES PRINTED	CU
BOSTON		
A-A	87,680,000	$3.00
A-★	6,400,000	5.00
NEW YORK		
B-A,B-B	198,999,998	3.00
B-C	19,200,000	75.00
B-★	15,040,000	4.00
PHILADELPHIA		
C-A	99,999,999	3.00
C-B	23,680,000	15.00
C-★	10,720,000	5.00
CLEVELAND		
D-A	99,999,999	3.00
D-B	8,200,000	100.00
D-★	8,160,000	5.00

RICHMOND
E-A	99,999,999	3.00
E-B	59,520,000	4.00
E-★	12,000,000	5.00

ATLANTA
F-A	99,999,999	3.00
F-B	99,999,999	8.00
F-C	21,120,000	20.00
F-★	18,880,000	4.00

CHICAGO
G-A,G-C	179,359,999	3.00
G-B	99,999,999	8.00
G-★	15,520,000	4.00

ST. LOUIS
H-A	99,840,000	3.00
H-A	9,600,000	4.00

MINNEAPOLIS
I-A	44,800,000	3.00
I-★	5,120,000	5.00

KANSAS CITY
J-A	88,960,000	3.00
J-★	8,960,000	4.00

DALLAS
K-A	85,760,000	3.00
K-★	8,960,000	4.00

SAN FRANCISCO
L-A	99,999,999	3.00
L-B	99,999,999	8.00
L-★	14,400,000	10.00

SERIES 1963A

SERIAL NUMBERS: All districts started both regular and star notes with serial 00 000 001.
SIGNATURES: Kathryn O'Hay Granahan, Henry H. Fowler

SERIAL NUMBERS	NOTES PRINTED	CU
BOSTON		
A-A	99,999,999	$3.00
A-B	99,999,999	5.00
A-C,A-D	119,839,999	3.00
A-★	8,360,000	4.00

NEW YORK		
B-A,B-E through,**B-G**	350,599,997	3.00
B-B	99,999,999	8.00

B-C,B-D	199,999,999	6.00
B-★	48,800,000	3.50

PHILADELPHIA

C-A,C-C,C-D	275,519,998	3.00
C-B	99,999,999	4.00
C-★	24,760,000	3.50

CLEVELAND

D-A through **D-D**	37,120,000	3.00
D-★	21,120,000	3.50

RICHMOND

E-A through **E-F**	631,999,994	3.00
E-★	41,600,000	3.50

ATLANTA

F-A through **F-G**	636,479,994	3.00
F-★	40,960,000	3.50

CHICAGO

G-A,G-D through **G-H,**	499,999,995	3.00
G-B,G-C	199,999,998	5.00
G-★	52,640,000	3.50

ST. LOUIS

H-A,H-C	117,919,999	3.00
H-B	99,999,999	5.00
H-★	17,920,000	3.50

MINNEAPOLIS

I-A	99,999,999	3.00
I-B	12,160,000	10.00
I-★	7,040,000	3.50

KANSAS CITY

J-A through **J-C**	219,199,998	3.00
J-★	14,720,000	3.50

DALLAS

K-A through **K-C**	288,959,998	3.00
K-★	19,184,000	3.50

SAN FRANCISCO

L-A through **L-F**	576,799,995	3.00
L-★	43,040,000	3.50

SERIES 1963B

SIGNATURES: Kathryn O'Hay Granahan, Joseph W. Barr

SERIAL NUMBERS	**NOTES PRINTED**	**CU**
NEW YORK		
B58137327**G** Known high	123,039,999	$3.50
B-H	80,640,000	3.50
B52113564* Known	3,680,000	4.50

	RICHMOND		
E-F	67,999,999		3.50
E-G	25,600,000		4.00
E-★	3,040,000		5.00
	CHICAGO		
G-H	15,519,999		4.00
G-I	75,520,000		3.50
G-★	2,400,000		4.50
	KANSAS CITY		
J-C	44,800,000		4.00
	SAN FRANCISCO		
L-F,L-G	106,399,999		4.00
L-★	3,040,000		4.50

SERIES 1969

SIGNATURES: Dorothy Andrews Elston, David M. Kennedy

SERIAL NUMBERS	NOTES PRINTED	VG/F	CU
	BOSTON		
A-A	99,200,000		$2.50
A-★	5,120,000		3.00
	NEW YORK		
B-A through B-C	269,119,998		2.50
B-★	13,760,000		3.00
	PHILADELPHIA		
C-A	68,480,000		2.50
C-★	3,776,000		3.00
C 05 120 00 ★C 05 753 000★	416,000	50.00	250.00

After completion of the printing of Series 1969A, 13,000 sheeets of Series 1969 without third printing were found. Rather than waste these sheets, the Bureau decided to overprint them as star notes. The production schedule called for star notes for Philadelphia, so the 13,000 sheets were scheduled for this district. Serial numbers up to 05 120 000 had already been used for 1969A Philadelphia star notes, so the first serial number assigned for this production was 05 120 001.

This special run was not realized by collectors until 15 to18 months after the notes had been issued, and locating even circulated examples of these high numbered, 1969 C-★'s, has been very difficult.

CLEVELAND

D-A,D-B	120,479,999	2.50
D-★	5,600,000	3.00

RICHMOND

E-A through **E-C**	250,559,998	2.50
E-★		3.00

ATLANTA

F-A,F-B	186,119,999	2.50
F-★	7,520,000	3.00

CHICAGO

G-A through **G-D**	359,519,997	2.50
G 11 317 973★ High known	7,840,000	3.00

ST. LOUIS

H-A	74,880,000	2.50
H-★	3,840,000	3.00

MINNEAPOLIS

I-A	48,000,000	2.50
I-★	1,920,000	4.00

KANSAS CITY

J-A	95,360,000	2.50
J-★	5,760,000	3.00

DALLAS

K.A	99,999,999	2.50
K-B	13,440,000	3.00
K-★	4,960,000	3.00

SAN FRANCISCO

L-A through **L-C**	226,239,998	2.50
L-★	9,280,000	3.50

SERIES 1969A

SIGNATURES: Dorothy Andrews Kabis, David M. Kennedy

SERIAL NUMBERS	NOTES PRINTED	CU
BOSTON		
A-A	799,999	$6.00
A-B	39,680,000	2.50
A-★	1,120,000	4.00

NEW YORK
B-C,B-D	122,399,999	2.50
B-★	6,240,000	3.00

PHILADELPHIA
C-A	31,519,999	2.50
C-B	13,440,000	3.00
C-★	1,760,000	3.50

CLEVELAND
D-B	30,080,000	2.50
D-★	1,280,000	4.00

RICHMOND
E 55 045 933 C Known	49,439,999	2.50
E-D	16,640,000	3.00
E-★	3,040,000	3.00

ATLANTA
F-B,F-C	70,559,999	2.50
F-★	2,400,000	3.00

CHICAGO
G-D,G-E	75,679,999	2.50
G-★	4,320,000	3.00

ST. LOUIS
H-A,H-B	41,419,999	2.50
H-★	1,200,000	3.50

MINNEAPOLIS
I-A	21,760,000	3.00
I-★	640,000	5.00

KANSAS CITY
J-A	4,639,999	3.00
J-B	35,840,000	2.50
J 06 428 723 ★ High known	1,120,000	4.00

DALLAS
K-B	27,520,000	3.00

SAN FRANCISCO
L-C	51,840,000	2.50
L-★	3,840,000	3.00

SERIES **1969B**

SIGNATURES: Dorothy Andrews Kabis, John B. Connally

SERIAL NUMBERS	NOTES PRINTED	CU
BOSTON		
A-A	94,720,000	$2.50
A-★	1,920,000	3.50
NEW YORK		
B-A through D	329,439,997	2.50
B-★	6,560,000	3.00

PHILADELPHIA		
C-A,C-B	133,279,999	2.50
C-★	3,040,000	3.00
CLEVELAND		
D-A	91,520,000	2.50
D-★	4,480,000	3.00
RICHMOND		
E-A,E-B	179,999,999	2.50
E-★	3,680,000	3.00
ATLANTA		
F-A,F-B	170,399,999	2.50
F-★	3,680,000	3.00
CHICAGO		
G-A,G-B	199,999,998	2.50
G-C	4,480,000	3.00
G-★	4,160,000	3.00
ST. LOUIS		
H-A	59,520,000	2.50
H-★	1,920,000	3.00
MINNEAPOLIS		
I-A	33,920,000	2.50
I-★	640,000	3.50
KANSAS CITY		
J-A	67,200,000	2.50
J-★	2,560,000	3.00
DALLAS		
K-A,K-B	116,639,999	2.50
K-★	4,960,000	3.00
SAN FRANCISCO		
L-A,L-B	199,999,998	2.50
L-C	8,960,000	3.00
L-★	5,440,000	3.00

SERIES **1969C**

SIGNATURES: Romana Acosta Banuelos, John B. Connally

SERIAL NUMBERS	NOTES PRINTED	CU
NEW YORK		
B-D	49,920,000	$2.50

	CLEVELAND	
D-A,D-B	15,520,000	2.50
D-★	480,000	5.00
	RICHMOND	
E-B,E-C	61,599,999	2.50
E-★	480,000	5.00
	ATLANTA	
F-B,F-C	60,959,999	2.50
F-★	3,600,000	3.50
	CHICAGO	
G-C,G-D	147,129,999	2.50
G-★	1,373,000	4.00
	ST. LOUIS	
H-A	23,680,000	2.50
H-★	640,000	4.00
	MINNEAPOLIS	
I-A	25,600,000	3.50
I-★	640,000	4.50
	KANSAS CITY	
J-A,J-B	38,559,999	2.50
J-★	1,120,000	4.00
	DALLAS	
K-B	29,440,000	2.50
K-★	640,000	4.00
	SAN FRANCISCO	
L-C,L-D	101,279,999	2.50
L-★	2,400,000	20.00

SERIES **1969D**

SIGNATURES: Romana Acosta Banuelos, George P. Shultz

SERIAL NUMBERS	NOTES PRINTED	CU
	BOSTON	
A-A,A-B	187,039,999	$2.50
A-★	1,840,000	3.50

NEW YORK
B-A through B-E	468,479,996	2.50
B-★	4,400,000	3.00

PHILADELPHIA
C-A through C-C	218,559,998	2.50
C-★	4,320,000	3.00

CLEVELAND
D-A,D-B	161,439,999	2.50
D-★	2,400,000	3.00

RICHMOND
E-A through E- D	374,239,997	2.50
E-★	8,480,000	3.00

ATLANTA
F-A through F-D	377,439,997	2.50
F-★	5,480,000	3.00

CHICAGO
G-A through G-D	378,079,997	2.50
G-★	4,560,000	3.00

ST. LOUIS
H-A,H-B	168,479,999	2.50
H-★	1,760,000	3.50

MINNEAPOLIS
I-A	83,200,000	2.50

KANSAS CITY
J-A,J-B	185,779,999	2.50
J-★	3,040,000	3.00

DALLAS
K-A,K-B	158,239,999	2.50
K-★	6,240,000	3.50

SAN FRANCISCO
L-A through L-D	399,999,996	2.50
L-E	640,000	10.00
L-★	6,400,000	3.50

SERIES 1974

SIGNATURES: Francine I. Neff, William E. Simon
PLATE SERIALS: Face check begins with #1. Back check continues from previous series. Back check 1472 is lowest observed. Back check 905 is an actual B.E.P. error, should be 1905.

SERIAL NUMBERS	NOTES PRINTED	CU
	BOSTON	
A-A through **A-C**	269,759,998	$2.00
A-★	1,828,000	3.00
	NEW YORK	
B-A through **B-H**	740,159,994	2.00
B-★	5,808,000	3.00
	PHILADELPHIA	
C-A through **C-C**	299,839,998	2.00
C-D	8,960,000	3.00
C-★	1,600,000	3.00
	CLEVELAND	
D-A through **D-C**	240,959,998	2.00
D-★	960,000	4.00
	RICHMOND	
E-A through **E-G**	644,159,994	2.00
E-★	4,960,000	3.00
	ATLANTA	
F-A through **F-F**	599,679,996	2.00
F-★	4,352,000	3.00
	CHICAGO	
G-A through **G-E**	473,599,996	2.00
G-★	4,992,000	3.00
	ST. LOUIS	
H-A through **H-C,**	291,519,998	2.00
H-★	2,880,000	3.00

SERIAL NUMBERS	NOTES PRINTED	CU
	MINNEAPOLIS	
I-A,I-B	144,159,999	2.00
I-★	480,000	10.00
	KANSAS CITY	
J-A through **J-C**	223,519,999	2.00
J-★	2,144,000	3.00
	DALLAS	
K-A,K-C,K-D	229,959,999	2.00
K-B	99,999,999	3.00
K-★	1,216,600	3.00
	SAN FRANCISCO	
L-A through **L-H**	736,959,994	2.00
L-★	3,520,000	3.00

SERIES 1977

SIGNATURES: Azie Taylor Morton, W. Michael Blumenthal
PLATE SERIALS: Check numbers continued from previous series.

SERIAL NUMBERS	NOTES PRINTED	CU
BOSTON		
A-A,A-B	188,160,000	$2.00
A-★	2,428,000	3.00
NEW YORK		
B-A through ,B-G	635,520,000	2.00
B-★	10,112,000	3.00
PHILADELPHIA		
C-A through C-C	217,279,998	2.00
C-★	3,840,000	3.00
CLEVELAND		
D-A through D-C	213,120,000	2.00
D-★	3,200,000	3.00
RICHMOND		
E-A through E-E	418,560,000	2.00
E-★	6,400,000	3.00
ATLANTA		
F-A through F-F	565,120,000	2.00
F-★	8,940,000	3.00

CHICAGO		
G-A through G-G	615,680,000	2.00
G-★	9,472,000	3.00
ST. LOUIS		
H-A,H-B	199,680,000	2.00
H-★	2,048,000	3.00
MINNEAPOLIS		
I-A,I-B	117,200,000	2.00
I-★	2,560,000	3.00
KANSAS CITY		
J-A through J-C	223,360,000	2.00
J-★	3,760,000	3.00
DALLAS		
K-A through K-C	289,280,000	2.00
K-★	4,704,000	3.00
SAN FRANCISCO		
L-A through,L-F	516,480,000	2.00
L-★	8,320,000	3.00

SERIES **1977A**

SIGNATURES: Azie Taylor Morton, J. William Miller
PLATE SERIALS: Highest face check #2185. Highest back check #3297.

SERIAL NUMBERS: All serials for this series continued from Series 1977, with the exception of the Richmond star which reverted to 00 000 001.

SERIAL NUMBERS	NOTES PRINTED	CU
BOSTON		
A-B through **A-D**	211,200,000	$2.00
A-★	2,668,000	3.00
NEW YORK		
B-G through **B-L**	592,000,000	2.00
B-★	9,984,000	2.50
PHILADELPHIA		
C-C through **C-E**	196,480,000	2.00
C-★	2,688,000	2.50
CLEVELAND		
D-C,D-D	174,720,000	2.00
D-★	2,560,000	2.50
RICHMOND		
E-E through **E-H**	377,560,000	2.00
E-★	6,360,000	2.50
ATLANTA		
F-F through **F-J**	396,160,000	2.00
F-★	5,376,000	2.50
CHICAGO		
G-G through **G-I**	250,880,000	2.00
G-★	2,560,000	2.50
ST. LOUIS		
H-C	99,840,000	2.00
H-D	3,840,000	2.50
H-★	5,760,000	2.50
MINNEAPOLIS		
I-B	38,400,000	2.50
I-★	1,024,000	5.00
KANSAS CITY		
J-C through **J-E**	275,840,000	2.00
J-★	4,864,000	2.50

DALLAS		
K-C through **K-F**	309,760,000	2.00
K-G	3,840,000	3.00
K-★	5,504,000	2.50

SAN FRANCISCO

L-F through **L-J**	433,280,000	2.00
L-★	5,888,000	2.50

SERIES 1981

SIGNATURES: Angela M. Buchanan, Donald T. Regan

PLATE SERIALS: Both front and back check numbers begin at 1, but some backs are found muled, using high numbered 1977A backs.

SERIAL NUMBERS: All districts begin at 00 000 001.

SERIAL NUMBERS	NOTES PRINTED	CU
BOSTON		
A-A through **A-C**,	299,520,000	2.00
A-D	9,600,000	2.50
A-★	4,480.00	3.50
NEW YORK		
B-A through **B-J**	965,760,000	2.00
B-★	12,800,000	3.50
PHILADELPHIA		
C-A through **C-D**	360,320,000	2.00
C-★	1,920,000	3.50
CLEVELAND		
D-A through **D-C**	295,680,000	2.00
D-H	160,000	10.00
D-★	3,200,000	3.50
RICHMOND		
E-A through	599,440,000	2.00
E-G	6,400,000	15.00
E-H	160,000	25.00
E-★	3,840,000	3.50
ATLANTA		
F-A through **F-H**	743,680,000	2.00
F-★	32,000,0000	3.50
CHICAGO		
G-A through **G-G**	631,040,000	2.00
G-★	5,760,000	3.50
ST. LOUIS		
H-A through **H-C**	263,680,000	2.00
H-D		
H-E		
H-★	1,619,000	3.50
MINNEAPOLIS		
I-A	99,840,000	2.00
I-B	35,200,000	3.00
I-★	1,920,000	3.50
KANSAS CITY		
J-A through **J-C**	299,620,000	2.00
J-D	3,200,000	50.00
J-★	3,840,000	3.50
DALLAS		
K-A through **K-D**	385 920,000	2.00
K-★	1,920,000	3.50

SAN FRANCISCO

L-A through **L-G**	679,040,000	2.00
L-★	6,400,000	3.50

SERIES **1981A**

SIGNATURES: Katherine Davalos Ortega, Donald T. Regan.

PLATE SERIALS: Both front and back check numbers begin at 1, but some backs are found muled using high numbered 1981 backs early in the run, and 1985 low numbered backs late in the run.

SERIAL NUMBERS	NOTES PRINTED	CU
BOSTON		
A-A,A-B	198,400,000	$3.00
A-C	6,400,000	6.00
NEW YORK		
B-A through **B-F**	595,200,000	2.50
B-★	3,328,000	3.50
PHILADELPHIA		
C-A	99,200,000	3.00
C 99 980 055 B Uncut sheets only see Appendix		
CLEVELAND		
D-A,D-B	188,800,000	2.50
RICHMOND		
E-A through **E-E**	496,000,000	3.00
E-★	8,320,000	2.50
ATLANTA		
F-A through ,**F-E**	483,200,000	2.50
CHICAGO		
G-A through **G-E**	432,000,000	2.50
G-★	3,200,000	3.50
ST. LOUIS		
H-A,H-B	182,400,600	3.00

MINNEAPOLIS

I-A	99,200,000	3.00
I-B	3,200,000	5.00

KANSAS CITY

J-A,J-B	176,000,000	3.00

DALLAS

K-A,K-B	188,800,000	3.00
K-★	3,200,000	35.00

SAN FRANCISCO

L-A through L-G	659,200,000	2.50
L-★	3,200,000	3.50

SERIES 1985

SIGNATURES: Katherine Davalos Ortega, John A. Baker III.

PLATE SERIALS: Both front and back check numbers begin at 1, through low backs are only seen in mid run.

SERIAL NUMBERS	NOTES PRINTED	CU
BOSTON		
A-A through A-F	553,600,000	$2.00
NEW YORK		
B-A through B-T	1,836,800.000	2.00
PHILADELPHIA		
C-A through C-E	422,400,000	2.00
CLEVELAND		
D-A through ,D-G	636,800,000	2.00
RICHMOND		
E-A through E-N	1,388,800,000	2.00
E-★	6,400,000	2.50
ATLANTA		
F-A through F-P	1,513,600,000	2.00

	CHICAGO	
G-A through G-L	1,190,400,000	2.00
G-★		2.50
	ST. LOUIS	
H-A through H-E	400,000,000	2.00
H-★	3,200,000	15.00
	MINNEAPOLIS	
I-A through I-C	297,600,000	2.00
I-D	96,000	12.00
I-★	3,200,000	3.00
	KANSAS CITY	
J-A through J-D	396,800,000	2.00
	DALLAS	
K-A through ,K-H	793,600,000	2.00
K -★	3,200,000	3.00
	SAN FRANCISCO	
L-A through L-T	1,980,800,000	2.00
L-★	9,600,000	2.50

SERIES 1988

SIGNATURES: Katherine Davalos Ortega, Nicholas F. Brady

SERIAL NUMBERS	NOTES PRINTED	CU
	BOSTON	
A-A through A-C	214,400,000	$3.00
A-★	3,200,000	5.00
	NEW YORK	
B-A through B-J	921,400,000	2.50
B-★	2,560,000	3.00
	PHILADELPHIA	
C-A	96,000,000	4.00
	CLEVELAND	
D-A,D-B	195,200,000	3.50
	RICHMOND	
E-A through E-G	458,480,000	3.00
E-★	2,688,000	4.50
	ATLANTA	
F-A through F-D	396,800,000	3.00
F-★	3,840,000	150.00

SERIAL NUMBERS	NOTES PRINTED	CU
CHICAGO		
G-A through **G-E**	422,400,000	3.00
ST. LOUIS		
H-A through **H-D**	384,000,000	3.00
MINNEAPOLIS		
I-A,I-B	124,800,000	3.00
KANSAS CITY		
J-A,J-B	137,600,000	3.00
J-★	3,200,000	4.50
DALLAS		
K-A	80,000,000	4.00
K-★	1,248,000	6.00
SAN FRANCISCO		
L-A, through **L-F**	585,600,000	3.00
L-★	3,200,000	6.00

SERIES **1988A**

(Series 1988A discontinued in April 1994; Series 1993 begun in April 1994.)

SIGNATURES: Catalina Vasquez Villalpando, Nicholas F. Brady
All printings in Washington unless otherwise indicated.

SERIAL NUMBERS	NOTES PRINTED	CU
BOSTON		
A-A through **A-G**	672,000,000	$2.00
A-★		
NEW YORK		
B-A through **B-X**	2,163,200,000	2.00
B 16 000 000 ★	14,080,000	2.50
PHILADELPHIA		
C-A through **C-E**	473,600,000	2.00
CLEVELAND		
D-A through **D-E**	454,400,000	2.00
D-★	6,400,000	2.50
RICHMOND		
E-A through **E-Q**	1,504,600,000	2.00
E-R	6,400,000	20.00
E-★	9,600,000	2.50
ATLANTA		
F-A through **F-M**,	1,248,000,000	2.00
F-N through **F-U W/FW**	672,000,000	2.00

F-P	FW		
F-Q	FW		
F-R	FW		
F-S	FW		
F-T	FW		
F-U	W/FW		
F-V through F-Y		371,200,000	2.00
F-W		96,000,000	2.00
F-X		96,000,000	2.00
F-Y		83,200,000	2.00
F-★		12,800,000	2.50

CHICAGO

G-A through G-G, G-J, G-K, G-R, G-X, G-Y		1,081,600,000	2.00
G-H	W/FW		
G-I	W/FW		
G-L	W/FW		
G-M	FW		
G-N	FW		
G-P	W/FW		
G-Q	W/FW		
G-S	F/FW		
G-T	FW		
G-U	F/FW		
G-V	W/FW		
G-W	W/FW		
G-★	W/FW	25,600,000	2.50

ST. LOUIS

H-A through H-C, H-G		339,200,000	2.00
H-D, H-F	W/FW	334,800,000	2.00
H-E	FW	96,000,000	2.00
H 57 852 078 H	FW		
H-I			
H-★		3,200,000	2.50

MINNEAPOLIS

I-A through I-J	W/FW	672,000,000	2.00
I-B	FW		
I-C	FW		
I-D	FW		
I-E	FW		
I-F	FW		
I-G	FW		
I-H	FW		
I-I			
I-J			
I-★	W/FW	12,800,000	2.50

KANSAS CITY

J-A		96,000,000	2.00
J-B, J-C	FW	185,600,000	2.00

DALLAS

K-A, K-B		195,200,000	2.00
K-C	W/FW	96,000,000	2.50
K-D through K-I	FW	576,000,000	2.00
K-★	FW	3,200,000	2.50

SAN FRANCISCO

L-A,L-B		192,000,000	2.00
L-C	W/FW	96,000,000	2.00
L-D through L-P FW		1,152,000,000	2.00

L-Q through L-Y FW		851,200,000	2.00
L-★	FW	19,200,000	2.50

SERIES 1988A WEB-FED Press Printings

With an initial press run in May, 1992, the Bureau of Engraving and printing began testing the high volume Web-Fed intaglio currency press in actual production. With this press, both sides of the note are printed in a single pass of a continuous roll of paper from a printing cylinder of 96 subjects or notes.

Some obvious face design changes including the removal of the face check letters and quadrant number. Check numbers begin a new sequence on both face and back with #1. The back check number has been relocated to the right of the word "TRUST".

Face check numbers used to press time include 1, 2, 3, 4, 5, 8, 9, 10.

Back check numbers in use include 1, 2, 4, 5, 6, 7, 8.

The compilation of the Web Fed Press production data was enabled by the research of Jim Hodgson and Bob Vandevender.

The printings are as follows:

SERIAL NUMBERS	NOTES PRINTED	VG/F	CU
BOSTON			
A25 600 001E – A32 000 000E	6,400,000		$25.00
A38 400 001E – A44 800 000E	6,400,000		10.00
A57 600 001E – A64 000 000E	6,400,000		10.00
A00 000 001F – A12 800 000F	12,800,000		10.00
A83 200 001F – A96 000 000F	12,800,000		10.00
A00 000 001G – A19 200 000G	19,200,000		10.00
NEW YORK			
B32 000 001L – B38 400 000L	1,920,000	250.00	500.00
PHILADELPHIA			
C64 000 001A – C76 800 000A	12,800,000		10.00
RICHMOND			
E44 800 001I – E64 000 000I	19,200,000		10.00
E44 800 001K – E64 000 000K	19,200,000		10.00
ATLANTA			
F70 400 001L – F76 800 000L	6,400,000		100.00
F83 200 001L – F89 600 000L	6,400,000		100.00
F00 000 001M – F06 400 000M	6,400,000		100.00
F57 600 001N – F76 800 000N	19,200,000		10.00
F51 200 001U – F57 600 000U	6,400,000		10.00
F64 000 001U – F70 400 000U	6,400,000		10.00
F89 600 001U – F96 000 000U	6,400,000		10.00
F06 400 001V – F12 800 000V	6,400,000		10.00
F19 200 001V – F25 600 000V	6,400,000		10.00
F38 400 001V – F44 800 000V	6,400,000		10.00
F57 600 001V – F64 000 000V	6,400,000		10.00
F76 800 001V – F83 200 000V	6,400,000		25.00
F89 600 001V – F96 000 000V	6,400,000		50.00
F06 400 001★ – F09 600 000★	640,000	450.00	750.00
CHICAGO			
G44 800 001P – G57 600 000P	12,800,000		150.00
G44 800 001Q – G51 200 000Q	6,400,000		50.00

SERIES 1993

SERIAL NUMBERS: All districts started numbering both regular and star notes with 00 000 001.

PLATE SERIALS: Face check numbers begin at #1. Back check letters are believed to have begun at #1 as # 2 has been observed on a 1993.

SIGNATURES: Mary Ellen Withrow, Lloyd Bentsen.

LOW SERIAL NUMBERS	HIGH		NOTES PRINTED	CU
BOSTON				
A-A, A-B	A44 800 000H		140,800,000	$2.00
NEW YORK				
B-A,-B-H	B44 800 000H		716,800,000	2.00
B-★	B09 600 000★		5,760,000	2.50
PHILADELPHIA				
C-A	C70 400 000A		70,400,000	2.00
C-★	C00 640 000★		640 000	5.00

CLEVELAND			
D-A,D-B	D12 800 000B	108,800,000	2.00
RICHMOND			
E-A,-E-E	E76 800 000E	460,800,000	2.00
ATLANTA			
F-A,-F-H	F51 200 000H	723,200,000	2.00
F-★	F09 600 000★	9,600,000	2.50
CHICAGO			
G-A through **G-G** W		96,000,000	2.00
G-B through **G-G** FW	G32 000 000G	512,000,000	2.00
G-★ FW	G06 400 000★	6,400,000	2.50
ST. LOUIS			
H-A W		96,000,000	
H-B through **H-C** FW	H25 600 000C	121,600,000	2.00
MINNEAPOLIS			
I-A FW	I25 600 000A	25,600,000	5.00
DALLAS			
K-A through **K-E** FW	K96 000 000E	480,000,000	2.00
K-★ FW	K12 800 000★	12,800,000	2.50
SAN FRANCISCO			
L-A through **L-K** W/FW	L89 600 000K	1,145,600,000	2.00

SERIES 1993 WEB-FED Press Printing

PLATE SERIALS: Face check number used: 1. Back check numbers used: 8, 9, 10.

SERIAL NUMBERS	NOTES PRINTED		CU
NEW YORK			
B19 200 001**H**	B25 600 000**H**	6,400,000	$6.00
B38 400 001**H**	B44 800 000**H**	6,400,000	6.00
PHILADELPHIA			
C38 400 001**A**	C44 800 000**A**	6,400,000	6.00
C51 200 001**A**	C57 600 000**A**	6,400,000	6.00

SERIES 1995

SIGNATURES: Mary Ellen Withrow, Robert E. Rubin.
PLATE SERIALS: Both face and back check numbers begin at #1.

SERIAL NUMBERS: Both regular and star notes begin at 00 000 0001.

LOW HIGH SERIAL NUMBERS		NOTES PRINTED	CU
BOSTON			
A-A through **A-I**	A83 200 000I	851,200,000	$2.00
A-★	A14 720 000★	9,600,000	2.50
NEW YORK			
B-A through **B-Q**	B51 200 000Q	1,491,200,000	2.00
B-★	B06 720 000★	3,520,000	3.00
PHILADELPHIA			
C-A through **C-C**	C57 600 000C	249,600,000	2.00
C-★	C03 200 000★	3,200,000	3.00
CLEVELAND			
D-A through **D-D**	D32 000 000D	320,000,000	2.00
RICHMOND			
E-A through **E-G**	E19 200 000G	595,200,000	2.00

ATLANTA

F-A through F-K	F64 000 000K	1,024,000,000	2.00
F-★	F14 080 000★	11,520,000	2.50

CHICAGO

G-A through G-H FW	G06 400 000H	678,400,000	2.00

ST. LOUIS

H-A through H-D FW	H06 400 000D	294,400,000	2.50

MINNEAPOLIS

I-A FW	I12 800 000A	12,800,000	2.50

KANSAS CITY

J-A through J-C FW	J70 400 000C	262,400,000	2.00

DALLAS

K-A through K-E FW	K12 800 000E	396,800,000	2.00

SAN FRANCISCO

L-A through L-J FW	L57 600 000J	921,600,000	2.00

SERIES 1995 WEB-FED Press Printings

PLATE SERIALS: Face check numbers used: 1, 2, 3, 4, 5, 6, 7. Back check numbers used: 8, 9, 10, 12.

SERIAL NUMBERS	NOTES PRINTED		CU

BOSTON

A32 000 001C	A38 400 000C	6,400,000	$6.00
A38 400 001C	A44 800 000C	6,400,000	6.00
A76 820 001D	A83 200 000D	5,760,000	15.00

NEW YORK

B32 000 001H	B38 400 000H	6,400,000	6.00
B44 800 001H	B51 200 000H	6,400,000	6.00

CLEVELAND

D64 000 001C	D70 400 000C	6,400,000	5.00

ATLANTA

F83 200 001D	F89 600 000D	6,400,000	6.00
F89 600 001D	F96 000 000D	6,400,000	6.00

The WEB-FED press trial operations were discontinued after the printing of the A-D run in December 1995, due to the bureau's inability to afford the resolution of problems in the peripheral issues connected to the printing operation.

TWO DOLLAR NOTES
LEGAL TENDER
Red Seal
12 Subject
SERIES 1928

PLATE SERIALS: Face check #1 was not used. Face check number ranges #2 through #103. Back check numbers are "micro" type and begin at #1. Some notes are known without a back number.

SIGNATURES: H.T. Tate, Andrew W. Mellon

SERIAL NUMBERS	NOTES PRINTED	VG/F	CU
A00 000 001A through			
A57 010 459A High observed	55,889 424	$12.50	$30.00
★00 000 001A –★00 68 584A observed		75.00	300.00
★00 000 579A			

SERIES 1928A

PLATE SERIALS: Face check #1 (master), #2 and #3 were not used. Face check number #4 through #93.

SIGNATURES: Walter O. Woods, Andrew W. Mellon

SERIAL NUMBERS		NOTES PRINTED	VG/F	CU
A51 112 758A	through A99 999 999A	46,859,136	$35.00	$150.00
B00 000 001A	through			
B08 965 670A	High observed		150.00	350.00
★00 745 016A –★01 055 379A Observed			550.00	2500.00

SERIES 1928B

PLATE SERIALS: Face check #1 through #6 not used. Face check numbers range #7 through #42.

SIGNATURES: Walter O. Woods, Ogden L. Mills

SERIAL NUMBERS		NOTES PRINTED	VG/F	CU
A87 522 908A	Low observed		$50.00	$425.00
B09 004 381A	High observed	9,001,632	45.00	375.00
★00 943 989A – ★01 053 286A observed			1750.00	3500.00

SERIES 1928C

PLATE SERIALS: Face check number range #1 through #181, excluding #56 through #75 which were not used.
Back check numbers end at #288 (high of the "micro" type).

SIGNATURES: W.A. Julian, Henry Morgenthau, Jr.

SERIAL NUMBERS		NOTES PRINTED	VG/F	CU
B09 008 001**A** **B**99 999 999**A**		86,584,008	$15.00	$75.00
C00 000 001**A** **C**05 594 680**A** High obsvd.			50.00	200.00
★01 082 940**A** ★01 990 816**A** Observed			100.00	400.00

SERIES **1928C MULE**

These are Series 1928C notes with larger back check numbers (#289 or higher), and are actually Series 1928C faces on Series 1928D backs.

SERIAL NUMBERS		NOTES PRINTED	VG/F
B98 473 577**A** **B**99 999 999**A**		see above	$500.00
C00 000 001**A** **C**02 199 891**A**		Observed	350.00

SERIES **1928D MULE**

These are series 1928D notes with the micro back check numbers (#288 or lower), and are actually Series 1928D faces on Series 1928C backs.

SERIAL NUMBERS		NOTES PRINTED	VG/F	CU
B88 695 447**A** **B**99 999 999**A**		Included in	$10.00	$25.00
C00 000 001**A** **C**55 064 693**A**		1928D Total	10.00	25.00
★01 911 287**A** ★02 505 945**A** Observed			25.00	175.00

SERIES **1928D**

PLATE SERIALS: Face check number range is #182 through #401. Back check numbers begin at #289.

SIGNATURES: W.A. Julian, Henry Morgenthau, Jr.

SERIAL NUMBERS		NOTES PRINTED	VG/F	CU
B83 988 001**A** B99 999 999**A**		146,381,364	$250.00	
CA & DA thru **D**35 443 700**A** Observed			4.00	$15.00
★020 300 51**A** − ★03 214 772**A** Observed			20.00	125.00

SERIES **1928E**

PLATE SERIALS: Face check number range #403 through #414.
SIGNATURES: W.A. Julian, Fred M. Vinson

SERIAL NUMBERS		NOTES PRINTED	VG/F	CU
D29 712 001**A** D39 591 186**A**		6,480,000	$15.00	$45.00
★03 212 775**A** ★03 227 372**A** Observed			1200.00	4500.00

SERIES **1928F**

PLATE SERIALS: Face check numbers #440 through #462.
SIGNATURES: W.A. Julian, John W. Snyder

SERIAL NUMBERS OFFICIAL		NOTES PRINTED	VG/F	CU
D36 192 001**A** D81 308 493**A**		42,360,000	$4.00	$18.00
★03 245 546**A** ★03 642 562**A** Observed			20.00	125.00

SERIES **1928G**

PLATE SERIALS: Face check numbers #483 through #516. Back check numbers end at #390 (high of 12 subject sheets)

SIGNATURES: Georgia Neese Clark, John W. Snyder

SERIAL NUMBERS OFFICIAL		NOTES PRINTED	VG/F	CU
D78 552 001**A** E30 760 000**A**		52,208,000	$5.00	$12.50
★03 688 936**A** ★04 152 000**A** Official High				
	★04 130 312**A** Observed	15.00	100.00

SERIES **1953**

PLATE SERIALS: Face check numbers begin at #1. (#8 was not used). Back check numbers begin at #391 (Low of 18 subject sheets).

SIGNATURES: Ivy Baker Priest, George M. Humphrey

SERIAL NUMBERS OFFICIAL		NOTES PRINTED	CU
A00 000 001**A** A45 360 000**A**		45,360,000	$7.50
★00 000 001**A** ★02 160 000**A**		2,160,000	24.00

SERIES **1953A**

SIGNATURES: Ivy Baker Priest, Robert B. Anderson

SERIAL NUMBERS OFFICIAL		NOTES PRINTED	CU
A45 360 001A	A63 360 000A	18,000,000	$5.00
★02 160 001A	★02 880 000A	720,000	35.00

SERIES **1953B**

SIGNATURES: Elizabeth Rudel Smith, C. Douglas Dillon

SERIAL NUMBERS OFFICIAL		NOTES PRINTED	CU
A63 360 001A	A74 160 000A	10,800,000	$5.50
★02 880 001A	★03 600 000A	720,000	18.00

SERIES **1953C**

SIGNATURES: Kathryn O'Hay Granahan, C. Douglas Dillon

PLATE SERIALS: Back check numbers used on 18 subject sheets end at #412. Face check numbers used on 18 subject sheets end at #16.

SERIAL NUMBERS OFFICIAL		NOTES PRINTED	CU
A74 160 001**A**	**A**79 920 000**A**	5,760,000	$6.50
★03 600 001**A**	★03 960 000**A**	360,000	30.00

SERIES 1963

PLATE SERIALS: Both face and back check numbers on 32 subject sheets begin at #1.

SIGNATURES: Kathryn O'Hay Granahan, C. Douglas Dillon

SERIAL NUMBERS OFFICIAL		NOTES PRINTED	CU
A00 000 001**A**	**A**15 360 000**A**	15,360,000	$5.00
★00 000 001**A**	★00 653 000**A** High observed	640,000	10.00

SERIES 1963A

PLATE SERIALS: Both face and back check numbers end at #3.

SIGNATURES: Kathryn O'Hay Granahan, Henry H. Fowler

SERIAL NUMBERS OFFICIAL		NOTES PRINTED	CU
A15 360 001**A**	**A**18 560 000**A**	3,200,000	$7.50
★00 640 001**A**	★01 280 000**A**	640,000	17.00

The printing of the $2 United States Note terminated with Series 1963A.

FEDERAL RESERVE NOTE

SERIES 1976

GREEN SEAL

SIGNATURES: Francine I. Neff, William E. Simon
PLATE SERIALS: Face check numbers 1 through 80, 93,94 and 98. Back check numbers 1 through 78, 84 and 100. These notes were not readily accepted by the public and therefore large stocks of unissued notes remain in the vaults of the Bureau and the Federal Reserve banks.

LOW SERIAL NUMBER	HIGH	NOTES PRINTED	VALUE CU
BOSTON			
A00 000 001A	A29 440 000A	29,440,000	$4.00
A00 000 001★	A01 280 000★	1,280,000	6.00

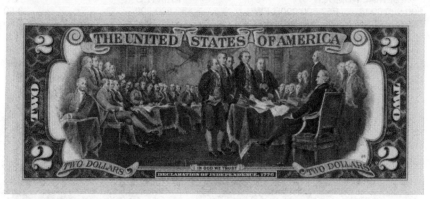

		NEW YORK	
B00 000 001A	B67 200 000A	67,200,000	4.00
B00 000 001★	B02 560 000★	2,560,000	5.00
		PHILADELPHIA	
C00 000 001A	C33 280 000A	33,800,000	4.00
C00 000 001★	C01 280 000★	1,280,000	6.00
		CLEVELAND	
D00 000 001A	D31 360 000A	31,630,000	4.00
D00 000 001★	D01 280 000★	1,280,000	6.00

RICHMOND

E00 000 001**A**	E56 960 000**A**	56,960,000	4.00
E00 000 001	E99 589 777**B**	99,000,000	4.00
E00 000 001★	E00 640 000★	640,000	6.00

ATLANTA

F00 000 001**A**	F60 800 000**A**	60,800,000	4.00
F00 000 001★	F01 280 000★	1,280,000	6.00

CHICAGO

G00 000 001**A**	G77 604 710**A**	84,480,000	4.00
G00 000 001★	G01 280 000★	1,280,000	6.00

ST. LOUIS

H00 000 001**A**	H39 040 000**A**	39,040,000	4.00
H00 000 001★	H01 280 000★	1,280,000	6.00

MINNEAPOLIS

I00 000 001**A**	I99 072 725**A**	99,000,000	4.00
I00 000 001★	I00 640 000★	640,000	6.00

KANSAS CITY

J00 000 001**A**	J24 960 000**A**	24,960,000	4.00
J00 000 001★	J00 640 000★	640,000	6.00

DALLAS

K00 000 001**A**	K41 600 000**A**	41,600,000	4.00
K00 000 001★	K01 280 000★	1,280,000	6.00

SAN FRANCISCO

L00 000 001**A**	L82 560 000**A**	82,560,000	4.00
L00 000 001★	L01 920 000★	1,920,000	6.00

SERIES **1995**

SIGNATURES: Mary Ellen Withrow, Robert E. Rubin
PLATE SERIALS: Both face and back check numbers start at #1.

LOW	HIGH	NOTES	VALUE
SERIAL NUMBER		**PRINTED**	**CU**
F00 000 000**A**	F57 600 000**B** FW	153,600,000	3.50
F00 000 001★	F05 760 000★ **FW**	1,280,000	7.50

FIVE DOLLAR NATIONAL BANK NOTES

Brown Seal

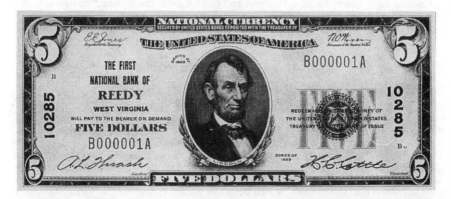

Type I has black serial numbers on the ends of the note. The left reading horizontally, the right reading vertically. Type II is similar, but the brown serial number is succeeded or preceded by the charter number also. All notes have facsimile signatures of E. E. Jones and W. O. Woods at the top. Signatures of the officers of the local bank appear at the bottom.

Note-Issuing National Banks
State-City Alphabetical Listing with Bank Rarity Rating

Bank and state rarity figures are based on data derived from the *Standard Catalog of National Bank Notes*, by John Hickman and Dean Oakes, the standard reference to this popularly-collected currency series.

R6 Very Rare — 0-2 notes known
R5 Rare — 3-5 notes known
R4 Very Scarce — 6-11 notes known
R3 Scarce — 12-25 notes known
R2 Common — 25-50 notes known
R1 Very Common — 50+ notes known

State/Bank Rarity Valuation Tables

The following tables provide approximate base figures for the value of any National Bank Note with a particular state/bank rarity combination. These tables may be used in conjunction with the bank rarity listings which follow to help determine a ballpark value.

While other factors, such as popularity of bank or city name, changing collector demand or the note's type/variety/denomination combination will affect value, the figures given in these tables can generally be regarded as a base value.

All valuations are for notes in Very Fine condition. Except in cases of the highest bank/state rarity combinations, notes in lesser grade will command a lower price. Notes in higher grade will command a higher price.

State Rarity Ranking — Small Size Nationals

Rarity 1
Pennsylvania
New York
California
Massachusetts
Illinois

Rarity 2
Wisconsin
Iowa
Kansas
New Jersey
Texas
Ohio

Rarity 3
Nebraska
Indiana
Minnesota
Michigan

Rarity 4
Alabama
Maryland

Colorado
Kentucky
Florida
Oklahoma
Tennessee
North Carolina
Missouri

Rarity 5
Virginia
West Virginia
Georgia
Washington
Mississippi
South Dakota
South Carolina
Wyoming
Connecticut
New Hampshire

Rarity 6
Louisiana
Oregon

Utah
North Dakota
Dist. Columbia

Rarity 7
Maine
Arkansas
Rhode Island

Rarity 8
New Mexico
Vermont

Rarity 9
Delaware
Idaho
Hawaii
Arizona
Montana
Nevada

Rarity 10
Alaska

NOTES IN VF CONDITIONS

Bank Rarity	1	2	3	4	5	6
State Rarity 1	20	25	30	35	60	175
State Rarity 2	20	25	30	35	65	195
State Rarity 3	25	30	35	40	70	200
State Rarity 4	25	30	35	40	80	230
State Rarity 5	30	35	40	50	95	280
State Rarity 6	35	40	45	55	110	315
State Rarity 7	35	40	45	55	125	350
State Rarity 8	40	50	65	75	150	440
State Rarity 9	125	165	175	200	330	960
State Rarity 10	—	—	5,000	5,000	—	—

National Bank, Year of Organization

Many collectors find it desirable to learn the year in which a particular National Bank was organized. The charter number which appears on the notes can yield that information when matched with the following list.

13160 to 13269 — 1928
13270 to 13412 — 1929
13413 to 13516 — 1930
13517 to 13586 — 1931

13587 to 13654 — 1932
13655 to 13920 — 1933
13921 to 14317 — 1934
14318 to 14348 — 1935

FIVE DOLLAR NOTES
FEDERAL RESERVE
BANK NOTES
Brown Seal
SERIES 1929

SERIAL NUMBERS: Figures shown below are the official high numbers. All districts started both regular and star notes with serial 00 000 001. Bureau of Engraving and Printing information is incomplete on star serial numbers, as are reports of High Observed Serial Numbers.

PLATE SERIALS: Face check numbers within the range, #1 through #910.

SIGNATURES: E.E. Jones, W.O. Woods, and the Federal Reserve Bank Cashier or Controller or the Deputy or Assistant Deputy Governor, with the Governor.

Collectors are requested to supply information on star serial numbers.

SERIAL NUMBERS		NOTES PRINTED	VF	CU
		BOSTON		
A00 000 001A	A03 180 000A	3,180,000	$22.50	$70.00
A00 012 190★		36,000	75.00	575.00
		NEW YORK		
B00 000 003A	B00 007 123A	2,100,000	22.50	60.00
B00 046 601★		24,000	75.00	400.00
		PHILADELPHIA		
C00 000 005A	C03 022 801A	3,096,000	22.50	70.00
C00 000 341★		36,000	75.00	575.00
		CLEVELAND		
D00 000 040A	D04 036 860A	4,236,000	22.50	60.00
D00 001 417★		60,000	60.00	475.00
		RICHMOND		
Not Printed.				
		ATLANTA		
F00 000 012A	F00 018 316A	1,884,000	27.50	100.00
F00 002 604★		24,000	60.00	600.00

CHICAGO				
G00 000 001A	G00 075 808A	5,988,000	20.00	75.00
G00 000 677★		84,000	40.00	500.00
ST. LOUIS				
H00 000 001A	H00 276 000A	276,000	150.00	750.00
H★		24,000	1000.00	4000.00
MINNEAPOLIS				
I00 000 020A	I00 00 5 774★	684,000	55.00	225.00
I00 005 512★		24,000	750.00	2000.00
KANSAS CITY				
J00 000 008A	J00 003 435A	2,460,000	25.00	85.00
J00 006 560★		48,000	50.00	700.00
DALLAS				
K00 000 034A	K00 996 000A	996,000	30.00	85.00
K00 003 021★		24,000	750.00	2000.00
SAN FRANCISCO				
L00 000 001A	L00 360 000A	360,000	500.00	2000.00
L★		24,000	2500.00	5000.00

US / LEGAL TENDER
Red Seal
SERIES 1928

PLATE SERIALS: Face check range is #5 through #408; face check #1 through #4 were not used. Back check numbers are micro type and begin at #1.

SIGNATURES: Walter O. Woods, Andrew W. Mellon

Serial numbers are those that have been observed.

SERIAL NUMBERS		NOTES PRINTED	VF	CU
A00 000 001A	through C-A	267,209,616	$8.00	$30.00
D14 577 286A	High Observed		50.00	100.00
★00 007 777A	★03 282 332A Observed		75.00	700.00

SERIES 1928A

PLATE SERIALS: Face check range is #3 through #122, #174 and #175. (Face check #1, #2 and #123 through #173 were not used).

SIGNATURES: Walter O. Woods, Ogden L. Mills

SERIAL NUMBERS		NOTES PRINTED	VF	CU
C29 334 214A	Low	58,194,600	$13.00	$60.00
D14 724 105A	High		20.00	75.00
★02 833 522A	★03 330 983A		750.00	3000.

SERIES **1928B MULE**

Macro back check numbers 939 or higher.

SERIAL NUMBERS		NOTES PRINTED	VF	CU
E09 764 160**A**	**E**79 039 659**A**	Included below	$30.00	$70.00
★04 795 133**A**	★05 187 780**A**		150.00	350.00

SERIES **1928B**

PLATE SERIALS: Face check range #1 through #287. Back check numbers end at #938 (High of the micro type).

SIGNATURES: W.A. Julian, Henry Morgenthau, Jr.

SERIAL NUMBERS		NOTES PRINTED	VF	CU
D15 228 001**A**	**E**68 016 167**A**	147,827,340	$9.00	$20.00
★03 409 465**A**	★05 042 742**A**		35.00	400.00

SERIES **1928C MULE**

PLATE SERIALS: Face check range #288 through #522.

Micro back check numbers 938 or lower.

SERIAL NUMBERS		NOTES PRINTED	VG/F	CU
E44 200 345**A**		Included below	$25.00	$60.00
F-**A**			100.00	250.00
G52 180 700**A**			200.00	
G45 604 67**A**				
★04 979 317**A**	★05 560 698**A**		75.00	350.00

SERIES **1928C**

PLATE SERIALS: Face check range #288 through #522. Back check numbers begin at #939.

SIGNATURES: W.A. Julian, Henry Morgenthau, Jr.

SERIAL NUMBERS	NOTES PRINTED	VF	CU
E45 568 545**A**, **F-A**, G57 877 893**A**	214,735,765	$9.00	$20.00
★04 994 858**A**　★07 074 007**A**		50.00	200.00

SERIES **1928D MULE**

PLATE SERIAL: Face check range #524 through #550. Micro back check number 637.

SERIAL NUMBERS	NOTES PRINTED	VG/F	CU
G58 008 072**A**　G65 998 334**A**	Included below	$250.00	$500.00

SERIES **1928D**

PLATE SERIALS: Face check range #524 through #550. Back check #939 or higher.

SIGNATURES: W.A. Julian, Fred M. Vinson

SERIAL NUMBERS	NOTES PRINTED	VG/F	CU
G50 628 001**A**　G66 675 309**A** (High Obs.)	9,297,120	$16.00	$150.00
★07 100 070**A**　★07 171 596**A**	96,000	250.00	1000.00

SERIES **1928E MULE**

PLATE SERIALS: Face check range #566 through #627. Micro back check numbers 629 and 637. 629 is at least 10 times as scarce as 637.

SERIAL NUMBERS	NOTES PRINTED	VG/F	CU
G70 465 356**A**　H39 373 460**A**	Included below	$100.00	$350.00

SERIES **1928E**

PLATE SERIALS: Face check range #566 through #627.

SIGNATURES: W.A. Julian, John W. Snyder

SERIAL NUMBERS		NOTES PRINTED	VG/F	CU
G62 496 001A	H77 577 770A	109,952,760	$9.50	$20.00
★07 187 321A	★08 697 470A		50.00	300.00

SERIES 1928F

SIGNATURES: Georgia Neese Clark, John W. Snyder

WIDE I

PLATE SERIALS: Back check number 2007 or lower.

SERIAL NUMBERS		NOTES PRINTED	VF	CU
H71 592 001A	I77 225 966A	104,194,704	$8.50	$32.00
★08 396 104A	★09 633 564A		50.00	200.00

NARROW

PLATE SERIALS: Back check number 2008 through 2066.

SERIAL NUMBERS		NOTES PRINTED	VF	CU
I51 902 306**A**	I75 479 000**A**	Included above	$35.00	$50.00
★09 419 479**A**	★09 641 024**A**		500.00	1500.00

WIDE II

PLATE SERIALS: Back check number 2067 through 2096.

SERIAL NUMBERS		NOTES PRINTED	VF	CU
I70 867 629**A**	I79 394 789**A**	Included above	$50.00	$100.00
★09 650 582**A**	★09 672 795**A**		1500.00	2500.00

Official ending serial numbers for 1928F are I79 468 000**A** and ★09 744 000**A**.

SERIES **1953**

PLATE SERIALS: Face check numbers begin at #1. Back check numbers begin at #2094 (low of 18 subject sheets).

SIGNATURES: Ivy Baker Priest, George M. Humphrey

SERIAL NUMBERS OFFICIAL		NOTES PRINTED	VG/F	CU
A00 000 001**A**	Low	120,880,000	$8.50	$25.00
B20 880 000**A**	High		10.00	35.00
★00 000 001**A**	★05 760 000**A**	5,760,000	15.00	75.00

SERIES **1953A**

SIGNATURES: Ivy Baker Priest, Robert B. Anderson

SERIAL NUMBERS OFFICIAL	NOTES PRINTED	VG/F	CU
B20 880 001**A**	90,280,000	$7.00	$22.00
C11 160 000**A**		10.00	25.00
★05 760 001**A** ★11 160 000**A**	5,400,000	15.00	35.00

SERIES **1953B**

SIGNATURES: Elizabeth Rudel Smith, C. Douglas Dillon

SERIAL NUMBERS OFFICIAL	NOTES PRINTED	VG/F	CU
C11 160 001**A** **C**55 800 000**A**	44,640,000	$7.00	$15.00
★11 160 001**A** ★13 320 000**A**	2,160,000	10.00	35.00

SERIES **1953C**

PLATE SERIALS: Face check numbers on 18 subject sheets end at #44. Back check numbers on 18 subject sheets end at #2587.

SIGNATURES: Kathryn O'Hay Granahan, C. Douglas Dillon

SERIAL NUMBERS OFFICIAL		NOTES PRINTED	VG/F	CU
C55 800 001A C64 440 000A		8,640,000	$7.50	$20.00
★13 320 001A ★13 653 373A High observed			10.00	60.00

SERIES **1963**

PLATE SERIALS: The range of the face check numbers made for 32 subject sheets is #1 through #10. Back check number range #1 through #9.

SIGNATURES: Kathryn O'Hay Granahan, C. Douglas Dillon

SERIAL NUMBERS OFFICIAL		NOTES PRINTED	VG/F	CU
A00 000 001A A63 360 000A		63,360,000	7.00	$12.00
★00 000 001A ★03 840 000A		3,840,000	$7.50	15.00

SILVER CERTIFICATES

Blue Seal

SERIES 1934

PLATE SERIALS: Face check number range #1 - #561. Back check numbers below #938 (micro size).

SIGNATURES: W.A. Julian, Henry Morgenthau, Jr.

SERIAL NUMBERS		NOTES PRINTED	VF	CU
A00 000 001A	D99 999 999A	356,352,000	$8.00	$20.00
E51 445 583A	High Observed		100.00	450.00
★00 003 991A	★03 954 635A	3,960,000	25.00	50.00

SERIES 1934 MULE

PLATE SERIALS: These are Series 1934 Notes with large back check numbers, and are 1934 faces on 1934A backs. Macro back check numbers #939 or higher.

SERIAL NUMBERS		NOTES PRINTED	VG/F	CU
E06 094 905A	E53 049 647A	Included above	$500.00	$1200.00

Lincoln Photo by Mathew Brady Feb. 9, 1864. Original glass plate negative presented to Library of Congress in 1953 by Louis Rabinowitz.

SERIES 1934A MULE

These are Series 1934A notes with micro back check numbers, and are actually Series 1934A faces on Series 1934 backs.

PLATE SERIAL: Back check numbers 938 or less (micro size).

SERIAL NUMBERS: O50 352 001A official low-Printed January 25, 1938.

SIGNATURES: W.A. Julian, Henry Morgenthau, Jr.

SERIAL NUMBERS	NOTES PRINTED	VG/F	CU
D56 173 786A E-A, F-A, & G-A	Included below	$12.50	$25.00
H-A		20.00	35.00
IA & JA Unknown			
K-A		100.00	200.00
L23 178 737A High Observed		150.00	250.00
★03 594 833A ★06 414 028A		50.00	125.00

SERIES 1934A

PLATE SERIALS: Face check number range #562 - #1765. Back check numbers begin at #939.

SERIAL NUMBERS	NOTES PRINTED	VF	CU
E28 924 120A Low Observed	740,128,000*	$10.00	$20.00
F-A through K-A		8.00	15.00
L26 399 685A High Observed		15.00	35.00
★04 837 313A ★11 656 719A		25.00	50.00
*Includes all types of 1934A Series			

SERIES 1934A LATE FINISHED FACE PLATE 307

SERIAL NUMBERS	NOTES PRINTED	VG/F	CU
K21 767 367A K52 928 748A	569,244*	$100.00	$300.00
*Includes 1934A North Africa			

NORTH AFRICA NOTES

SERIES 1934A

Yellow Seal
North Africa

PLATE SERIALS: Back check numbers begin at 939.

SERIAL NUMBERS		NOTES PRINTED	VG/F	CU
K34 188 001A	K34 508 000A	320,000	$50.00	$200.00
K36 420 001A	K36 740 000A	320,000	50.00	200.00
K37 464 001A	K37 784 000A	320,000	50.00	200.00
K40 068 001A	K42 068 000A	2,000,000	25.00	125.00
K43 152 001A	K44 852 000A	1,700,000	25.00	125.00
K53 984 001A	K65 984 000A	12,000,000	17.50	100.00
★10 548 001A	★10 568 000A	20,000	50.00	200.00
★10 716 001A	★10 764 000A	48,000	35.00	150.00
★10 884 001A	★11 016 000A	32,000	40.00	175.00
★10 549 061A	★11 015 131A Low and High observed		35.00	150.00

SERIES 1934A LATE FINISHED FACE PLATE 307

North Africa
Yellow Seal

SERIAL NUMBERS		NOTES PRINTED	VG/F	CU
K40 927 103A	K63 071 799A		$50.00	$150.00
★10 896 399A	Low observed	See 1934A		
		Plate 307		
★11 010 487A	High observed		50.00	200.00

SERIES 1934B MULE

These are Series 1934B notes with micro back check numbers, and are actually Series 1934B faces on Series 1934 backs.

PLATE SERIALS: Back check number used #637 (micro size)

SIGNATURES: W.A. Julian, Fred M. Vinson

SERIAL NUMBERS		NOTES PRINTED	VG/F	CU
K90 480 001A	Low	Included below	$125.00	$300.00
L84 069 273A	High		100.00	200.00
★11 665 559A	★12 397 170A Observed		250.00	500.00

SERIES **1934B**

PLATE SERIALS: Face check number range #1769 - #1826. Back check #939 and higher.

SERIAL NUMBERS		NOTES PRINTED	VG/F	CU
K90 375 110**A** Low Observed		60,328,000	$25.00	$100.00
L00 000 001**A**	**L**99 999 999**A**		10.00	35.00
M33 301 809**A** High Observed			150.00	300.00
★12 416 940**A**			50.00	150.00

SERIES **1934C MULE**

These are Series 1934C notes with micro back check numbers, and are actually Series 1934C faces on Series 1934 backs.

PLATE SERIALS: Primary back check number used #637 (micro size). Back check number 629 is at least 10 times as scarce as 637.

SERIAL NUMBERS OBSERVED		NOTES PRINTED	VG/F	CU
L51 435 522**A**	**P**72 850 478**A**	Included below	$35.00	$75.00
★13 803 080**A**	★15 047 154**A**		250.00	500.00

SERIES **1934C**

PLATE SERIALS: Face check number range #1875 - #2031. Back check number 939 and higher.

SIGNATURES: W.A. Julian, John W. Snyder

SERIAL NUMBERS OBSERVED		NOTES PRINTED	VG/F	CU
L49 546 170**A**	**Q**65 450 107**A**	372,328,000	$25.00	$75.00
M-A			10.00	20.00
★12 004 318**A**	★17 687 718**A**		17.50	75.00

SERIES 1934D

SERIAL NUMBERS OFFICIAL		NOTES PRINTED
Q23 136 001**A**	**V**14 796 000**A**	491,666,000
★16 884 788**A**	★23 088 000**A**	
(Low Observed)		

SIGNATURES: Georgia Neese Clark, John W. Snyder

WIDE I

PLATE SERIALS: Back check number 2007 or lower.

SERIAL NUMBERS OBSERVED		NOTES PRINTED	VG/F	CU
Q45 838 633**A**	**V**13 492 055**A**	See above	$8.00	$20.00
★16 884 788**A**	★23 052 212**A**		15.00	35.00

NARROW

PLATE SERIALS: Back check number 2008 through 2066.

SERIAL NUMBERS OBSERVED		NOTES PRINTED	VG/F	CU
T43 892 772A	V13 942 627A	See above	$15.00	$30.00
★17 687 712A	★23 033 545A		30.00	60.00

WIDE II

PLATE SERIALS: Back check number 2067 through 2096.

SERIAL NUMBERS OBSERVED		NOTES PRINTED	VG/F	CU
U37 326 477A	V12 325 327A	See above	$25.00	$50.00
★22 017 567A	★23 034 317A		100.00	250.00

SERIES 1953

PLATE SERIALS: Face check numbers begin at #1. Back check numbers begin at #2097 (low of 18 subject sheets).

SIGNATURES: Ivy Baker Priest, George M. Humphrey

SERIAL NUMBERS OFFICIAL		NOTES PRINTED	CU
A00 000 001A	D39 600 000A	339,600,000	$17.50
★00 000 039A	★15 120 000A	15,120,000	30.00

SERIES 1953A

SIGNATURES: Ivy Baker Priest, Robert B. Anderson

SERIAL NUMBERS OFFICIAL		NOTES PRINTED	CU
D39 600 001A	F72 000 000A	232,400,000	$12.00
★15 120 001A	★28 080 000A	12,960,000	20.00

SERIES 1953B

SIGNATURES: Elizabeth Rudel Smith, C. Douglas Dillon

SERIAL NUMBERS OFFICIAL		NOTES PRINTED	VG/F	CU
F72 000 001A	G45 000 000A	73,000,000		$12.50
★28 080 001A	★31 320 000A	3,240,000	350.00	2000.00

This series was only released in part. **G-A** printed but not released.

★28 428 881A Highest observed   500.00

SERIES 1953C

PLATE SERIALS: Face check numbers of 18 subject sheets end at #97. Back check numbers on 18 subject sheets end at #2587.

SIGNATURES: Kathryn O'Hay Granahan, C. Douglas Dillon

NOTE: This series was printed but not released. The Bureau actually exhibits an uncut sheet of star notes.

SERIAL NUMBERS OFFICIAL

G45 000 001**A**	H35 640 000**A**	90,640,000
★31 320 001**A**	★35 640 000**A**	4,320,000

FEDERAL RESERVE NOTES

Green Seal

SERIES 1928

SERIAL NUMBERS: All districts started both regular and star notes with serial 00 000 001. Bureau of Engraving and Printing information is incomplete on ending serial numbers.

PLATE SERIALS: Both face and back check numbers begin at #1.

SIGNATURES: H.T. Tate, A.W. Mellon

LOW SERIAL NUMBERS	HIGH	NOTES PRINTED	VG/F	CU

BOSTON

A00 000 049A	A07 452 161A	8,025,300	$12.50	$60.00
A00 000 741★	A00 283 715★		50.00	250.00

NEW YORK

B00 787 007A	B50 764 007A	14,701,884	12.50	60.00
B00 099 527★			50.00	250.00

PHILADELPHIA

C00 000 063A	C27 758 611A	11,819,712	12.50	60.00
C00 000 002★	C00 217 187★		50.00	250.00

CLEVELAND

D00 000 385A	D13 179 914A	9,049,000	12.50	60.00
D00 086 861★	D00 088 287★		50.00	250.00

RICHMOND

E03 854 699A	E06 022 463A	6,027,660	12.50	60.00
E00 022 434★	E00 085 392★		50.00	250.00

ATLANTA

F01 886 364A	F11 087 392A	10,964,400	12.50	50.00
F00 000 284★	F00 211 885★		50.00	250.00

CHICAGO

G00 000 001A	G23 387 298A	12,326,052	12.50	50.00
G00 000 393★	G00 445 680★		40.00	250.00

ST. LOUIS

H00 000 001A	H04 220 853A	4,675,200	12.50	60.00
H00 020 486★	H00 113 707★		50.00	250.00

MINNEAPOLIS

I00 000 001A	I03 818 066A	4,284,300	12.50	75.00
I-★			150.00	500.00

KANSAS CITY

J00 134 821A	J05 245 344A	4,480,800	12.50	60.00
J00 017 998★	J00 137 993★		40.00	250.00

DALLAS

K00 000 001A	K08 438 568A	8,137,824	12.50	40.00
K00 014 742★	K00 102 068★		50.00	250.00

SAN FRANCISCO

L00 000 025A	L11 189 914A	9,792,000	12.50	100.00
L00 377 573★			150.00	500.00

SERIES **1928A**

SERIAL NUMBERS: All districts continued sequence from previous series with regular and star notes.

PLATE SERIALS: Face check numbers begin with #1.

SIGNATURES: Walter O. Woods, A.W. Mellon

LOW SERIAL NUMBERS	HIGH	NOTES PRINTED	VG/F	CU
BOSTON				
A06 494 819A	A16 638 789A	7,404,352	$12.50	$40.00
	A00 406 454★		50.00	300.00
NEW YORK				
B10 828 275A	B54 038 970A	43,210,696	12.50	40.00
B00 827 434★			50.00	300.00
PHILADELPHIA				
C06 466 940A	C32 769 554A	10,806,012	12.50	40.00
C00 218 478★	C00 350 766★		50.00	300.00
CLEVELAND				
D07 510 464A	D14 225 044A	6,822,000	12.50	40.00
D00 243 855★			40.00	300.00
RICHMOND				
	E07 580 362A	2,409,900	20.00	75.00
	E00 126 303★		40.00	300.00
ATLANTA				
F08 928 700A	F17 171 469A	3,537,600	12.50	40.00
F★			50.00	300.00

		CHICAGO		
G23 163 229A	G49 855 759A	37,882,176	12.50	40.00
G00 247 663★	G00 649 815★		40.00	275.00
ST. LOUIS				
H05 117 274A	H09 947 974A	2,731,824	20.00	60.00
H00 162 702★			50.00	300.00
MINNEAPOLIS				
I04 188 101A	I04 924 161A	652,800	40.00	200.00
I-★			100.00	450.00
KANSAS CITY				
J04 822 495A	J080 772 20A	3,572,400	20.00	60.00
J-★			50.00	300.00

DALLAS

K05 632 501A	K08 234 307A	2,564,400	20.00	75.00
	K00 134 737★		50.00	500.00

SAN FRANCISCO

L09 694 201A	L14 362 130A	6,565,500	12.50	50.00
L00 275 230★	L00 350 766★		50.00	300.00

Dark Green Seal

SERIES 1928B

SERIAL NUMBERS: All districts continued sequence from previous series with regular and star notes.

PLATE SERIALS: Face check numbers begin with #1.

SIGNATURES: Walter O. Woods, A.W. Mellon

LOW SERIAL	HIGH NUMBERS	EST NOTES PRINTED	VG/F	CU
BOSTON				
A15 921 412A	A29 010 354A	28,430,724	$10.00	$40.00
	A00 425 259★		50.00	200.00
NEW YORK				
B54 042 182A	B81 942 241A	51,157,536	10.00	40.00
B★			50.00	200.00
PHILADELPHIA				
C21 695 184A	C27 999 003A	25,698,396	10.00	40.00
C00 401 030★	C00 450 649★		50.00	200.00
CLEVELAND				
D15 828 264A	D30 400 320A	24,874,272	10.00	40.00
	D00 364 555★		50.00	200.00
RICHMOND				
E08 343 197A	E13 568 780A	15,151,932	10.00	40.00
	E00 085 392★		50.00	200.00
ATLANTA				
F14 337 964A	F22 522 512A	13,386,420	10.00	40.00
F00 272 092★	F00 333 663★		50.00	200.00

CHICAGO

G45 649 832A	G48 671 639A	17,157,036	10.00	40.00
G★			50.00	200.00

ST. LOUIS

H06 221 967A	H20 529 387A	20,251,716	10.00	40.00
H00 216 303★	H00 299 543★		50.00	200.00

MINNEAPOLIS

I04 692 029A	I08 295 799A	6,954,060	10.00	40.00
I00 101 208★	I00 101 557★		50.00	200.00

KANSAS CITY

J08 602 028A	J09 380 977A	10,677,636	10.00	40.00
J★			50.00	200.00

DALLAS

K09 827 819A	K12 115 181A	4,334,400	10.00	40.00
K★			50.00	200.00

SAN FRANCISCO

L17 719 957A	L25 562 221A	28,840,080	10.00	40.00
L00 377 571★	L00 419 041★		50.00	200.00

Light Green Seal
SERIES 1928B

SERIAL NUMBERS: All districts continued sequence from dark green seal variety above.

TOTAL NOTES PRINTED: This information is found in previous section and includes both light and dark seal varieties of Series 1928B. High official star serial numbers are listed, but only a fraction of these were actually used.

LOW	HIGH	NOTES		
SERIAL NUMBERS		PRINTED	VG/F	CU

BOSTON

A-A			$22.50	$75.00
A-★	A00 612 000★		50.00	300.00

NEW YORK

B-A			22.50	75.00
B★	B01 284 000★		50.00	300.00

PHILADELPHIA

	C39 044 023A		22.50	75.00
C★	C00 636 000★		50.00	300.00

CLEVELAND

D21 250 688A	D25 055 270A		22.50	75.00
D00 571 523★	D00 576 000★		50.00	300.00

RICHMOND

E38 269 080A			22.50	75.00
E★	E00 288 000★		50.00	300.00

ATLANTA

F23 227 169A	F28 452 147A		22.50	75.00
F00 359 273★	F00 372 000★		50.00	350.00

CHICAGO

G47 473 955A	G48 487 082A		22.50	100.00
G★	G00 852 000★		50.00	300.00

ST. LOUIS

H24 139 801A	H27 716 788A		22.50	60.00
H00 315 765★	H00 360 000★		50.00	250.00

MINNEAPOLIS

I07 684 974A			22.50	100.00
I★	I00 144 000★		50.00	300.00

KANSAS CITY

J09 774 705A			22.50	100.00
J★	J00 240 000★		50.00	300.00

DALLAS

K10 827 231A	K11 403 644A		22.50	100.00
K★	K00 180 000★		50.00	300.00

SAN FRANCISCO

L18 566 372A	L39 700 819A		22.50	75.00
L★	L00 576 000★		50.00	300.00

SERIES **1928C**

SERIAL NUMBERS: Districts printed continued sequence from previous series. Of those printed, only 1.2 million were released.

PLATE SERIALS: Face check numbers begin with #1. High Observed #7.

SIGNATURES: Walter O. Woods, Ogden L. Mills

LOW SERIAL NUMBERS	HIGH	NOTES PRINTED	VG/F	CU
		CLEVELAND		
D-A Unknown		3,293,640	$500.00	$1000.00

		ATLANTA		
F23 825 359A	F28 424 033A	2,056,200	200.00	575.00
F★ Unknown				
		SAN FRANCISCO		
L-A Unknown		266,304	500.00	1000.00

SERIES **1928D**

SERIAL NUMBERS: District printed continued sequence from previous series.

PLATE SERIALS: Face check range #1 through #9.

SIGNATURES: Walter O. Woods, W.H. Woodin

LOW SERIAL NUMBERS	HIGH	NOTES PRINTED	VG/F	CU
		ATLANTA		
F26 282 729A	F28 617 186A	1,281,600	$350.00	$1000.00
F★ Unknown				

Light Green Seal
SERIES 1934

SERIAL NUMBERS: All districts started both regular and star notes with 00 000 001.

PLATE SERIALS: Face check numbers begin at #1. Back check numbers continue from Series 1928D. Back check #938 and lower. All Serial numbers start with #1.

SIGNATURES: W.A. Julian, Henry Morgenthau, Jr.

LOW	HIGH	NOTES		
SERIAL NUMBERS		**PRINTED**	**VG/F**	**CU**
		BOSTON		
A00 166 741A	A06 000 000A	30,510,036	$12.50	$37.50
	A00 021 382★		30.00	150.00
		NEW YORK		
B00 000 003A	B14 832 000A	47,888,760	11.00	20.00
B00 007 363★	B00 129 358★		30.00	150.00
		PHILADELPHIA		
C00 840 196A	C06 756 383A	47,327,760	11.50	20.00
C00 007 356★	C00 043 755★		30.00	150.00
		CLEVELAND		
D00 000 002A	D05 400 000A	62,237,508	11.00	20.00
D★			30.00	150.00
		RICHMOND		
E00 054 350A	E04 992 000A	62,128,000	11.00	20.00
E★			30.00	150.00
		ATLANTA		
F03 641 100A	F12 000 000A	22,811,916	11.50	20.00
F00 012 697★			30.00	150.00
		CHICAGO		
G00 020 996A	G09 732 000A	31,299,156	12.00	20.00
G00 033 590★	G00 080 750★		30.00	150.00
		ST. LOUIS		
H00 000 003A	H10 368 000A	48,737,280	12.50	20.00
H00 010 633★	H00 084 202★		30.00	150.00
		MINNEAPOLIS		
I00 196 641A	I04 920 000A	16,795,392	15.00	20.00
I00 028 690★			30.00	150.00
		KANSAS CITY		
J00 004 451A	J03 000 000A	31,854,432	13.50	20.00
	J60 002 861★			30.00 150.00
		DALLAS		
K00 000 001A	K08 352 000A	33,332,208	13.50	20.00
K-★			30.00	150.00

SAN FRANCISCO

L02 718 182**A**	**L**12 396 000**A**	39,324,168	12.50	20.00
L00 005 324★			30.00	150.00

Dark Green Seal
SERIES 1934

PLATE SERIALS: Back check number 938 and lower.

LOW	HIGH	NOTES		
SERIAL NUMBERS		**PRINTED**	**VG/F**	**CU**

BOSTON

A-A		See above	100.00	250.00
A00 063 562★	**A**00 088 170★			

NEW YORK

B15 260 338**A**	**B**15 480 140**A**		25.00	75.00
	B00 520 457★		75.00	150.00

PHILADELPHIA

C06 891 512**A**	**C**08 029 264**A**		35.00	75.00
C00 095 026★	**C**00 095 717★		100.00	250.00

CLEVELAND

D-A			35.00	75.00
D00 074 656★			100.00	250.00

RICHMOND

E-A			35.00	75.00
E00 021 980★	**E**00 640 402★		100.00	250.00

ATLANTA

F12 119 799**A**			35.00	75.00
F00 129 590★			100.00	275.00

CHICAGO

G10 265 578**A**	**G**10 875 488**A**		35.00	75.00
G00 113 174★			100.00	250.00

ST. LOUIS

H10 643 526**A**	**H**10 718 116**A**		100.00	250.00

MINNEAPOLIS

I04 949 402**A**	**I**06 257 433**A**		35.00	75.00
I00 083 077★	**I**00 091 074★		150.00	300.00

KANSAS CITY

J-A	**J**27 040 900**A**			35.00 75.00

DALLAS

K00 091 232★	**K**00 091 576★		100.00	250.00

SAN FRANCISCO

L12 748 235**A**   35.00   75.00

Dark Green Seal
SERIES **1934 MULE**

PLATE SERIALS: Back check number 939 and higher. These are series 1934 notes with larger back check numbers and are 1934 faces on 1934A backs.

Quantities included with 1934 Light Green Seal.

LOW SERIAL	HIGH NUMBERS	NOTES PRINTED	VG/F	CU
BOSTON				
A06 190 178**A**	**A**37 361 644**A**	See above	$11.50	$35.00
A00 178 682★	**A**00 275 471★		40.00	85.00
NEW YORK				
B17 676 495**A**			10.00	30.00
	B72 677 449**B**		10.00	30.00
B00 238 289★	**B**00 667 641★		35.00	80.00
PHILADELPHIA				
C07 732 843**A**	**C**64 460 348**A**		10.00	32.50
C00 086 921★	**C**00 626 791★		35.00	85.00
CLEVELAND				
D07 651 389**A**	**D**57 994 447**A**		10.00	30.00
D00 140 234★	**D**00 728 450★		40.00	85.00
RICHMOND				
E10 784 859**A**	**E**60 059 991**A**		10.00	30.00
E00 139 846★	**E**00 694 542★		40.00	100.00
ATLANTA				
F16 845 339**A**	**F**68 164 863**A**		10.00	32.50
F00 201 702★	**F**00 766 242★		35.00	100.00
CHICAGO				
G12 120 900**A**	**G**58 557 297**A**		11.00	35.00
G00 186 010★	**G**00 565 215★		35.00	90.00
ST. LOUIS				
H15 045 606**A**	**H**50 974 371**A**		11.00	32.50
H00 244 341★	**H**00 656 124★		40.00	90.00
MINNEAPOLIS				
I06 143 948**A**	**I**15 302 244**A**		12.00	37.50
I00 166 514★			50.00	100.00
KANSAS CITY				
J09 085 694**A**	**J**31 057 520**A**		11.50	36.00
J00 087 675★	**J**00 346 983★		50.00	100.00
DALLAS				
K08 990 097**A**	**K**31 181 830**A**		14.00	36.00
K00 348 303★	**K**00 366 164★		35.00	85.00
SAN FRANCISCO				
L14 996 001**A**	**L**77 547 571**A**		11.00	35.00
L★	**L**00 314 954**A**		50.00	100.00

HAWAII NOTES

Brown Seal

The word "Hawaii" is overprinted in black on both face and back. Seals and serial numbers are printed in brown ink.

OFFICIAL PRINT RUNS - ALL VARIETIES INCLUDED

LOW SERIAL	HIGH NUMBERS	NOTES PRINTED
L12 396 001A	L14 996 000A	2,600,000
L19 776 001A	L20 176 000A	400,000
L46 404 001A	L47 804 000A	1,400,000
L54 072 001A	L56 088 000A	2,016,000
L66 132 001A	L69 132 000A	3,000,000
L00 120 001★	L00 192 000★	72,000
L00 852 001★	L00 856 000★	4,000
L00 892 001★	L00 896 000★	4,000

SERIES 1934 HAWAII

PLATE SERIALS: Back check numbers 938 or lower.

SIGNATURES: Same as Series 1934 Green Seal notes.

LOW SERIAL	HIGH NUMBERS	VG/F	CU
L12 511 327★	L12 748 233★	$40.00	$125.00
L00 129 365★	L00 138 037★	500.00	3000.00

SERIES 1934 MULE HAWAII

PLATE SERIALS: Back check numbers 939 or higher.

LOW SERIAL	HIGH NUMBERS	VG/F	CU
L12 396 001A	L47 287 281A	$35.00	$110.00
L00 148 473★	L00 190 469★	250.00	1000.00

SERIES 1934A HAWAII

PLATE SERIALS: Back check numbers 939 or higher.

SIGNATURES: Same as Series 1934A Green Seal notes.

LOW	HIGH	NOTES		
SERIAL NUMBERS		PRINTED	VG/F	CU
L46 623 977A	L69 132 000A		$25.00	$90.00
L00 854 313★			1500.00	6000.00
L00 892 353★	L00 894 083★		1500.00	6000.00

SERIES 1934A MULE

Green Seal

SERIAL NUMBERS: All districts continued sequence from previous series.

PLATE SERIALS: All are back check #637.

LOW	HIGH	NOTES		
SERIAL NUMBERS		PRINTED	VG/F	CU
		NEW YORK		
B00 374 463A	B69 708 310B	See below	$40.00	$75.00
		PHILADELPHIA		
C69 052 070A			40.00	75.00
		CHICAGO		
	G80 536 253A		40.00	75.00
		ST. LOUIS		
	H39 621 679A		40.00	75.00
		SAN FRANCISCO		
L32 664 147A			40.00	75.00
L01 212 949★			75.00	250.00

SERIES 1934A

Green Seal

SERIAL NUMBERS: All districts continued sequence from previous series.

PLATE SERIALS: Back check numbers begin at 939.

SIGNATURES: W.A. Julian, Henry Morgenthau, Jr.

LOW	HIGH	NOTES		
SERIAL NUMBERS		PRINTED	VG/F	CU
		BOSTON		
A21 342 253A	A51 153 931A	23,231,568	$11.00	$20.00
A00 391 563★	A00 597 573★		22.00	100.00
		NEW YORK		
B26 490 000A		143,199,336	15.00	35.00
	B89 640 063B		11.00	20.00
B00 493 247★	B02 153 093★		22.00	100.00

PHILADELPHIA

C27 010 066A	C73 940 411A	30,691,632	11.00	20.00
C00 554 825★	C00 925 000★		22.00	100.00

CLEVELAND

D18 311 621A	D63 150 769A	1,610,676	20.00	50.00
D-★			22.00	100.00

RICHMOND

E46 685 672A	E66 003 920A	6,555,168	11.00	20.00
E00 782 182★			22.00	120.00

ATLANTA

F17 523 826A	F47 978 632A	22,811,916	11.00	20.00
F00 299 341★			22.00	100.00

CHICAGO

G22 168 431A			11.00	20.00
	G16 084 199B	88,376,376	11.00	20.00
G00 382 596★	G01 449 391★		22.00	100.00

ST. LOUIS

H40 698 437A	H53 000 511A	7,843,852	11.00	20.00
H00 521 917★			22.00	120.00

SAN FRANCISCO

L24 794 934A			11.00	20.00
	L00 793 914B	72,118,452	15.00	50.00
L00 799 203★	L01 219 181★		22.00	100.00

No regular or star notes were printed for Minneapolis, Kansas City or Dallas.

SERIES 1934B

SERIAL NUMBERS: All districts continued sequence from previous series.

PLATE SERIALS: Back check number 939 and higher.

SIGNATURES: W.A. Julian, Fred M. Vinson

LOW	HIGH	NOTES	VG/F	CU
SERIAL NUMBERS		**PRINTED**		
BOSTON				
A51 927 351A	A56 200 677A	3,457,800	$11.00	$40.00
A00 695 512★			75.00	250.00
NEW YORK				
B75 425 469B	B95 741 965B	14,099,580	11.00	40.00
B02 263 343★	B02 312 902★		60.00	200.00
PHILADELPHIA				
C72 036 121A	C80 574 996A	8,306,820	11.00	40.00
C00 938 264★	C01 026 003★		75.00	200.00
CLEVELAND				
D57 994 351A	D69 833 028A	11,348,184	11.00	40.00
D00 756 699★	D01 022 514★		60.00	200.00
RICHMOND				
E67 499 771A	E72 106 406A	5,902,848	11.00	30.00
E-★			75.00	250.00
ATLANTA				
F69 413 365A	F72 120 482A	4,314,048	11.00	40.00
F-★			75.00	250.00
CHICAGO				
G13 186 858B	G25 042 572B	9,070,932	11.00	40.00
G-★			75.00	250.00
ST. LOUIS				
H53 492 931A	H71 547 955A	4,307,712	11.00	40.00
H00 682 009★	H00 753 479★		75.00	200.00
MINNEAPOLIS				
I15 477 261A	I17 833 985A	2,482,500	11.00	40.00

I00 219 664★	I00 232 537★		75.00	250.00

KANSAS CITY

J31 854 433A	J32 227 785A	64,000	100.00	500.00
J-★			250.00	Rare

SAN FRANCISCO

L95 336 592A			11.00	45.00
	L03 750 526B	9,910,296	11.00	40.00
L-★			75.00	250.00

SERIES **1934B** LATE FINISHED FACE PLATE 212

PLATE SERIAL: Face check number 212.

LOW SERIAL NUMBERS	HIGH	NOTES PRINTED	VG/F	CU
B73 706 585B		Included above	$175.00	$500.00

BLOCKS KNOWN: Twenty-two
No regular or star notes were printed for Dallas.

SERIES **1934B** MULE

(Back Check #637)

These are actually Series 1934B faces on Series 1934 backs.
SERIAL NUMBERS: All districts continued sequence from previous series.

LOW SERIAL NUMBERS	HIGH	NOTES PRINTED	VG/F	CU
BOSTON				
A54 375 901A		Included above	$25.00	$100.00
NEW YORK				
B58 021 649A				
B80 851 374B	B94 911 759B	Included above	25.00	100.00
CLEVELAND				
D60 641 001A		Included above	25.00	100.00
D00 761 254★			75.00	250.00

CHICAGO				
G21 370 363B		Included above	25.00	100.00
ST. LOUIS				
H54 567 383A		Included above	25.00	100.00
MINNEAPOLIS				
I18 105 713A		Included above	25.00	100.00
SAN FRANCISCO				
L01 597 562B	L02 967 122B		25.00	100.00
L01 359 866★	L01 359 867★	Included above	50.00	250.00

SERIES **1934C MULE**

These are actually Series 1934C faces on Series 1934 backs. (Back check #629 and 637)

LOW	HIGH	NOTES		
SERIAL NUMBERS		PRINTED	VG/F	CU
BOSTON				
A54 870 831A	A60 476 989A	Included below	$25.00	$100.00
NEW YORK				
B22 594 851C	B45 409 229C	Included below	25.00	100.00
PHILADELPHIA				
C95 791 219A		Included below	40.00	150.00
	C00 036 000B		75.00	300.00
CLEVELAND				
D76 605 379A	D77 184 218A	Included below	25.00	100.00
CHICAGO				
G31 475 153B	G64 633 087B	Included below	25.00	100.00
ST. LOUIS				
H70 831 511A		Included below	25.00	100.00
MINNEAPOLIS				
I20 058 699A		Included below	25.00	100.00
KANSAS CITY				
J31 266 251A		Included below	25.00	100.00
SAN FRANCISCO				
L07 782 787A		Included below	25.00	100.00

SERIES **1934C**

SERIAL NUMBERS: All districts continued sequence from previous series.

PLATE SERIALS: Back check number 939 and higher.

SIGNATURES: W.A. Julian, John W. Snyder

LOW	HIGH	NOTES		
SERIAL NUMBERS		PRINTED	VG/F	CU
BOSTON				
A54 946 387A	A69 278 685A	14,332,299	$11.00	$45.00
A00 904 062★			35.00	125.00
NEW YORK				
B98 488 573B		74,383,248	15.00	30.00
	B61 890 091C		11.00	30.00
B02 795 441★	B03 314 656★		22.00	85.00
PHILADELPHIA				
C82 464 358A		22,879,212	11.00	30.00
	C05 721 259B		11.00	35.00
C01 083 169★	C01 211 270★		22.00	85.00
CLEVELAND				
D69 301 787A	D88 716 575A	19,898,256	11.00	30.00
D00 933 393★	D01 060 906★		22.00	85.00
RICHMOND				
E59 821 773A	E93 983 925A	23,800,524	11.00	30.00
E00 988 099★	E01 176 380★		22.00	85.00
ATLANTA				
F74 457 032A	F95 223 927A	23,572,968	11.00	30.00
F01 156 544★			22.00	125.00

		CHICAGO		
G23 755 809B	G80 425 385B	60,598,812	11.00	30.00
G01 709 522★	G02 763 794★		22.00	85.00
		ST. LOUIS		
H60 311884A		20,393,340	11.00	30.00
	H07 551 780B		11.00	30.00
H00 784 303★	H01 556 190★		22.00	85.00
		MINNEAPOLIS		
I18 659 627	I22 393 332A	5,089,200	11.00	30.00
			22.00	125.00
		KANSAS CITY		
J31 066 284A	J37 473 472A	8,313,504	11.00	30.00
J00 453 442★	J00 527 874★		22.00	100.00
		DALLAS		
K31 819 270A	K37 276 203A	5,107,800	11.00	30.00
			22.00	125.00
		SAN FRANCISCO		
L05 994 335B	L12 353862B	9,451,944	11.00	30.00
L01 431 170★			25.00	100.00

SERIES **1934D**

SERIAL NUMBERS: All districts continued sequence from previous series. High star numbers shown indicate official end of print run.

SIGNATURES: Georgia Neese Clark, John W. Snyder

LOW	HIGH	NOTES		
SERIAL NUMBERS		**PRINTED**	**VF**	**CU**
		BOSTON		
A68 486 900A	A80 384 786A	12,660,552	$10.00	$30.00
A01 037 183★	A01 052 000★		30.00	110.00
		NEW YORK		
B57 783 928C		50,976,576	10.00	30.00
	B12 352 539D		10.00	30.00
B03 377 501★	B03 888 000★		30.00	110.00
		PHILADELPHIA		
C02 491 319B	C14 815 746B	12,106,740	10.00	30.00
	C01 500 000★		30.00	110.00
		CLEVELAND		
D65 673 725A	D96 448 810A	8,969,052	10.00	30.00
D01 033 988★	D01 284 000★		60.00	200.00

RICHMOND

E94 054 703A		13,333,032	10.00	30.00
	E06 944 636B		10.00	30.00
	E01 428 000★		35.00	150.00

ATLANTA

F95 002 632A		9,599,352	100.00	350.00
	F03 093 944B		100.00	300.00
	F01 380 000★		350.00	750.00

CHICAGO

G80 874 865B		36,601,680	10.00	30.00
	G16 249 094C		10.00	30.00
G02 622 609★	G02 916 000★		35.00	110.00

ST. LOUIS

H76 423 572A		8,093,412	10.00	30.00
	H18 892 698B		15.00	50.00
H01 033 988★	H01 176 000★		30.00	110.00

MINNEAPOLIS

I23 569 492A	I26 000 935A	3,594,900	10.00	30.00
	I00 372 000★		40.00	150.00

KANSAS CITY

J38 882 384A	J44 891 392A	6,538,740	10.00	30.00
	J00 568 000★		45.00	150.00

DALLAS

K33 950 138A	K40 668 433A	4,139,016	10.00	30.00
K00 493 278★	K00 496 000★		45.00	150.00

SAN FRANCISCO

L12 681 010B	L21 664 370B	11,704,200	10.00	30.00
	L01 644 000★		45.00	150.00

SERIES 1950 WIDE

SERIAL NUMBERS: All districts started both regular and star notes with serial 00 000 001. High numbers shown are official for Series 1950 (All varieties).

PLATE SERIALS: Face Check numbers begin at #1. Back check numbers 2007 or lower.

SIGNATURES: George Neese Clark, John W. Snyder

LOW SERIAL NUMBERS	HIGH	NOTES PRINTED	VF	CU
BOSTON				
A00 000 024A	A30 672 000A	30,672,000	$10.00	$30.00
	A00 408 000★	408,000	12.00	110.00
NEW YORK				
B00 000 003A		106,768,000	10.00	30.00
	B06 768 000B		15.00	50.00
B00 866 227★	B01 464 000★	1,464,000	12.00	85.00
PHILADELPHIA				
C04 809 907A	C44 784 000A	44,784,000	10.00	30.00
C00 237 838★	C00 600 000★	600,000	12.00	110.00
CLEVELAND				
D00 000 005A	D54 000 000A	54,000,000	10.00	30.00
D00 459 954★	D00 744 000★	744,000	12.00	100.00
RICHMOND				
E00 000 099A	E47 088 000A	47,088,000	10.00	30.00
E00 446 933★	E00 684 000★	684,000	12.00	100.00
ATLANTA				
F36 059 982A	F52 416 000A	52,416,000	10.00	30.00
F00 003 967★	F00 696 000★	696,000	12.00	110.00
CHICAGO				
G00 000 500A	G85 104 000A	85,104,000	10.00	30.00
G00 408 074★	G01 176 000★	1,176,000	12.00	85.00
ST. LOUIS				
H00 000 013A	H36 864 000A	36,864,000	10.00	30.00
H00 000 486★	H00 552 000★	552,000	20.00	150.00
MINNEAPOLIS				
I00 000 007A	I11 796 000A	11,796,000	10.00	30.00
I00 024 470★	I00 144 000★	144,000	12.00	150.00
KANSAS CITY				
J00 006 000A	J25 428 000A	25,428,000	12.00	30.00
J00 001 106★	J00 360 000★	360,000	10.00	85.00

		NOTES PRINTED	VF	CU
DALLAS				
K03 116 659A	K22 848 000A	22,848,000	10.00	30.00
	K00 372 000★	372,000	12.00	110.00
SAN FRANCISCO				
L00 000 100A	L55 008 000A	55,008,000	10.00	30.00
L00 400 917★	L00 744 000★	744,000	12.00	85.00

SERIES **1950 NARROW**

PLATE SERIALS: Back check number range #2008-2066.

LOW	HIGH	NOTES PRINTED	VF	CU
SERIAL NUMBERS				
BOSTON				
A17 738 425A	A29 017 643A	Included above	$12.00	$45.00
NEW YORK				
B68 131 945A		Included above	12.50	45.00
	B05 445 534 B		15.00	50.00
B00 824 357★	B01 375 357★		17.50	85.00
PHILADELPHIA				
C25 191 174A	C43 652 958A	Included above	12.00	45.00
C00 429 930★	C00 481 081★		17.50	100.00
CLEVELAND				
D25 967 165A	D53 997 798A	Included above	12.00	45.00
D00 556 749★	D00 717 430★		17.50	100.00

RICHMOND

E27 648 294A	E46 969 425A	Included above	12.00	45.00

ATLANTA

F36 965 675A	F36 965 676A	Included above	12.00	45.00

CHICAGO

G52 807 564A	G81 018 210A	Included above	12.00	45.00
G52 807 564★	G00 964 200★		17.50	100.00

ST. LOUIS

H21 533 064A	H36 639 659A	Included above	12.00	45.00

MINNEAPOLIS

I06 328 008A	I11 527 084A	Included above	12.00	45.00

KANSAS CITY

J12 455 195A	J24 466 242A	Included above	12.00	45.00

DALLAS

K17 147 340A	K22 220 544A	Included above	12.00	45.00

SAN FRANCISCO

L38 391 131A	L52 328 092A	Included above	12.00	45.00
L00 640 807★	L00 667 972★		17.50	85.00

SERIES **1950 WIDE II**

PLATE SERIALS: Face check numbers end at #144. Back check number range #2067 - #2096. Both are highest of 12 subject sheets.

LOW	HIGH	NOTES		
SERIAL NUMBERS		PRINTED	VF	CU
BOSTON				
A24 311 603A	A25 366 951A	Included above	$14.00	$30.00
NEW YORK				
B72 080 268A		Included above	17.50	30.00
	B04 905 193B		20.00	50.00
PHILADELPHIA				
C38 068 000A	C41 833 294A		20.00	40.00
CLEVELAND				
D35 864 001A	D50 973 519A	Included above	14.00	30.00
RICHMOND				
E36 507 409A	E46 170 089A	Included above	14.00	30.00
ATLANTA				
F42 342 238A		Included above	14.00	30.00

CHICAGO

G57 723 984A	G81 917 195A	Included above	13.00	30.00

ST. LOUIS

H25 443 568A	H36 596 446A	Included above	14.00	30.00

MINNEAPOLIS

I11 111 108A		Included above	14.00	30.00

KANSAS CITY

J15 960 799A	J21 041 939A	Included above	15.00	32.00

DALLAS

	K20 575 016A	Included above	15.00	32.00

SAN FRANCISCO

L39 841 232A	L52 328 098A	Included above	14.00	30.00

SERIES 1950A

SERIAL NUMBERS: All numbers shown are official.

PLATE SERIALS: Face check numbers begin at #145. Back check numbers begin at #2097. Both lowest of 18 subject sheets.

SIGNATURES: Ivy Baker Priest, George M. Humphrey

LOW	HIGH	NOTES	VALUE
SERIAL NUMBERS		PRINTED	CU
BOSTON			
A30 672 001A	A84 240 000A	53,568,000	$16.00
A00 432 001★	A03 240 000★	2,808,000	26.00
NEW YORK			
B06 768 001B		186,472,000	16.00
	B93 240 000C		16.00
B01 584 001★	B10 800 000★	9,216,000	24.00
PHILADELPHIA			
C44 784 001A		79,616,000	16.00
	C14 400 000B		16.00
C00 720 001★	C05 040 000★	4,320,000	26.00
CLEVELAND			
D54 000 001A	D99 360 000A	45,360,000	16.00
D00 864 001★	D03 240 000★	2,376,000	30.00
RICHMOND			
E47 088 001A		76,672,000	16.00
	E23 760 000B		16.00
E00 720 001★	E06 120 000★	5,400,000	26.00
ATLANTA			
F52 416 001A		86,464,000	16.00
	F38 880 000B		16.00
F00 720 001★	F05 760 000★	5,040,000	24.00

CHICAGO

G85 104 001**A**		129,296,000	16.00
G-B			16.00
	G14 400 000**C**		16.00
G01 296 001★	G07 560 000★	6,284,000	24.00

ST. LOUIS

H36 864 001**A**	H91 800 000**A**	54,936,000	16.00
H00 576 001★	H03 960 000★	3,384,000	30.00

MINNEAPOLIS

I11 808 001**A**	I23 040 000**A**	11,232,000	16.00
I00 144 001★	I01 008 000★	864,000	40.00

KANSAS CITY

J25 488 001**A**	J55 440 000**A**	29,952,000	16.00
J00 432 001★	J02 520 000★	2,088,000	35.00

DALLAS

K22 896 001**A**	K47 880 000**A**	24,984,000	16.00
K00 432 001★	K00 974 069★	542,069	35.00

SAN FRANCISCO

L55 008 001**A**		90,712,000	16.00
	L45 720 000**B**		16.00
L00 864 001★	L07 200 000★	6,336,000	30.00

SERIES **1950B**

SERIAL NUMBERS: All numbers shown are official.

SIGNATURES: Ivy Baker Priest, Robert B. Anderson

LOW	HIGH	NOTES	
SERIAL NUMBERS		**PRINTED**	**CU**

BOSTON

A84 240 001**A**		30,880,000	$15.00
	A15 120 000**B**		15.00
A03 240 001★	A05 760 000★	2,520,000	30.00

NEW YORK

B93 240 001**C**		85,960,000	15.00
	B79 200 000**D**		15.00
B10 800 001★	B15 480 000★	4,680,000	30.00

PHILADELPHIA

C14 400 001**B**	C57 960 000**B**	43,560,000	15.00
C05 040 001★	C07 920 000★	2,880,000	30.00

CLEVELAND

D99 360 001**A**		38,800,000	50.00
	D38 160 000**B**		15.00
D03 240 001★	D06 120 000★	2,880,000	30.00

RICHMOND

E23 760 001B	E76 680 000B	52,920,000	15.00
E06 120 001★	E09 000 000★	2,880,000	30.00

ATLANTA

F38 880 001B		80,560,000	15.00
	F19 440 000C		15.00
F05 760 001★	F09 720 000★	3,960,000	30.00

CHICAGO

G14 400 001C		104,320,000	15.00
	G18 720 000D		15.00
G07 560 001★	G13 680 000★	6,120,000	30.00

ST. LOUIS

H91 800 001A		25,840,000	15.00
	H17 640 000B		15.00
H03 960 001★	H05 400 000★	1,440,000	30.00

MINNEAPOLIS

I23 040 001A	I43 920 000A	20,880,000	15.00
I01 008 001★	I01 800 000★	792,000	40.00

KANSAS CITY

J55 440 001A	J87 840 000A	32,400,000	15.00
J02 520 001★	J05 040 000★	2,520,000	30.00

DALLAS

K47 880 001A	K99 999 999A	52,119,999	15.00
K01 800 001★	K05 040 000★	3,240,000	30.00

SAN FRANCISCO

L45 720 001B		56,080,000	15.00
	L01 800 000C		25.00
L07 200 001★	L10 800 000★	3,600,000	30.00

SERIES 1950C

SERIAL NUMBERS: All numbers shown are official.

SIGNATURES: Elizabeth Rudel Smith, C. Douglas Dillon

LOW	HIGH	NOTES	
SERIAL NUMBERS		PRINTED	CU

BOSTON

A15 120 001B	A36 000 000B	20,880,000	$15.00
A05 760 001★	A06 480 000★	720,000	35.00

NEW YORK

B79 200 001D		47,440,000	15.00
	B26 640 000E		15.00
B15 480 001★	B18 360 000★	2,880,000	30.00

PHILADELPHIA

C57 960 001B	C87 480 000B	29,520,000	15.00
C07 920 001★	C09 720 000★	1,800,000	30.00

CLEVELAND

D38 160 001B	D72 000 000B	33,840,000	15.00
D06 120 001★	D07 920 000★	1,800,000	30.00

RICHMOND

E76 680 001B		33,400,000	15.00
	E10 080 000C		15.00
E09 000 001★	E11 160 000★	2,160,000	30.00

ATLANTA

F19 440 001C	F76 500 000C	57,060,000	15.00
F09 720 001★	F12 960 000★	3,240,000	30.00

CHICAGO

G18 720 001D	G75 600 000D	56,880,000	15.00
G13 680 001★	G16 920 000★	3,240,000	30.00

ST. LOUIS

H17 640 001B	H40 320 000B	22,680,000	15.00
H05 400 001★	H06 120 000★	720,000	50.00

MINNEAPOLIS

I43 920 001A	I56 880 000A	12,960,000	15.00
I01 800 001★	I02 520 000★	720,000	50.00

KANSAS CITY

J87 840 001A		24,760,000	15.00
	J12 600 000B		15.00
J05 040 001★	J06 840 000★	1,800,000	30.00

DALLAS

K00 000 001B	K03 960 000B	3,960,000	35.00
K05 040 001★	K05 400 000★	360,000	80.00

SAN FRANCISCO

L01 800 001C	L27 720 000C	25,920,000	15.00
L10 800 001★	L12 240 000★	1,440,000	30.00

SERIES 1950D

SERIAL NUMBERS: All numbers shown are official.

SIGNATURES: Kathryn O'Hay Granahan, C. Douglas Dillon

LOW	HIGH	NOTES	
SERIAL NUMBERS		PRINTED	CU

BOSTON

A36 000 001B	A61 200 000B	25,200,000	$15.00
A06 480 001★	A07 560 000★	1,080,000	30.00

NEW YORK

B26 640 001E		102,160,000	15.00
	B28 800 000F		15.00
B18 360 001★	B23 400 000★	5,040,000	30.00

PHILADELPHIA

C87 480 001B		21,520,000	15.00
	C09 000 000C		15.00
C09 720 001★	C10 800 000★	1,080,000	30.00

CLEVELAND

D72 000 001B	D95 400 000B	23,400 000	15.00
D07 920 001★	D09 000 000★	1,080,000	30.00

RICHMOND

E00 000 099C	E52 560 000C	42,480,000	15.00
E11 160 001★	E12 960 000★	1,800,000	30.00

ATLANTA

F73 800 001C		35,200,000	15.00
	F09 000 000D		15.00
F12 960 001★	F14 760 000★	1,800,000	30.00

CHICAGO

G75 600 001D		67,240,000	15.00
	G42 840 000E		15.00
G16 920 001★	G20 520 000★	3,600,000	30.00

ST. LOUIS

H40 320 001B	H60 480 000B	20,160,000	15.00
H06 120 001★	H06 840 000★	720,000	35.00

MINNEAPOLIS

I56 880 001A	I64 800 000A	7,920,000	15.00
I02 520 001★	I02 880 000★	360,000	50.00

KANSAS CITY

J12 600 001B	J23 760 000B	11,160,000	15.00
J06 840001★	J07 560 000★	720,000	35.00

DALLAS

K02 201 078B	K11 160 000B	7,200,000	15.00
K05 400 001★	K05 760 000★	360,000	40.00

SAN FRANCISCO

L27 720 001C	L81 000 000C	53,280,000	15.00
L12 240 001★	L15 840 000★	3,600,000	30.00

SERIES 1950E

SERIAL NUMBERS: All numbers shown are official.

PLATE SERIALS: Face check numbers on 18 subject sheets end at #436. Back check numbers of 18 subject sheets end at #2587.

SIGNATURES: Kathryn O'Hay Granahan, Henry H. Fowler

LOW SERIAL NUMBERS	HIGH	NOTES PRINTED	CU
NEW YORK			
B28 800 001F		82,000,000	$20.00
	B10 800 000G		20.00
B23 400 001★	B30 100 552★ observed		35.00
CHICAGO			
G42 840 001E	G57 600 000E	14,760,000	25.00
G20 520 001★	G21 600 000★	1,080,000	50.00
SAN FRANCISCO			
L81 000 001C		24,400,000	20.00
	L05 400 000D		25.00
L15 840 001★	L17 640 000★	1,800,000	50.00

SERIES 1963

SERIAL NUMBERS: All districts started both regular and star notes with serial 00 000 001.

PLATE SERIALS: Both face and back check numbers begin at #1 with 32 subject sheets. Motto IN GOD WE TRUST added to back.

SIGNATURES: Kathryn O'Hay Granahan, C. Douglas Dillon.

SERIAL NUMBERS	NOTES PRINTED	CU
BOSTON		
A-A	4,480,000	$14.00
A-★	640,000	45.00
NEW YORK		
B-A	12,160,000	14.00
B-★	1,280,000	20.00
PHILADELPHIA		
C-A	8,320,000	14.00
C-★	1,920,000	20.00
CLEVELAND		
D-A	10,240,000	14.00
D-★	1,920,000	20.00
ATLANTA		
F-A	17,920,000	14.00
F-★	2,560,000	20.00
CHICAGO		
G-A	22,400,000	14.00
G-★	3,200,000	16.00
ST. LOUIS		
H-A	14,080,000	14.00
H-★	1,920,000	20.00
KANSAS CITY		
J-A	1,920,000	14.00
J-★	640,000	45.00
DALLAS		
K-A	5,760,000	14.00
K-★	1,920,000	20.00
SAN FRANCISCO		
L-A	18,560,000	14.00
L-★	1,920,000	20.00

SERIES 1963A

SERIAL NUMBERS: All districts continued sequence from previous series.

SIGNATURES: Kathryn O'Hay Granahan, Henry F. Fowler

LOW SERIAL NUMBERS	HIGH	NOTES PRINTED	CU
BOSTON			
A04 480 001A	A81 920 000A	77,440,000	$12.00
A00 640 001★	A06 400 000★	5,760,000	17.00

NEW YORK

B12 160 001A	B12 160 001A	85,160,000	12.00
B-B	B10 240 000B	10,240,000	12.00
B01 280 001★	B08 960 000★	7,040,000	17.00

PHILADELPHIA

C08 320 001A		91,680,000	12.00
C-B	C14 720 000B	14,720,000	12.00
C01 920 001★	C12 160 000★	8,320,000	17.00

CLEVELAND

D10 240 001A	D94 080 000A	83,840,000	12.00
D01 920 001★	D08 960 000★	7,040,000	17.00

RICHMOND

E00 000 001A		99,999,999	12.00
E-B	E18 560 000B	18,560,000	12.00
E00 000 001★	E10 880 000★	10,880,000	17.00

ATLANTA

F17 920 001A		82,080,000	12.00
F-B	F35 840 000B	35,840,000	12.00
F02 560 001★	F12 160 000★	9,600,000	17.00

CHICAGO

G22 400 001A		77,600,000	12.00
G-B		99,999,999	12.00
G-C	G35 840 000C	35,840,000	12.00
G03 200 001★	G19 840 000★	16,640,000	17.00

ST. LOUIS

H14 080 001A	H71 040 000A	56,960,000	12.00
H01 920 001★	H07 040 000★	5,120,000	17.00

MINNEAPOLIS

I00 000 001A	I32 640 000A	32,640,000	12.00
I00 000 001★	I03 200 000★	3,200,000	17.00

KANSAS CITY

J01 920 001A	J56 960 000A	55,040,000	12.00
J00 640 001★	J06 400 000★	5,760,000	17.00

DALLAS

K05 760 001A	K67 760 000A	64,000,000	12.00
K01 920 001★	K05 760 000★	3,340,000	17.00

SAN FRANCISCO

L18 560 001A		81,440,000	12.00
L-B	L47 360 000B	47,860,000	12.00
L01 920 001★	L14 073 000★	12,153,000	17.00

SERIES **1969**

SERIAL NUMBERS: All districts started both regular and star notes with serial 00 000 001.

PLATE SERIALS: Face check numbers begin at # 1. Back check numbers continue from previous series.

SIGNATURES: Dorothy Andrews Elston, David M. Kennedy

SERIAL NUMBER	NOTES PRINTED	CU
BOSTON		
A-A	51,200,000	$10.00
A-★	1,920,000	20.00
NEW YORK		
B-A	99,999,999	10.00
B-B	98,560,000	10.00
B-★	8,800,000	18.00
PHILADELPHIA		
C-A	60,120,000	10.00
C-★	2,560,000	20.00
CLEVELAND		
D-A	56,320,000	10.00
D-★	2,560,000	20.00

SERIAL NUMBER	NOTES PRINTED	CU
RICHMOND		
E-A	84,480,000	10.00
E-★	3,200,000	20.00
ATLANTA		
F-A	84,480,000	10.00
F-★	3,840,000	20.00
CHICAGO		
G-A	99,999,999	10.00
G-B	25,600,000	10.00
G-★	5,120,000	20.00
ST. LOUIS		
H-A	27,520,000	10.00
H-★	1,280,000	20.00

MINNEAPOLIS

I-A	16,640,000	10.00
I-★	640,000	25.00

KANSAS CITY

J-A	48,640,000	10.00
J-★	3,192,000	20.00

DALLAS

K-A	39,680,000	10.00
K-★	1,920,000	20.00

SAN FRANCISCO

L-A	99,999,999	10.00
L-B	3,840,000	15.00
L-★	4,480,000	20.00

SERIES 1969A

SERIAL NUMBERS: All districts continued sequence from previous series.

SIGNATURES: Dorothy Andrews Kabis, John B. Connally

LOW SERIAL NUMBERS	HIGH	NOTES PRINTED	CU
BOSTON			
A51 200 001A	A74 240 000A	23,040,000	$12.00
A01 920 001★	A03 200 000★	1,280,000	30.00
NEW YORK			
B98 560 001B		1,440,000	35.00
	B60 800 000C	60,800,000	12.00
B09 120 001★	B10 880 000★	1,760,000	25.00
PHILADELPHIA			
C60 120 001A		39,880,000	12.00
	C01 280 000B	1,280,000	25.00
C02 650 001★	C04 480 000★	1,760,000	25.00
CLEVELAND			
D56 320 001A	D77 440 000A	21,120,000	12.00
D02 560 001★	D03 200 000★	640,000	35.00
RICHMOND			
E84 480 001A		15,520,000	12.00
	E22 400 000B	22,400,000	12.00
E03 360 001★	E04 480 000★	1,120,000	30.00
ATLANTA			
F84 480 001A		15,520,000	12.00
	F09 600 000B	9,600,000	12.00
F04 000 001★	F04 480 000★	480,000	35.00
CHICAGO			
G25 600 001B	G86 400 000B	60,800,000	12.00
G05 120 001★	G07 040 000★	1,920,000	25.00
ST. LOUIS			
H27 520 001A	H42 880 000A	15,360,000	12.00
H01 280 001★	H01 920 000★	640,000	35.00
MINNEAPOLIS			
I16 640 001A	I25 600 000A	8,960,000	12.00
I00 640 001★	I01 280 000★	640,000	35.00

KANSAS CITY

J48 640 001A	J66 560 000A	17,920,000	12.00
J03 200 001★	J03 840 000★	640,000	35.00

DALLAS

K39 680 001A	K60 800 000A	21,120,000	12.00
K01 920 001★	K02 560 000★	640,000	35.00

SAN FRANCISCO

L03 840 001B	L48 640 000B	44,800,000	12.00
L04 480 001★	L06 400 000★	1,920,000	25.00

SERIES 1969B

SIGNATURES: Romana Acosta Banuelos, John B. Connally

SERIAL NUMBERS		NOTES PRINTED	CU

BOSTON

A74 240 001A	A80 000 000A	5,760,000	$20.00
A-★		None printed	

NEW YORK

B60 800 001C	B95 360 000C	34,560,000	14.00
B10 880 001★	B11 520 000★	640,000	50.00

PHILADELPHIA

C01 280 001B	C06 400 000B	5,120,000	20.00
C-★		None printed	

CLEVELAND

D77 440 001**A**	**D**89 600 000**A**	12,160,000	20.00
D-★		None printed	

RICHMOND

E22 400 001**B**	**E**37 760 000**B**	15,360,000	20.00
E04 480 001★	**E**05 120 000★	640,000	50.00

ATLANTA

F09 600 001**B**	**F**28 160 000**B**	18,560,000	20.00
F04 480 001★	**F**05 120 000★	640,000	50.00

CHICAGO

G86 400 001**B**		13,600,000	18.00
G-**C**	**G**13 440 000**C**	13,440,000	18.00
G07 200 000★	**G**07 680 000★	480,000	50.00

ST. LOUIS

H42 880 001**A**	**H**48 000 000**A**	5,120,000	20.00
H-★		None printed	

MINNEAPOLIS

I25 600 001**A**	I33 920 000**A**	8,320,000	20.00
I-★		None printed	

KANSAS CITY

J66 560 001**A**	**J**74 880 000**A**	8,320,000	20.00
J03 840 001★	**J**04 448 000★	640,000	50.00

DALLAS

K60 800 001**A**	**K**72 960 000**A**	12,160,000	20.00
K-★		None printed	

SAN FRANCISCO

L48 640 001**B**	**L**72 320 000**B**	23,680,000	20.00
L06 400 001★	**L**07 040 000★	640,000	50.00

SERIES 1969C

SIGNATURES: Romana Acosta Banuelos, George P. Shultz

SERIAL NUMBERS		NOTES PRINTED	CU

BOSTON

A80 000 001**A**		20,000,000	$10.00
	A30 720 000**B**	30,720,000	10.00
A03 200 001★	**A**05 120 000★	1,920,000	25.00

NEW YORK

B95 536 001**C**		4,640,000	25.00
B-**D**		99,840,000	10.00
	B15 360 000**E**	15,360,000	10.00
B11 520 001★	**B**13 920 000★	2,400,000	25.00

PHILADELPHIA

C06 400 001B	C60 160 000B	53,760,000	10.00
C04 480 001★	C05 760 000★	1,280,000	25.00

CLEVELAND

D89 600 001A		10,400,000	10.00
	D33 280 000B	33,280,000	10.00
D03 200 001★	D03 680 000★	480,000	40.00

RICHMOND

E37 760 001B		62,240,000	10.00
	E11 520 000C	11,520,000	10.00
E05 150 000★	E05 760 000★	640,000	35.00

ATLANTA

F28 160 001B		71,840,000	10.00
	F09 600 000C	9,600,000	10.00
F05 120 001★	F08 320 000★	3,200,000	25.00

CHICAGO

G13 440 001C	G67 840 000C	54,400,000	10.00
G-★		None printed	

ST. LOUIS

H48 000 000A	H86 400 000A	38,400,000	10.00
H01 920 001★	H03 200 000★	12,800,000	25.00

MINNEAPOLIS

I33 920 001A	I45 400 000A	11,520,000	10.00
I-★		None printed	

KANSAS CITY

J74 880 001A		25,120,000	10.00
	J16 000 000B	16,000,000	10.00
J04 480 001★	J06 400 000★	1,920,000	25.00

DALLAS

K72 960 001A		27,040,000	10.00
	K14 080 000B	14,080,000	10.00
K02 560 001★	K04 480 000★	1,920,000	25.00

SAN FRANCISCO

L72 320 001B		27,680,000	10.00
	L57 120 000C	57,120,000	10.00
L07 040 001★	L10 080 000★	3,040,000	25.00

SERIES 1974

SIGNATURES: Francine I. Neff, William E. Simon

SERIAL NUMBERS: All districts continue in sequence from previous series.

PLATE SERIALS: Check numbers continue from previous series.

SERIAL NUMBERS		NOTES PRINTED	CU

BOSTON

A30 720 001B	A88 960 000B	58,240,000	$10.00
A05 120 001★	A06 588 000★	1,468,000	20.00

NEW YORK

B15 600 001E		84,640,999	10.00
	B68 480 000F	68,480,000	10.00
B13 920 001★	B16 736 000★	2,816,000	15.00

PHILADELPHIA

C60 160 001B		39,840,999	10.00
	C14 800 000C	14,080,000	10.00
C05 760 001★	C08 320 000★	2,560,000	15.00

CLEVELAND

D33 280 001B		66,200,000	10.00
	D11 520 000C	11,520,000	10.00
D03 840 001★	D05 760 000★	1,920,000	20.00

RICHMOND

E11 520 001C		88,480,000	10.00
	E46 720 000D	46,720,000	10.00
E05 760 001★	E07 680 000★	1,920,000	20.00

ATLANTA

F09 600 001C		90,400,000	10.00
	F37 120 000D	37,120,000	10.00
F08 320 001★	F11 520 000★	3,200,000	15.00

CHICAGO

G67 840 001C		32,160,000	10.00
	G63 360 000D	63,360,000	10.00
G07 680 001★	G14 080 000★	6,400,000	15.00

ST. LOUIS

H-86 400 001A		14,720,000	10.00
	H51 200 000B	51,200,000	10.00
H03 200 001★	H03 400 000★	640,000	25.00

MINNEAPOLIS

| I45 440 001A | I87 040 000A | 41,600,000 | 10.00 |
| I01 280 001★ | I03 840 000★ | 2,560,000 | 15.00 |

KANSAS CITY

| J16 000 001B | J58 240 000B | 42,240,000 | 10.00 |
| J06 400 001★ | J08 448 000★ | 2,048,000 | 15.00 |

DALLAS

| K14 080 001B | K71 800 000B | 57,600,000 | 10.00 |
| K04 480 001★ | K06 260 000★ | 1,782,000 | 20.00 |

SAN FRANCISCO

L57 120 001C		43,880,000	10.00
	L92 800 000D	92,800,000	10.00
L10 080 001★	L14 688 000★	4,608,000	15.00

SERIES 1977

SIGNATURES: Azie Taylor Morton, W. Michael Blumenthal
SERIAL NUMBERS: All districts, regular and stars begin at 00 000 001.

PLATE SERIALS: Face and back check numbers continue from previous series.

SERIAL NUMBER	NOTES PRINTED	CU
BOSTON		
A-A	60,800,000	$10.00
A-★	256,000	25.00
NEW YORK		
B-A	99,840,000	10.00
B-B	83,200,000	10.00
B-★	2,560,000	15.00
PHILADELPHIA		
C-A	78,280,000	10.00
C-★	1,280,000	15.00
CLEVELAND		
D-A	76,160,000	10.00
D-★	864,000	20.00

	RICHMOND	
E-A	99,840,000	10.00
E-B	10,880,000	10.00
E-★	2,816,000	15.00
ATLANTA		
F-A	99,840,000	10.00
F-B	27,520,000	10.00
F-★	1,792,000	20.00
CHICAGO		
G-A	99,840,000	10.00
G-B	77,440,000	10.00
G-★	2,944,000	15.00
ST. LOUIS		
H-A	46,080,000	10.00
H-★	128,000	30.00
MINNEAPOLIS		
I-A	21,760,000	10.00
I-★	None printed	
KANSAS CITY		
J-A	78,080,000	10.00
J-★	1,024,000	25.00

DALLAS

K-A	60,800,000	10.00
K-★	1,024,000	20.00

SAN FRANCISCO

L-A	99,840,000	10.00
L-B	44,800,000	10.00
L-★	1,816,000	20.00

SERIES 1977A

SIGNATURES: Azie Taylor Morton, G. William Miller
SERIAL NUMBERS: Continue from previous series.

PLATE SERIALS: Continue from previous series.

SERIAL NUMBER	NOTES PRINTED	CU
BOSTON		
A-A	39,040,000	$10.00
A-B	8,960,000	10.00
A-★	512,000	25.00
NEW YORK		
B-B	16,640,000	10.00
B-C	97,280,000	10.00
B-★	2,304,000	15.00
PHILADELPHIA		
C-A	21,120,000	10.00
C-B		10.00
C-★	2,048,000	15.00
CLEVELAND		
D-A	27,744,000	10.00
D-B	32,000,000	10.00
D-★	1,024,000	25.00
RICHMOND		
E-B	77,440,000	10.00
E-★	128,000	25.00
ATLANTA		
F-B	72,320,000	10.00
F-C	3,840,000	10.00
F-★	1,152,000	15.00
CHICAGO		
G-B	22,800,000	10.00
G-C	58,880,000	10.00
G-★	1,536,000	15.00
ST. LOUIS		
H-A	32,000,000	10.00
H-★	640,000	25.00
MINNEAPOLIS		
I-A	10,240,000	10.00
I-★	128,000	25.00
KANSAS CITY		
J-A	21,760,000	10.00
J-B	30,720,000	10.00
J-★	1,152,000	25.00
DALLAS		
K-A	39,040,000	10.00
K-B	37,120,000	10.00
K-★	2,166,000	20.00

SAN FRANCISCO

L-B	55,040,000	10.00
L-C	42,240,000	10.00
L-★	1,152,000	15.00

SERIES **1981**

SIGNATURES. Angela M. Buchanan, Donald T. Regan

SERIAL NUMBERS: All blocks begin at 00 000 001.

PLATE SERIALS: Back check numbers continue from previous series. Face check numbers begin at #1.

SERIAL NUMBER	NOTES PRINTED	CU
	BOSTON	
A-A	99,400,000	$10.00
A-B	9,600,000	14.00
A-★	None printed	

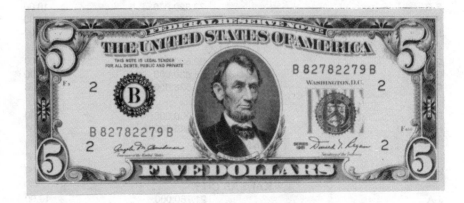

	NEW YORK	
B-A	99,840,000	10.00
B-B	99,840,000	10.00
B-C	51,200,000	10.00
B-★	4,464,000	20.00

PHILADELPHIA

C-A	99,840,000	10.00
C-B	12,800,000	10.00
C-★	640,000	20.00

CLEVELAND

D-A	99,840,000	10.00
D-B	22,400,000	10.00
D-★	1,268,000	20.00

RICHMOND

E-A	99,840,000	10.00
E-B	99,840,000	10.00
E-C	35,200,000	10.00
E-★	640,000	20.00

ATLANTA

F-A	99,840,000	10.00
F-B	99,840,000	10.00
F-C	35,200,000	10.00
F-★	640,000	20.00

CHICAGO

G-A	99,840,000	10.00
G-B	99,840,000	10.00
G-C	41,600,000	10.00
G-★	640,000	20.00

ST. LOUIS

H-A	99,840,000	10.00
H-B	99,840,000	10.00
H-★	628,000	20.00

MINNEAPOLIS

I-A	99,840,000	10.00
I-B	9,600,000	10.00
I-★	640,000	20.00

KANSAS CITY

J-A	99,840,000	10.00
J-B	25,600,000	10.00
J-★	960,000	20.00

DALLAS

K-A	99,840,000	10.00
K-B	38,400,000	10.00
K-★	640,000	20.00

SAN FRANCISCO

L-A	99,840,000	10.00
L-B	99,840,000	10.00
L-C	64,000,000	10.00
L-★	2,560,000	20.00

SERIES 1981A

SIGNATURES: Katherine Davalos Ortega, Donald T. Regan
SERIAL NUMBERS: All blocks begin at 00 000 001.
PLATE SERIALS: Face and back check numbers continue from previous series.

SERIAL NUMBER	NOTES PRINTED	CU
	BOSTON	
A-A	99,200,000	$10.00
A-B	92,800,000	10.00
A-★	Printing not verified	

NEW YORK

B-A	99,200,000	10.00
B-B	99,200,000	10.00
B-C	99,200,000	10.00
B-D	99,200,000	10.00
B-E	51,200,000	10.00
B02 481 592★ **B**02 855 433★		25.00

PHILADELPHIA

C-A	99,200,000	10.00
C-B	70,400,000	10.00
C-★	None printed	

CLEVELAND

D-A	99,200,000	10.00
D-B	99,200,000	10.00
D-C	16,000,000	10.00
D-★	None printed	

RICHMOND

E-A	99,200,000	10.00
E-B	99,200,000	10.00
E-C	99,200,000	10.00
E-D	35,200,000	10.00
E-★	3,200,000	20.00

ATLANTA

F-A	99,200,000	10.00
F-B	99,200,000	10.00
F-C	99,200,000	10.00
F-D	54,400,000	10.00
F-★	none printed	

CHICAGO

G-A	99,200,000	10.00
G-B	99,200,000	10.00
G-C	99,200,000	10.00
G-D	48,000,000	10.00
G-★	none printed	

ST. LOUIS

H-A	99,200,000	10.00
H-B	28,800,000	10.00
H-★	none printed	

MINNEAPOLIS			
I-A		73,800,000	10.00
I-★		none printed	
KANSAS CITY			
J-A		99,200,000	10.00
J-B		35,200,000	10.00
J-★		none printed	
DALLAS			
K-A		99,200,000	10.00
K-B		76,800,000	10.00
K-★		3,200,000	20.00
SAN FRANCISCO			
L-A		99,200,000	10.00
L-B		99,200,000	10.00
L-C		99,200,000	10.00
L-D		99,200,000	10.00
L-E		41,600,000	10.00
L-★		3,200,000	20.00

SERIES 1985

SERIAL NUMBERS: All districts started numbering notes with 00 000 001.

PLATE SERIALS: Back check numbers continue from previous series. Face check numbers begin at #1.

SIGNATURES: Katherine Davalos Ortega, James A. Baker III.

SERIAL NUMBER		NOTES PRINTED	CU
		BOSTON	
A-A		192,800,000	$10.00
	A92 800 000B		10.00
		NEW YORK	
B-A		451,200,000	10.00
B-B			10.00
B-C			10.00
B-D			10.00
	B51 200 000E		10.00
	B03 200 000★	3,200,000	20.00
		PHILADELPHIA	
C-A		170,400,000	10.00
	C70 400 000B		10.00
	C00 416 307★		25.00

CLEVELAND

D-A		116,000,000	10.00
D-B			10.00
	D16 000 000**C**		10.00

RICHMOND

E-A		335,200,000	10.00
E-B			10.00
E-C			10.00
	E35 200 000**D**		10.00
	E03 200 000★	3,200,000	20.00

ATLANTA

F-A		354,400,000	10.00
F-B			10.00
F-C			10.00
	F54 400 000**D**		10.00
	F06 400 000★	6,400,000	20.00

CHICAGO

G-A		348,000,000	10.00
G-B			10.00
G-C			10.00
	G48 000 000**D**		10.00
	G06 400 000★	6,400,000	20.00

ST. LOUIS

H-A		128,800,000	10.00
	H28 800 000**B**		10.00

MINNEAPOLIS

I-A		173,600,000	10.00
	I73 600 000**B**		10.00

KANSAS CITY

J-A		135,200,000	10.00
	J35 200 000**B**		10.00

DALLAS

K-A		176,800,000	10.00
	K76 800 000**B**		10.00

SAN FRANCISCO

L-A		460,800,000	10.00
L-B			10.00
L-C			10.00
L-D			10.00
	L60 800 000**E**		10.00
	L03 200 000★	3,200,000	20.00

SERIES 1988

SIGNATURES: Katherine D. Ortega, Nicholas F. Brady
SERIAL NUMBERS: All districts, regulars and stars, begin at 00 000 001.
PLATE SERIALS: Back check numbers continue from previous series. Face check numbers begin at #1.

SERIAL NUMBER	NOTES PRINTED	CU
BOSTON		
A-A	86,400,000	$10.00
A-★	768,000	20.00
NEW YORK		
B-A	99,200,000	10.00
B-B	86,400,000	10.00
B-★	3,200,000	15.00
PHILADELPHIA		
C-A	54,400,000	10.00

CLEVELAND

D-A	99,200,000	10.00
D-B	12,000,000	10.00

RICHMOND

E-A	99,200,000	10.00
E-B	32,000,000	10.00

ATLANTA

F-A	99,200,000	10.00
F-B	38,000,000	10.00
F-★	6,400,000	15.00

CHICAGO

G-A	99,200,000	10.00
G-B	35,200,000	10.00

ST. LOUIS

H-A	51,200,000	10.00

MINNEAPOLIS

I-A	9,600,000	10.00

KANSAS CITY

J-A	44,800,000	10.00

DALLAS

K-A	54,400,000	10.00

SAN FRANCISCO

L-A	70,400,000	10.00

SERIES 1988A

SERIAL NUMBERS: All districts started numbering notes with 00 000 001. Fort Worth printings are interspersed with standard Washington D.C. issues.

PLATE SERIALS: Face check numbers begin at #1. Back check numbers continue from previous series.

SIGNATURES: Catalina Vasquez Villalpando, Nicholas F. Brady.

SERIAL BLOCK	PTG. LOC.		NOTES PRINTED	CU
		BOSTON		
A-A	W		96,000,000	$10.00
A-B			44,800,000	10.00
A-★	W	A03 200 000★	3,200,000	20.00

NEW YORK

B-A	W		96,000,000	10.00
B-B	W		96,000,000	10.00
B-C	W		96,000,000	10.00
B-D	W		96,000,000	10.00
B-E	W		96,000,000	10.00
B-F	W		96,000,000	10.00
B-G	W		64,000,000	10.00
B-★	W	B06 400 000★	4,608,000	20.00

PHILADELPHIA

C-A	W/FW		96,000,000	10.00
C-B	W		25,000,000	10.00

CLEVELAND

D-A	W		96,000,000	10.00
D-B	W		32,000,000	10.00
D-C	W		38,000,000	10.00
D-★	W	D00 640 000★	4,864,000	20.00

RICHMOND

E-A,-E-E	High observed		480,000,000	10.00
E-F	W		6,400,000	25.00
E-★	W	E09 600 000★	3,020,000	20.00

ATLANTA

F-A	W		96,000,000	10.00
F-B	W/FW		96,000,000	10.00
F-C	FW		96,000,000	10.00
F-D	FW		96,800,000	10.00
F-E	W/FW		89,600,000	10.00
F-★	W/FW	F09 600 000★	3,280,000	20.00

CHICAGO

G-A through G-H			633,600,000	10.00
G-★	FW		1,280,000	20.00

ST. LOUIS

H-A,H-B	W		185,600,000	10.00
H-★	W	H03 200 000★	1,280,000	20.00

MINNEAPOLIS

I-A	W		73,600,000	10.00
I-★	W	I03 200 000★	3,200,000	20.00

KANSAS CITY

J-A	W/FW	96,000,000	10.00
J-B	W	44,800,000	10.00

DALLAS

K-A	W/FW	96,000,000	10.00
K-B	W/FW	76,800,000	10.00

SAN FRANCISCO

L-A,L-H	W/WF		672,000,000	10.00
L-★	FW	L03 200 000★	2,560,000	20.00

SERIES 1993

SERIAL NUMBERS: All districts started numbering both regular and star notes with 00 000 001.

PLATE SERIALS: Face check numbers begin at #1. Back check numbers continue from previous series.

SIGNATURES: Mary Ellen Withrow, Lloyd Bentsen.

LOW		HIGH	NOTES	
	SERIAL NUMBERS		PRINTED	CU

BOSTON

A-A		A19 200 000A	19,200,000	$10.00

NEW YORK

B-A			96,000,000	10.00
B-B		B06 400 000B	6,400,000	15.00
B-★		B03 206 000★	3,200,000	20.00

PHILADELPHIA

C-A		C38 400 000A	38,400,000	10.00

RICHMOND

E-A		E76 800 000A	76,800,000	10.00
E-★		E03 200 000★	1,920,000	10.00

ATLANTA

F-A		F70 400 000A	70,400,000	10.00

CHICAGO

G-A	FW	G 64 000 000A	64,000,000	10.00
G-★	FW	G01 280 000★	1,280,000	20.00

ST. LOUIS

H-A	FW	H64 000 000A	64,000,000	10.00
H-★	FW	H03 200 000★	3,200,000	20.00

MINNEAPOLIS

I-A	FW	I06 400 000A	6,400,000	15.00

KANSAS CITY

J-A	FW	J32 000 000A	32,000,000	10.00

DALLAS

K-A	FW	K57 600 000A	57,600,000	10.00

SAN FRANCISCO

L-A, L-B	FW	L89 600 000B	185,600,000	10.00
L-★	FW	L02 560 000★	2,560,000	20.00

SERIES **1995**

SIGNATURES: Mary Ellen Withrow, Robert E. Rubin

PLATE SERIALS: Face check numbers begin at #1. Back check numbers continue from previous series, creating mules, then start #1 in mid-series.

SERIAL NUMBERS: Both regular and star notes begin at 00 000 001.

LOW SERIAL NUMBERS		HIGH	NOTES PRINTED	CU
BOSTON				
A-A,A-B		A57 600 000B	153,600,000	$10.00
A-★		A00 640 000B	640,000	25.00
N EW YORK				
B-A,-B-C		B76 800 000C	364,800,000	10.00
B-★		B05 120 000★	3,840,000	20.00
PHILADELPHIA				
C-A		C76 800 000A	76,800,000	10.00
CLEVELAND				
D-A	W/FW	D57 600 000A	57,600,000	10.00
D-★	FW	D03 200 000★	3,200,000	20.00
RICHMOND				
E-A,E-B	FW	E64 000 000B	256,000,000	10.00
ATLANTA				
F-A	W		96,000,000	10.00
F-B	W/WF		96,000,000	10.00
F-C	FW	F83 200 000C	83,200,000	10.00
CHICAGO				
G-A,-G-B	FW	G64 000 000B	160,000,000	10.00
ST. LOUIS				
H-A	FW	H89 600 000A	89,600,000	10.00
MINNEAPOLIS				
I-A	FW	I38 400 000A	38,400,000	10.00
KANSAS CITY				
J-A	FW	J44 800 000A	44,800,000	10.00
DALLAS				
K-A	FW	K64 000 000A	64,000,000	10.00
SAN FRANCISCO				
L-A,-L-C	FW	L89 600 000A	281,600,000	10.00

SERIES 1995 Remains in production at press time.

TEN DOLLAR NATIONAL BANK NOTES

Brown Seal

Type I has black serial numbers on the ends of the note. The left reading horizontally, the right reading vertically. Type II is similar, but the brown serial number is succeeded or preceded by the charter number also. All notes have facsimile signatures of E. E. Jones and W. O. Woods at the top. Signatures of the officers of the local bank appear at the bottom.

See listings under Five Dollar denomination for detailed information as to rarity and value.

TEN DOLLAR NOTES
FEDERAL RESERVE
BANK NOTES
Brown Seal
SERIES 1929

SERIAL NUMBERS: Figures shown below are the official high numbers. All districts started both regular and star notes with serial 00 000 001. Bureau of Engraving and Printing information is incomplete on star serial numbers, as are reports of high observed serial numbers.

PLATE SERIALS: Face check numbers within the range #1 through #290.

SIGNATURES: E.E. Jones, W.O. Woods

Also the Federal Reserve Bank Cashier or Controller or the Deputy or Assistant Deputy Governor, with the Governor.

SERIAL NUMBER		NOTES PRINTED	VF	CU
BOSTON				
A00 485 578A	A01 680 000A	1,680,000	$20.00	$60.00
A00 001 088★		24,000	400.00	1500.00
NEW YORK				
B00 010 039A	B05 556 000A	5,556,000	15.00	42.50
B00 001 634★	B00 067 879★	76,000	150.00	1000.00
PHILADELPHIA				
C00 213 248A	C01 416 000A	1,416,000	18.00	55.00
C00 007 359★	C00 012 526★	24,000	200.00	1250.00
CLEVELAND				
D00 000 010A	D02 412 000A	2,412,000	18.00	60.00
D00 015 541★	D00 023 401★	36,000	250.00	1250.00
RICHMOND				
E00 000 006A	E01 356 000A	1,356,000	22.00	85.00
E00 015 295★	E00 018 228★	24,000	250.00	1500.00
ATLANTA				
F00 080 689A	F01 056 000A	1,056,000	22.00	65.00
F00 002 270★	F00 003 158A	36,000	400.00	1500.00

		CHICAGO		
G00 213 072A	G03 156 000A	3,156,000	18.00	45.00
G00 002 151★	G00 006 988★	12,000	250.00	1500.00

ST. LOUIS

H00 302 369A	H01 584 000A	1,584,000	18.00	55.00
H00 000 547★	H00 029 408★	36,000	200.00	1000.00

MINNEAPOLIS

I00 174 847A	I00 588 000A	588,000	20.00	70.00
I00 000 547★	I00 020 529★	24,000	250.00	1500.00

KANSAS CITY

J00 000 010A	J01 284 000A	1,284,000	20.00	60.00
J00 000 582★	J00 025 816★	36,000	175.00	750.00

DALLAS

K00 178 892A	K00 504 000A	504,000	400.00	1000.
K00 000 183★	K00 000 189★	12,000	1000.00	2500.00

SAN FRANCISCO

L00 017 495A	L01 080 000A	1,080,000	22.00	90.00
L00 000 889★	L00 015 245★	36,000	200.00	1200.00

LEGAL TENDER
Red Seal
SERIES 1928

SERIAL NUMBERS: No Bureau record of printing.

PLATE SERIALS: Face and back check number 1.

SIGNATURES: Walter O. Woods, W.H. Woodin

One specimen of this note was displayed at the Chicago Worlds Fair in 1933 (along with a $20).

GOLD CERTIFICATE
Gold Seal
SERIES 1928

PLATE SERIALS: Face check #1 through #290.

SIGNATURES: Walter O. Woods, Andrew W. Mellon

SERIAL NUMBER		NOTES PRINTED	VG/F	CU
A00 000 001A	A99 999 999A	99,999,999	$25.00	$250.00
B00 000 001A	B30 812 000A	30,812,000	75.00	350.00
★00 025 276A	★01 473 261A		150.00	750.00

GOLD CERTIFICATE

Gold Seal

SERIES 1928A

SERIAL NUMBER	NOTES PRINTED	VG/F	CU
B30 802 001**A** B33 346 000**A**	2,544,000		Unknown

SIGNATURES: Walter O. Woods, Ogden L. Mills

NOTE: Although BEP records indicate that 2,544,000 notes were DELIVERED, it is believed that all are in storage vaults in the basement of the Main Treasury Building, Washington, D.C. and that none were released to the public.

TREASURY REMOVES RESTRICTIONS ON UNITED STATES

GOLD CERTIFICATES ISSUED BEFORE 1934

On April 24, 1964, the Secretary of the Treasury issued Regulations removing all restrictions on the acquisition or holding of gold certificates which were issued by the United States Government prior to January 30, 1934. The main effect of this action will be to permit collectors to hold this type of currency.

The restrictions which are being eliminated are considered no longer necessary or desirable. Under the laws enacted in 1934, these pre-1934 gold certificates are not redeemable in gold. They will, of course, continue to be exchangeable at face value for other currency of the United States.

The new Regulation authorizing the holding of gold certificates applies only to United States gold certificates issued prior to January 30, 1934. The holding of any other type of gold certificates, including any issued by foreigners against gold held on deposit abroad, continues to be prohibited. Also, the status of the special series gold certificates issued by the U.S. Treasury only to the Federal Reserve system for reserve purposes is not affected.

SILVER CERTIFICATE

Blue Seal

SERIES 1933

PLATE SERIALS: Face check #1 only.

SIGNATURES: W.A. Julian, W.H. Woodin

SERIAL NUMBER	NOTES PRINTED	VF	CU
A00 000 001**A** A00 216 000**A**	216,000	$2500.00	$6500.00
★00 000 002**A**	ONE KNOWN	7500.00	30,000.

Blue Seal

SERIES 1933A

PLATE SERIALS: Face check #1 only.

SIGNATURES: W.A. Julian, Henry Morgenthau, Jr.

SERIAL NUMBER	NOTES PRINTED	VF	CU
A00 216 001A A00 552 000A	336,000		Unknown

In November 1935, 368,000 $10.00 silver certificates were destroyed. Reports indicate that 156,000 Series 1933 and 60,000 Series 1933A were released and that the balance of 60,000 1933 and 308,000 of the 1933A were destroyed, however these reports are believed to be inaccurate since NO 1933A regular notes have ever been reported. It is likely that the destruction included the entire printing of 1933A.

Perhaps the most desired notes in the small series Silver Certificates are Series of 1933 and 1933A $10.00 notes. Issued in the year 1933, their manufacture was cut short by the Administration's change in the silver policy. These two (1933 and 1933A) are the only certificates mentioning the word "coin" as such. The Series of 1933 were issued just prior to Woodin's retirement (signatures W.A. Julian and W.H. Woodin). This $10.00 differs from all other Silver Certificates, being inscribed "The United States of America-Ten Dollars-payable in silver coin to bearer on demand." No mention is made of the deposit of the silver. Only a few plates were prepared and only face check #1 is known. Later in the year Series 1933A was printed, Morgenthau's name replacing that of Woodin. A proof of a 12 subject sheet is in the Smithsonian Archives. The bureau occasionally exhibits its 12-subject sheet of specimen notes, but no one has ever verified the existence of an issued note.

Blue Seal

SERIES 1934

PLATE SERIALS: Back check numbers #584 (micro size) and lower.

SIGNATURES: W.A. Julian, Henry Morgenthau, Jr.

DESIGN: Face design for series 1934 through 1934D shows large blue 10 to left of portrait of Hamilton, blue Treasury seal at right. Back design same as 1933. Face and back check number doubled in size for series 1934A and beyond.

LOW	HIGH	NOTES		
SERIAL NUMBERS		PRINTED	VF	CU
A00 000 001A	A84 946 579A	88,692,864	$20.00	$50.00
★00 000 111A	★00 939 068A	All Types	50.00	350.00
		of Series 1934		

Blue Seal

SERIES 1934 MULE

These are series 1934 notes with the larger back check numbers (585 or higher), and are actually Series 1934 Face on Series 1934A Back.

LOW	HIGH	NOTES		
SERIAL NUMBERS		PRINTED	VF	CU
A34 998 118A	A91 044 000A	Included above	$22.00	$55.00
B00 904 000A	B16 924 554A		100.00	200.00
★00 000 111A	★01 007 810A		50.00	350.00

NORTH AFRICA
Yellow Seal
SERIES 1934 Mule

PLATE SERIALS: Back check number 585 or higher. Face check numbers 116, 122, 123, 125, 126, and 127.

SIGNATURES: W.A. Julian, Henry Morgenthau, Jr.

SERIAL NUMBER		NOTES PRINTED	VF	CU
A91 061 041A	Low Observed		$2000.00	$6000.00
B07 560 760A	High Observed		2000.00	7500.00
★01 122 388A			7500.00	

Only 12 CU specimens are known. One circulated star note is known.

SERIES 1934A

Blue Seal

SERIAL NUMBER		NOTES PRINTED	VG/F	CU
A74 862 042A	A91 044 000A	42,346,428	$22.00	$80.00
B00 904 001A	B26 053 155A		50.00	200.00
★00 951 347A	★01 547 059A		65.00	350.00

SERIES 1934A MULE

These are Series 1934A notes with the Micro Back Check Numbers (#584 or lower) and are actually Series 1934A Faces on Series 1934 Backs.
PLATE SERIALS: Back check numbers used #404, 523, 553, and 578.

SERIAL NUMBER		NOTES PRINTED	VF	CU
A74 452 813A	A90 577 124A	Included above	$50.00	$125.00

NORTH AFRICA
SERIES 1934A
Yellow Seal

PLATE SERIALS: Face check #129-209. Back check #585 and higher.

SIGNATURES: Same as Series 1934

LOW	HIGH	NOTES		
SERIAL NUMBERS		PRINTED	VF	CU
A91 044 001A	B00 904 000A		$20.00	$175.00
B00 653 775A	B13 564 000A	21,000,000	20.00	175.00
★01 008 001A	★01 284 000A	276,000	20.00	175.00
★01 008 704A	★01 282 762A		30.00	300.00

Blue Seal

SERIES 1934A LATE FINISHED FACE PLATE 86

SERIAL NUMBER		NOTES PRINTED	VG/F	CU
A84 958 136A	B19 469 564A	Included above	$30.00	$200.00
★00 985 192A	★01 485 388A		50.00	500.00

SERIES 1934A MULE LATE FINISHED FACE PLATE 86

PLATE SERIALS: Face check number 86. Back check used 404, 553, and 578.

LOW	HIGH	NOTES		
	SERIAL NUMBERS	PRINTED	VF	CU
A84 899 119A	A90 853 724A	Included above	250.00	$500.00

SERIES 1934A LATE FINISHED FACE PLATE 87

SERIAL NUMBERS	NOTES PRINTED	VF	CU
A77 166 221A	Included above	$100.00	$1000.00

SERIES 1934A MULE LATE FINISHED FACE PLATE 87

PLATE SERIALS: Face check number 87. Back check: 404, 553 and 578.

LOW	HIGH	NOTES		
	SERIAL NUMBERS	PRINTED	VF	CU
A77 425 715A	A78 491 508A	Included above	250.00	$2500.00

SERIES 1934A NORTH AFRICA LATE FINISHED FACE - PLATE 86

Yellow Seal

SERIAL NUMBER		NOTES PRINTED	VF	CU
A91 816 519A	B11 643 235A	Included above	$75.00	$175.00
★01 010 325A	★01 226 656A		90.00	300.00

SERIES 1934B

Blue Seal

PLATE SERIALS: Face check #211 only.

SIGNATURES: W.A. Julian, Fred M. Vinson

LOW	HIGH	NOTES		
	SERIAL NUMBERS	PRINTED	VF	CU
B15 432 001A	B21 521 396A	337,740	$200.00	$1250.00
★01 333 331A	★01 505 683A		700.00	2400.00

SERIES **1934C**

PLATE SERIALS: Face check number range #214-#232.
SIGNATURES: W.A. Julian, John W. Snyder

SERIAL NUMBERS		NOTES PRINTED	VG/F	CU
B16 848 001A	B43 158 586A	20,032,632	$25.00	$80.00
★01 410 277A	★01 787 573A		40.00	120.00

SERIES **1934D WIDE**

PLATE SERIALS: Face check number range (both groups) #233-#252. Back check numbers #1389 or lower.
SIGNATURES: Georgia Neese Clark, John W. Snyder

LOW	OFFICIAL HIGH	NOTES		
SERIAL NUMBERS		**PRINTED**	**VG/F**	**CU**
B38 556 671A	B50 196 000A	11,801,112	$25.00	$90.00
★01 788 051A	★01 938 558A High observed		35.00	125.00

SERIES **1934D NARROW**

PLATE SERIALS: Back check number range #1390-1456 (Highest of 12 subject sheets).

LOW	OFFICIAL HIGH	NOTES		
SERIAL NUMBERS		**PRINTED**	**VF**	**CU**
B47 556 045A	B50 196 000A	Included above	$100.00	$200.00
★01 932 430A	★01 980 000A		Rare	
★01 939 976A	is high observed.			

$10.00 Wide   **$10.00 Narrow**

SERIES 1953

PLATE SERIALS: Face check numbers begin at #1. Back check numbers begin at #1448 (low of 18 subject sheets).

SIGNATURES: Ivy Baker Priest, George M. Humphrey

LOW	HIGH	NOTES		
SERIAL NUMBERS		**PRINTED**	**VF**	**CU**
A00 000 001A	A10 440 000A	10,440,000	$25.00	$100.00
★00 000 001A	★00 576 000A	576,000	25.00	200.00

SERIES **1953A**

SIGNATURES: Ivy Baker Priest, Robert B. Anderson

LOW SERIAL NUMBERS	HIGH	NOTES PRINTED	VF	VALUE CU
A10 440 001A	A11 520 000A	1,080,000	$30.00	$125.00
★00 576 001A	★00 720 000A	144,000		225.00

SERIES **1953B**

PLATE SERIALS: Face check numbers on 18 subject sheets end at #5. Back check numbers on 18 subject sheets end at #1839.

SIGNATURES: Elizabeth Rudel Smith, C. Douglas Dillon

LOW SERIAL NUMBERS	HIGH	NOTES PRINTED	VF	VALUE CU
A11 520 001A	A12 240 000A	720,000	25.00	$75.00
No star notes printed.				

FEDERAL RESERVE NOTES

Dark Green Seal

SERIES 1928

SERIAL NUMBERS: All serial numbers both regular and star notes begin with 00 000 001.
PLATE SERIALS: All face and back check numbers begin with 1.
SIGNATURE: H.T. Tate, A.W. Mellon

LOW SERIAL NUMBER	HIGH	NOTES PRINTED	VG/F	CU
BOSTON				
A00 000 019**A**	**A**08 690 316**A**	9,804,552	$30.00	$150.00
A00 066 470★	**A**00 236 667★		60.00	350.00

NEW YORK				
B00 172 246**A**	**B**10 035 592**A**	11,295,796	30.00	150.00
B00 012 823★	**B**00040 714★		60.00	350.00
PHILADELPHIA				
C00 005 389**A**	**C**10 847 487**A**	8,114,412	30.00	150.00
C00 099 477★			60.00	350.00
CLEVELAND				
D00 000 032**A**	**D**10 155 855**A**	7,570,680	30.00	150.00
D00 000 996★	**D**00 158 996★		60.00	350.00

RICHMOND

E01 144 031A	E04 378 311A	4,534,800	32.50	150.00
E00 091 579★			60.00	350.00

ATLANTA

F00 002 821A	F08 682 361A	6,807,720	30.00	150.00
			40.00	375.00

CHICAGO

G00 335 365A	G10 778 287A	8,130,000	30.00	140.00
G00 000 042★	G00 304 040★		50.00	325.00

ST. LOUIS

H00 000 012A	H05 157 636A	4,124,400	32.50	150.00
H00 015 245★	H00 146 517★		55.00	350.00

MINNEAPOLIS

I00 000 001A	I03 679 793A	3,874,440	35.00	155.00
I00 044 344★	I00 067 287★		85.00	375.00

KANSAS CITY

J00 000 088A	J04 655 326A	3,620,400	35.00	150.00
J00 004 660★	J00 096 514★		60.00	375.00

DALLAS

K00 000 010A	K04 557 496A	4,855,500	32.50	150.00
K★	K00 096 000★ Official high		60.00	350.00

SAN FRANCISCO

L01 788 631A	L04 918 586A	7,086,900	30.00	160.00
L00 136 294A			45.00	475.00

SERIES 1928A

SERIAL NUMBERS: All districts continued sequence from previous series. Face plates start with #1 Backs continue from previous series.

SIGNATURES: Walter O. Woods, A.W. Mellon

LOW SERIAL NUMBER	HIGH	NOTES PRINTED	VG/F	CU
BOSTON				
A08 555 834A	A11 117 094A	2,893,440	$32.50	$190.00
A00 256 761★			150.00	500.00
NEW YORK				
B08 442 103A	B27 585 371A	18,631,056	30.00	190.00
B00 233 440★	B00 668 377★		150.00	500.00
PHILADELPHIA				
C07 083 912A	C09 798 033A	2,710,680	35.00	190.00
C★			225.00	500.00
CLEVELAND				
D07 270 530A	D15 256 075A	5,610,000	30.00	190.00
D00 138 930★	D00 200 157★		125.00	500.00
RICHMOND				
E05 457 947A		552,300	50.00	250.00
E00 124 932★			250.00	500.00
ATLANTA				
F04 771 055A	F09 362 464A	3,033,780	35.00	190.00
F00 159 856★			200.00	500.00

		CHICAGO			
G08 294 214A	G15 855 210A		8,715,000	30.00	190.00
G00 250 073★	G00 302 346★			200.00	500.00
		ST. LOUIS			
H03 967 681A	H05 151 623A		531,600	50.00	190.00
H00 062 759★	H00 113 789★			300.00	500.00
		MINNEAPOLIS			
I03 649 469A	I03 998 386A		102,600	85.00	300.00
I★				350.00	650.00
		KANSAS CITY			
J03690 438A	J04 286 834A		410,400	60.00	250.00
J★				300.00	450.00
		DALLAS			
K04 650 160A			961,800	60.00	200.00
		SAN FRANCISCO			
L07 629 700A	L09 734 683A		2,547,900	50.00	200.00
L00 149 457★				275.00	400.00

Dark Green Seal

SERIES 1928B

SERIAL NUMBERS: All districts continued sequence from previous series.

SIGNATURES: Walter O. Woods, A.W. Mellon

LOW	HIGH	NOTES		
SERIAL NUMBER		PRINTED	VG/F	CU
	BOSTON			
A13 166 578A	A36 123 650A	33,218,088	$15.00	$75.00
A00 323 424★			60.00	450.00
	NEW YORK			
B27 480 893A	B50 604 105A	44,458,308	15.00	55.00
B★			75.00	450.00
	PHILADELPHIA			
C10 062 953A	C22 944665A	22,689,216	15.00	65.00
C00 239 922★			75.00	450.00
	CLEVELAND			
D12 800 819A	D26 585 122A	17,418,024	15.00	65.00
D00 218 393★	D00 271 636★		50.00	300.00
	RICHMOND			
E05 323 470A	E13 569 609A	12,714,504	15.00	75.00
E00 124 932★	E00 152 097★		50.00	450.00

ATLANTA

F09 563 762A	F13 862 358A	5,246,700	15.00	75.00
F00 176 034★		36,000	75.00	450.00

CHICAGO

G15 708 491A	G35 533 388A	38,035,000	15.00	55.00
G00 316 826★	G00 559 530★		50.00	300.00

ST. LOUIS

H04 350 546A	H09 917 580A	10,814,664	15.00	50.00
H★			75.00	450.00

MINNEAPOLIS

I03 927 054A		5,294,460	15.00	75.00
I00 077 380★			75.00	450.00

KANSAS CITY

J04 478 358A	J08 820 387A	7,748,040	15.00	50.00
J★		48,000	75.00	450.00

DALLAS

K07 487 466A	K08 319 882A	3,396,096	15.00	75.00

SAN FRANCISCO

L09 279 596A	L18 289 932A	22,695,300	15.00	60.00
L00 208 244★			60.00	450.00

Light Green Seal
SERIES 1928B

SERIAL NUMBERS: All districts continue sequence from 1928 dark green seal variety. High official star serial numbers are listed just right of the high observed star serial numbers.

LOW	HIGH	NOTES		
SERIAL NUMBER		PRINTED	VG/F	CU
BOSTON				
	A42 392 748A	Included above	$15.00	$75.00
A00 524 128★	A00 568 003★		75.00	400.00
	A00 624 000★			
NEW YORK				
B53 719 374A	B73 268 799A	Included above	15.00	50.00
B00 783 499★	B00 780 597★		60.00	400.00
	B00 852 000★			
PHILADELPHIA				
C30 514 705A	C39 744 939A	Included above	15.00	50.00
	C00 328 478★		75.00	400.00
	C00 372 000★			

	D29 268 477**A**		
D00 346 433★	**D**00 353 207★		
	D00 420 000★		

CLEVELAND
Included above	15.00		75.00
	60.00		400.00

E08 979 390**A**	**E**16 894 828**A**
E00 161 132★	**E**00 162 811★
	E00 216 000★

RICHMOND
Included above	15.00	75.00
	100.00	400.00

F12 449 218**A**	**F**14 176 964**A**
	F00 180 922★
	F00 024 000★

ATLANTA
Included above	15.00	75.00
	100.00	400.00

G39 810 816**A**	**G**54 564 239**A**
G00 563 830★	**G**00 635 486★
	G00 672 000★

CHICAGO
Included above	15.00	45.00
	50.00	300.00

H11 116 605**A**	**H**15 104 217**A**
H00 131 528★	**H**00 161 189★
	H00 192 000★

ST. LOUIS
Included above	15.00	60.00
	75.00	400.00

I05 285 001**A**	**I**08 830 262**A**
I00 085 944★	**I**00 086 956★
	I00 120 000★

MINNEAPOLIS
Included above	15.00	75.00
	100.00	400.00

J08 842 745**A**	**J**11 625 049**A**
	J00 192 000★

KANSAS CITY
Included above	15.00	75.00
	100.00	400.00

K-A

DALLAS
Included above	15.00	100.00

SAN FRANCISCO
Included above	15.00	75.00
	75.00	400.00

L20 679 234**A**	**L**23 275 830**A**
L00 271 330★	**L**00 274 127★
	L00 312 000★

SERIES 1928C

SERIAL NUMBERS: Districts printed continued sequence from previous series.
SIGNATURES: Walter O. Woods, Ogden L. Mills

LOW SERIAL NUMBER	HIGH	NOTES PRINTED	VG/F	CU
		NEW YORK		
B69 216 300**A**	**B**73 537 758**A**	2,902,678	$30.00	$150.00

CLEVELAND

D29 233 933A	D30 400 271A	4,230,428	50.00	300.00
D00 405 891★	D00 405 892★		1500.00	6000.00
	D00 420 000★ Official high			

RICHMOND

	E16 922 036A	304,800	250.00	1000.00

ATLANTA

None reported	688,380	

CHICAGO

G44 181 072A	G54 852 746A	2,423,400	30.00	120.00

Light Green Seal
SERIES 1934

SERIAL NUMBERS: Both regular and star notes begin at 00 000 001.

PLATE SERIALS: Face check numbers begin with number 1. Back check numbers continue from previous series.

SIGNATURES: W.A. Julian, Henry Morgenthau, Jr.

Total 1934 quantities printed listed under dark green seal series 1934.

LOW SERIAL NUMBER	HIGH	NOTES PRINTED	VG/F	CU
BOSTON				
A00 060 273A	A00 259 758A		$12.50	$25.00
A00 147 546★	A00 260 375★		35.00	150.00
NEW YORK				
B00 000 003A	B28 909 950A		12.50	25.00
B00 043 761★			35.00	150.00
PHILADELPHIA				
C00 000 005A	C00 392 664A		12.50	25.00
C00 074 117★	C00 020 020★		25.00	150.00
CLEVELAND				
D00 000 003A	D03 021 804A		12.50	25.00
D00 007 123★	D00 116 193★		35.00	150.00
RICHMOND				
E01 157 355A			12.50	25.00
E00 023 280★			50.00	200.00
ATLANTA				
F01 217 223A	F10 509 569A		12.50	25.00
F00 023 031★	F00 052 036★		35.00	150.00

CHICAGO

G03 397 370**A**	G19 222 113**A**	12.50	25.00
G00 040 505★	G00 045 461★	25.00	150.00

ST. LOUIS

H00 030 906**A**	H07 266 526**A**	12.50	25.00
H00 005 348★	H00 074 716★	35.00	150.00

MINNEAPOLIS

I00 040 238**A**	I06 637 971**A**	12.50	25.00
I00 008 963★	I00 046 302★	50.00	200.00

KANSAS CITY

J00 921 349**A**	J01 268 426**A**	12.50	25.00
J00 012 904★	J00 026 312★	35.00	150.00

DALLAS

K00 309 695**A**		12.50	25.00
K-★		50.00	200.00

SAN FRANCISCO

L00 242 668**A**	L12 311 394**A**	12.50	25.00
L00 108 655★		35.00	150.00

Dark Green Seal
SERIES 1934

SERIAL NUMBERS: All districts continue sequence from 1934 light green seal variety.

PLATE SERIALS: Face check numbers and back check numbers continue from 1934 light green seals up to back check number 584.

Quantities include all types & variations.

SIGNATURES: W.A. Julian, Henry Morgenthau, Jr.

LOW	HIGH	NOTES		
SERIAL NUMBER		PRINTED	VG/F	CU
BOSTON				
A25 225 731**A**	A43 886 186**A**	46,276,152	$13.00	$32.50
A00 404 208★	A00 587 303★		30.00	150.00
NEW YORK				
B02 716 197**A**	B09 971 355**B**	117,298,008	25.00	85.00
B00 511 809★	B01 307 634★	795,826	30.00	150.00
PHILADELPHIA				
C22 923 114**A**	C40 023 082**A**	34,770,768	13.00	32.50
C00 226 168★	C00 360 756★		30.00	150.00
CLEVELAND				
D10 258 013**A**	D25 667 442**A**	28,764,108	13.00	32.50
D00 296 968★			30.00	200.00
RICHMOND				
E12 104 720**A**	E15 181 156**A**	16,437,252	13.00	32.50
E-★			30.00	200.00
ATLANTA				
F28 851 008**A**		20,656,872	13.00	32.50
F-★			45.00	200.00
CHICAGO				
G26 600 761**A**	G73 692 498**A**	69,972,064	13.00	32.50
G00 204 995★	G00 680 441★		25.00	125.00
ST. LOUIS				
H07 296 150**A**	H20 299 417**A**	22,593,204	13.00	32.50
H-★			40.00	200.00

MINNEAPOLIS

I07 405 455A	I10 805 935A	16,840,980	13.00	32.50
I00 123 464★			40.00	150.00

KANSAS CITY

J02 882 622A	J26 262 020A	22,627,824	13.00	32.50
J00 174 654★	J00 891 972★		35.00	150.00

DALLAS

K02 879 500A	K07 952 929A	21,403,488	13.00	32.50
	K00 091 216★		40.00	150.00

SAN FRANCISCO

L19 241 988A	L32 120 664A	37,402,308	13.00	32.50
L00 491 987★			30.00	150.00

Dark Green Seal
SERIES 1934 MULE

PLATE SERIALS: Back check number 585 and higher.

LOW	HIGH	NOTES		
SERIAL NUMBER		PRINTED	VG/F	CU
BOSTON				
A33 222 723A	A35 041 268A	See above	$20.00	$35.00
A-★			40.00	200.00
NEW YORK				
B99 259 354A	B99 975 344A		35.00	100.00
B03 735 856B			35.00	100.00
B-★			40.00	200.00
PHILADELPHIA				
C26 564 773A	C35 839 892A		20.00	35.00
C-★			40.00	200.00
CLEVELAND				
D47 320 233A			20.00	35.00
D-★			40.00	200.00
RICHMOND				
E-A			20.00	35.00
E-★			50.00	225.00
ATLANTA				
F28 849 873A	F89 702 759A		20.00	35.00
F00 336 930★	F01 186 761★		40.00	200.00
CHICAGO				
G54 397 265A	G73 911 416A		20.00	35.00
G00 778 732★	G00 812 693★		40.00	200.00
ST. LOUIS				
H18 338 834A	H21 382 640A		20.00	35.00
H00 245 528★			40.00	200.00
MINNEAPOLIS				
I09 243 549A	I30 223 367A		20.00	35.00
I-★			40.00	200.00
KANSAS CITY				
J14 209 664A	J45 772 513A		20.00	35.00
J00 251 400★	J00 623 946★		40.00	200.00
DALLAS				
K09 964 715A	K39 837 504A		20.00	35.00
K00 297 430★			40.00	200.00
SAN FRANCISCO				
L32 029 459A	L36 866 420A		20.00	35.00
L00 393 872★			40.00	200.00

Green Seal
SERIES 1934A MULE

SERIAL NUMBERS: All districts continued sequence from previous series.
PLATE SERIALS: Back check number 584 and lower.
SIGNATURES: W. A. Julian, Henry Morgenthau, Jr.

LOW	HIGH	NOTES		
SERIAL NUMBER		**PRINTED**	**VG/F**	**CU**
		BOSTON		
A43 438 366A	A62 535 662A	see above	$15.00	$30.00
A-★			40.00	200.00
		NEW YORK		
B07 635 340B	B39 751 390B		15.00	30.00
B01 117 228★	B01 439 995★		40.00	350.00
		PHILADELPHIA		
C32 512 371A	C40 083 516A		15.00	30.00
C00 457 415★			40.00	350.00
		CLEVELAND		
D31 289 689A	D50 366 255A		15.00	30.00
D-★			40.00	200.00
		RICHMOND		
E17 721 419A	E22 665 433A		15.00	30.00
E-★			40.00	200.00
		ATLANTA		
F15 852 438A	F16 661 865A		15.00	75.00
F-★			40.00	200.00
		CHICAGO		
G58 564 719A	G75 743 248A		15.00	30.00
G00 880 374★	G00 974 185★		30.00	300.00
		ST. LOUIS		
H-A			15.00	30.00
H-★			40.00	200.00
		MINNEAPOLIS		
I10 866 264A	I15 365 852A		15.00	30.00
I-★			40.00	200.00
		KANSAS CITY		
J-A			15.00	30.00
J-★			40.00	200.00
		DALLAS		
K-A			15.00	30.00
K-★			40.00	200.00
		SAN FRANCISCO		
L-A			15.00	30.00
L-★			40.00	200.00

Green Seal
SERIES 1934A

SERIAL NUMBERS: All districts continued sequence from previous series.
PLATE SERIALS: Back check numbers begin at 585
SIGNATURES: W.A. Julian, Henry Morgenthau, Jr.

LOW SERIAL NUMBER	HIGH	NOTES PRINTED	VG/F	CU
BOSTON				
A50 101 123A			$11.00	$25.00
	A44 222 363B		11.00	25.00
A00 605 352★	A01 801 501★		20.00	100.00
NEW YORK				
B17 895 318B			11.00	25.00
B-C			11.00	25.00
	B90 870 463D		11.00	25.00
B01 558 862★	B05 097 302★		20.00	100.00
PHILADELPHIA				
C32 791 370A			11.00	25.00
	C27 992 286B		11.00	25.00
C00 376 834★	C01 523 585★		20.00	100.00
CLEVELAND				
D38 939 570A			11.00	25.00
	D12 473 923B		15.00	30.00
D00 501 989★	D01 420 239★		20.00	100.00
RICHMOND				
E17 288 754A			11.00	25.00
	E14 497 070B		12.50	25.00
E00 369 502★	E01 257 554★		20.00	100.00
ATLANTA				
F15 665 042A	F97 932 586A	85,478,160	11.00	25.00
F03 611 159B	F03 361 160B		75.00	250.00
F00 428 796★	F01 186 759★		20.00	80.00

CHICAGO				
G70 175 527A		177, 295, 960	11.00	25.00
G-B			11.00	25.00
	G37 851 417C		11.00	25.00
G00 783 328★	G03 144 001★		20.00	100.00
ST. LOUIS				
H23 167 634A	H68 071 995A	50,694,312	11.00	25.00
H00 354 606★	H00 857 792★		20.00	100.00
MINNEAPOLIS				
I09 243 570A	I27 799 792A	16,340,016	11.00	25.00
I00 182 459★	I00 379 905★		20.00	100.00
KANSAS CITY				
J18 160 353A	J52 984 711A	31,069,978	11.00	25.00
J00 237 441★	J00 623 948★		20.00	100.00

DALLAS

K13 954 086A	K46 508 148A	28,263,156	11.00	25.00
K00 439 248★	K00 490 413★		20.00	100.00

SAN FRANCISCO

L39 870 377A		125,537,592	11.00	25.00
	L49 236 587B		11.00	25.00
L00 876 051★	L01 987 502★		20.00	100.00

HAWAII NOTE

Brown Seal

SERIES 1934A

SIGNATURES: Same as Series 1934A.

OFFICIAL LOW SERIAL NUMBER	HIGH	NOTES PRINTED	VF	CU
L65 856 001A	L66 456 000A	600,000	$50.00	$325.00
L67 476 001A	L69 076 000A	1,600,000	50.00	325.00
L69 736 001A	L71 336 000A	1,600,000	50.00	325.00
L77 052 001A	L77 172 000A	120,000	50.00	325.00
L11 160 001B	L12 664 000B	1,504,000	50.00	325.00
L28 212 001B	L29 712 000B	1,500,000	50.00	275.00
L43 032 001B	L45 532 000B	2,500,000	50.00	275.00
L50 292 001B	L51 292 000B	1,000,000	50.00	275.00
L00 900 001★	L00 916 000★	16,000	1000.00	3000.00
L00 924 001★	L00 928 000★	4,000	1500.00	3500.00
L00 952 001★	L00 960 000★	8,000	1000.00	3000.00
L00 964 001★	L00 968 000★	4,000	1500.00	3500.00
L00 972 001★	L00 996 000★	24,000	750.00	2500.00
L02 008 001★	L02 012 000★	4,000	1000.00	3000.00
L02 040 001★	L02 048 000★	8,000	1000.00	3000.00

SERIES 1934B

SERIAL NUMBERS: All districts continued sequence from previous series.

SIGNATURES: W.A. Julian, Fred M. Vinson

LOW SERIAL NUMBER	HIGH	NOTES PRINTED	VG/F	CU
BOSTON				
A38 659 831B	A46 068 132B	3,999,600	$15.00	$35.00
A01 820 686★	A01 897 603★		25.00	125.00
NEW YORK				
B49 119 571C			12.00	25.00
B75 316 369D			12.00	30.00
	B17 311 144E	34,815,948	12.00	60.00
B05 092 596★	B05 660 947★		20.00	175.00
PHILADELPHIA				
C22 408 785B	C35 564 386B	10,339,020	12.00	35.00
C01 588 547★	C01 660 619★		20.00	175.00
CLEVELAND				
D17 711 381B	D29 697 457B	1,394,700	15.00	35.00
D-★			30.00	150.00
RICHMOND				
E11 800 489B	E17 995 646B	4,018,272	12.00	25.00
E-★			30.00	150.00
ATLANTA				
F00 012 420B	F08 240 462B	6,746,076	12.00	25.00
F-★			30.00	150.00
CHICAGO				
G32 848 555C	G48 703 986C	18,130,836	12.00	25.00
G03 032 893★	G03 181 803★		20.00	100.00
ST. LOUIS				
H69 891 088A	H78 814 225A	6,849,348	12.50	30.00
H00 949 250★	H00 952 702★		20.00	100.00

MINNEAPOLIS

I32 139 319A	I33 647 397A	2,254,800	12.00	25.00
I-★			20.00	150.00

KANSAS CITY

J50 864 742A	J54 513 824A	3,835,764	12.00	25.00
J00 729 624★			20.00	150.00

DALLAS

K46 673 651A	K49 034 542A	3,085,200	12.00	25.00
K-★			30.00	150.00

SAN FRANCISCO

L55 870 023B	L63 525 795B	9,076,800	12.00	25.00
L02 270 807★	L02 274 853★		25.00	150.00

SERIES 1934C

SIGNATURES: W.A. Julian, John W. Snyder

LOW SERIAL NUMBER	HIGH	NOTES PRINTED	VG/F	CU
BOSTON				
A46 727 409B	A89 241 775B	42,431,404	$12.00	$20.00
A01 991 691★	A02 188 164★		30.00	125.00
NEW YORK				
B14 341 429E			12.00	20.00
	B79 629 354F	115,675,644	12.00	20.00
B05 695 448★	B07 813 576★		15.00	125.00
PHILADELPHIA				
C34 226 174B	C81 049 029B	46,874,760	12.00	20.00
C01 651 127★	C03 260 509★		15.00	125.00
CLEVELAND				
D19 581 685B	D58 664 062B	33,240,000	12.00	20.00
D00 145 476★	D02 175 697★ High observed		20.00	125.00
RICHMOND				
E18 515 459B	E60 388 949B	37,422,600	12.00	20.00
E01 615 677★	E02 123 769★		15.00	125.00
ATLANTA				
F10 012 993B	F51 072 323B	44,838,264	12.00	20.00
F01 347 295★	F01 758 281★		15.00	125.00

LOW	HIGH	NOTES		
SERIAL NUMBER		PRINTED	VG/F	CU
CHICAGO				
G52 580 795**C**		105,875,412	12.00	20.00
	G52 249 411**D**		12.00	20.00
G03 438 172★	G05 361 175★		15.00	100.00
ST. LOUIS				
H75 861 252**A**			12.00	20.00
	H08 645 013**B**	36,541,404	12.00	20.00
H01 139 716★	H01 556 190★		15.00	100.00
MINNEAPOLIS				
I33 985 183**A**	I43 165 262**A**	11,944,848	12.00	20.00
I00 474 694★	I00 526 641★		25.00	150.00
KANSAS CITY				
J54 943 948**A**	J76 918 162**A**	20,874,072	12.00	20.00
J00 833 311★	J00 911 599★		15.00	100.00
DALLAS				
K50 804 411**A**	K74 108 012**A**	25,642,620	12.00	20.00
K00 926 999★	K01 007 384★		25.00	150.00
SAN FRANCISCO				
L64 548 208**B**			12.00	20.00
	L07 215 023**C**	49,164,480	12.00	20.00
L02 454 243★	L02 501 521★		15.00	100.00

SERIES **1934D**

SERIAL NUMBERS: All districts continued sequence from previous series.

SIGNATURES: Georgia Neese Clark, John W. Snyder

LOW	HIGH	NOTES		
SERIAL NUMBER		PRINTED	VG/F	CU
BOSTON				
A89 660 775**B**			$12.00	$25.00
	A08 687 876**C**	9,917,900	12.00	25.00
A02 798 792★	A02 938 568★		20.00	100.00
NEW YORK				
B24 706 302**F**	B82 977 478**F**	64,067,904	12.00	25.00
B07 813 576★	B08 337 511★		20.00	100.00
PHILADELPHIA				
C75 769 379**B**	C94 609 249**B**	18,432,000	12.00	25.00
C02 424 486★	C02 596 068★		20.00	100.00

CLEVELAND

D63 592 856B	D77 777 777B	20,291,316	12.00	25.00
D02 353 097★	D02 550 742★		20.00	100.00

RICHMOND

E53 277 056B	E68 657 787B	18,090,312	12.00	25.00
			20.00	150.00

ATLANTA

F50 388 847B	F65 958 230B	17,064,816	12.00	25.00
F02 137 363★	F02 270 202★		20.00	100.00

CHICAGO

G47 665 115D			12.00	50.00
	G01 426 854E	55,943,844	12.00	50.00
G05 182 143★	G05 665 693★		20.00	125.00

ST. LOUIS

H09 348 201B	H21 503 566B	15,828,048	12.00	50.00
H01 587 975★	H01 767 546★		20.00	125.00

MINNEAPOLIS

I44 420 066A	I47 071 181A	5,237,220	12.00	50.00
I00 606 556★	I00 662 768★		20.00	125.00

KANSAS CITY

J75 180 729A	J81 778 613A	7,992,000	12.00	50.00
J01 166 212★			20.00	125.00

DALLAS

K73 073 191A	K80 705 334A	7,178,196	12.00	50.00
K-★			30.00	175.00

SAN FRANCISCO

L07 328 128C	L27 559 874C	23,956,584	12.00	50.00
L-★			30.00	175.00

SERIES 1950

WIDE

SERIAL NUMBERS: All districts both regular and star notes begin with 00 000 001A.

PLATE SERIALS: Face check numbers begin at #1. Back check 1389 and lower.

SIGNATURES: Georgia Neese Clark, John W. Snyder

Serial numbers shown below include both Wide and Narrow varieties of this series.

OFFICIAL LOW SERIAL NUMBER	HIGH	NOTES PRINTED	VG/F	CU
		BOSTON		
A00 000 001A	A70 992 000A	70,992,000	$12.00	$50.00
A00 520 093★	A01 008 000★		20.00	150.00

NEW YORK

B00 000 001A		99,999,999	12.00	50.00
B-B		99,999,999	12.00	50.00
	B18 576 000C	18,576,000	12.00	50.00
	B03 168 000★	2,568,000	20.00	150.00

PHILADELPHIA

C00 000 001A	C76 320 000A	76,320,000	12.00	50.00
C00 455 096★	C01 008 000★	1,008,000	20.00	150.00

CLEVELAND

D00 000 001A	D76 320 000A	76,320,000	12.00	50.00
	D01 008 000★	1,008,000	20.00	150.00

RICHMOND

E00 000 001A	E61 776 000A	61,776,000	12.00	50.00
	E00 876 000★	876,000	20.00	150.00

ATLANTA

F00 000 001A	F63 792 000A	63,792,000	12.00	50.00
	F00 864 000★	864,000	20.00	150.00

CHICAGO

G00 000 001A	G50 894 721A	99,999,999	12.00	50.00
	G61 056 000B	61,056,000	12.00	50.00
	G02 088 000★	2,088,000	20.00	150.00

ST. LOUIS

H00 000 001A	H47 808 000A	47,808,000	12.00	225.00
H00 185 738★	H00 648 000★	648,000	40.00	175.00

MINNEAPOLIS

I00 000 001A	I18 864 000A	18,864,000	12.00	50.00
	I00 252 000★	252,000	20.00	150.00

KANSAS CITY

J00 000 001A	J36 332 000A	36,332,000	12.00	60.00
J00 236 168★	J00 456 000★	456,000	20.00	150.00

DALLAS

K00 000 001A	K33 264 000A	33,264,000	12.00	50.00
K00 214 040★	K00 480 000★	480,000	20.00	150.00

SAN FRANCISCO

L00 000 001A	L76 896 000A	76,896,000	12.00	50.00
L00 076 479★	L01 152 000★	1,152,000	20.00	150.00

SERIES **1950**
NARROW
PLATE SERIALS: Back check numbers 1390-1456 (highest of 12 subject sheets).

$10.00 Wide		$10.00 Narrow		
LOW	HIGH	NOTES		
SERIAL NUMBER		PRINTED	VG/F	CU
BOSTON				
A41 691 014A	A65 931 748A	see above	$12.00	$50.00
A00 738 597★			50.00	250.00
NEW YORK				
B41 715 573B			12.00	50.00
	B15 969 729C		12.50	50.00
PHILADELPHIA				
C45 571 678A	C74 610 569A		50.00	50.00
C00 612 404★			50.00	250.00
CLEVELAND				
D48 081 316A	D65 686 894A		12.00	50.00
RICHMOND				
E43 772 722A	E53 905 422A		12.00	50.00
E00 765 688★			50.00	250.00
ATLANTA				
F46 651 804A			12.00	50.00
CHICAGO				
G19 614 029B	G44 702 685B		12.00	50.00
G01 191 814★	G01 413 337★		25.00	125.00
ST. LOUIS				
H27 407 447A	H46 127 726A		12.00	50.00
H00 443 068★	H00 516 252★		50.00	250.00
MINNEAPOLIS				
I16 828 975A	I17 068 904A		12.00	50.00
KANSAS CITY				
J20 978 619A	J29 574 837A		12.00	50.00
J00 375 239★			50.00	250.00
DALLAS				
K18 202 369A	K31 415 982A		12.00	50.00
K00 214 035★			50.00	250.00
SAN FRANCISCO				
L54 597 305A	L66 999 612A		12.00	50.00
L00 850 039★			50.00	250.00

SERIES **1950A**

SERIAL NUMBERS: All numbers shown are official.
SIGNATURES: Ivy Baker Priest, George M. Humphrey

SERIAL NUMBERS		NOTES PRINTED	VG/F	CU
BOSTON				
A70 992 001A		104,248,000	$12.00	$35.00
	A75 240 000B		12.00	35.00
A01 008 001★	A06 120 000★	5,112,000	20.00	100.00
NEW YORK				
B18 576 001C	B-D, B-E	356,664,000	12.00	35.00
	B75 240 000F		12.00	35.00
B03 168 001★	B20 160 000★	16,992,000	20.00	100.00
PHILADELPHIA				
C76 320 001A		73,920,000	12.00	35.00
	C48 240 000B		12.00	35.00
C01 008 001★	C04 680 000★	3,672,000	20.00	100.00
CLEVELAND				
D76 032 001A		75,088,000	12.00	35.00
	D51 120 000B		12.00	35.00
D01 008 001★	D04 680 000★	3,672,000	20.00	100.00
RICHMOND				
E61 776 001A		82,144,000	12.00	35.00
	E43 920 000B		12.00	35.00
E01 008 001★	E05 400 000★	4,392,000	20.00	100.00
ATLANTA				
F63 792 0001A		73,288,000	12.00	35.00
	F37 080 000B		12.00	35.00
F00 864 001★	F04 680 000★	3,816,000	20.00	100.00

		CHICAGO		
G61 056 001B	G-C	235,064,000	12.00	35.00
	G96 120 000D		12.00	35.00
G02 160 001★	G13 320 000★	11,160,000	20.00	100.00
		ST. LOUIS		
H47 808 001A	H94 320 000A	46,512,000	12.00	35.00
H00 720 001★	H03 600 000★	2,880,000	20.00	100.00
		MINNEAPOLIS		
I18 864 001A	I27 000 000A	8,136,000	12.00	35.00
I00 288 001★	I00 720 000★	482,000	20.00	100.00
		KANSAS CITY		
J36 432 001A	J61 920 000A	25,488,000	12.00	35.00
J00 576 001★	J02 880 000★	2,304,000	20.00	100.00

DALLAS

K33 264 001**A**	K55 080 000**A**	21,816,000	12.00	35.00
K00 576 001★	K02 160 000★	1,584,000	20.00	100.00

SAN FRANCISCO

L76 896 001**A**		101,584,000	12.00	35.00
	L78 480 000**B**		12.00	35.00
L07 152 001★	L07 560 000★	6,408,000	20.00	100.00

SERIES **1950B**

SIGNATURES: Ivy Baker Priest, Robert B. Anderson

SERIAL NUMBERS		NOTES PRINTED	CU
BOSTON			
A75 240 001**B**		49,240,000	$30.00
	A24 480 000**C**		30.00
A06 120 001★	A09 000 000★	2,880,000	60.00
NEW YORK			
B75 240 001**F**	B-G	170,840,000	30.00
	B46 080 000**H**		30.00
B20 160 001★	B28 440 000★	8,280,000	60.00
PHILADELPHIA			
C48 240 001**B**		66,880,000	30.00
	C15 120 000**C**		30.00
C04 680 001★	C07 920 000★	3,240,000	60.00
CLEVELAND			
D51 120 001**B**		55,360,000	35.00
	D06 480 000**C**		30.00
D04 680 001★	D07 560 000★	2,880,000	60.00

RICHMOND

E43 920 001**B**	E95 040 000**B**	51,120,000	30.00
E05 400 001★	E08 286 000★	2,880,000	60.00

ATLANTA

F37 080 001**B**		66,520,000	25.00
	F03 600 000**C**		30.00
F04 680 001★	F07 560 000★	2,880,000	60.00

CHICAGO

G96 120 001**D**	G-E	165,080,000	30.00
	G61 200 000**F**		25.00
G13 680 001★	G20 160 000★	6,480,000	60.00

ST. LOUIS

H94 320 001A		33,040,000	30.00
	H27 360 000B		20.00
H03 600 001★	H05 400 000★	1,800,000	60.00

MINNEAPOLIS

I27 000 001A	I40 320 000A	13,320,000	30.00
I00 720 001★	I01 440 000★	720,000	60.00

KANSAS CITY

J61 920 001A	J95 400 000A	33,480,000	30.00
J02 880 001★	J05 400 000★	2,520,000	60.00

DALLAS

K55 080 001A	K81 360 000A	26,280,000	30.00
K02 160 001★	K03 600 000★	1,440,000	60.00

SAN FRANCISCO

L78 480 001B		55,000,000	30.00
	L33 480 000C		30.00
L07 560 001★	L10 440 000★	2,880,000	60.00

SERIES 1950C

SIGNATURES: Elizabeth Rudel Smith, C. Douglas Dillon

SERIAL NUMBERS		NOTES PRINTED	CU

BOSTON

A24 480 001C	A75 600 000C	51,120,000	$35.00
A09 000 001★	A11 160 000★	2,160,000	50.00

NEW YORK

B46 080 001H		120,520,000	35.00
	B66 600 000I		35.00
B28 440 001★	B35 280 000★	6,840,000	50.00

PHILADELPHIA

C15 120 001C	C40 320 000C	25,200,000	35.00
C07 920 001★	C08 640 000★	720,000	60.00

CLEVELAND

D06 480 001C	D39 600 000C	33,120,000	35.00
D07 560 001★	D09 360 000★	1,800,000	40.00

RICHMOND

E95 040 001B		45,640,000	40.00
	E40 680 000C		35.00
E08 280 001★	E10 080 000★	1,800,000	40.00

ATLANTA

F03 600 001C	F42 480 000C	38,800,000	35.00
F07 560 001★	F09 360 000★	1,800,000	40.00

CHICAGO

G61 200 001F		69,400,000	35.00
	G30 600 000G		35.00
G20 160 001★	G23 760 000★	3,600,000	40.00

ST. LOUIS

H27 360 001B	H50 400 000B	23,040,000	35.00
H05 400 001★	H06 480 000★	1,080,000	40.00

MINNEAPOLIS

I40 320 001A	I49 320 000A	9,000,000	40.00
I01 440 001★	I02 160 000★	720,000	40.00

KANSAS CITY

J95 400 001A		23,320,000	45.00
	J18 720 000B		35.00
J05 680 001★	J06 480 000★	800,000	60.00

DALLAS

K81 360 001A	K99 000 000A	17,640,000	40.00
K03 600 001★	K04 320 000★	720,000	60.00

SAN FRANCISCO

L33 480 001C	L69 120 000C	35,640,000	35.00
L10 440 001★	L12 240 000★	1,800,000	40.00

SERIES 1950D

SIGNATURES: Kathryn O'Hay Granahan, C. Douglas Dillon

SERIAL NUMBERS		NOTES PRINTED	CU
BOSTON			
A75 600 001C		38,800,000	$35.00
	A14 400 000D		35.00
A11 160 001★	A12 960 000★	1,800,000	40.00

NEW YORK

B66 600 001I	B-J	150,320,000	35.00
	B16 920 000K		35.00
B35 280 001★	B42 120 000★	6,840,000	40.00

PHILADELPHIA

| C40 320 001C | C59 400 000C | 19,080,000 | 35.00 |
| C08 640 001★ | C09 7209 000★ | 1,080,000 | 40.00 |

CLEVELAND

| D39 600 001C | D63 720 000C | 24,120,000 | 35.00 |
| D09 360 001★ | D10 800 000★ | 360,000 | 60.00 |

RICHMOND

| E40 680 001C | E74 520 000C | 33,840,000 | 35.00 |
| E10 080 001★ | E10 800 000★ | 720,000 | 50.00 |

ATLANTA

| F42 480 001C | F78 480 000C | 36,000,000 | 35.00 |
| F09 360 001★ | F10 800 000★ | 1,440,000 | 40.00 |

CHICAGO

G30 600 001G		115,480,000	35.00
	G46 080 000H		35.00
G23 760 001★	G28 800 000★	5,040,000	40.00

ST. LOUIS

| H50 400 001B | H60 840 000B | 10,440,000 | 40.00 |
| H06 480 001★ | H07 200 000★ | 720,000 | 50.00 |

MINNEAPOLIS

None printed

KANSAS CITY

| J18 720 001B | J34 200 000B | 15,480,000 | 35.00 |
| J06 480 001★ | J07 560 000★ | 1,080,000 | 50.00 |

DALLAS

K99 000 001A		18,280,000	50.00
	K17 280 000B		35.00
K04 600 001★	K05 400 000★	800,000	50.00

SAN FRANCISCO

L69 120 001C		62,560,000	35.00
	L31 680 000D		35.00
L12 240 001★	L15 840 000★	3,600,000	40.00

SERIES **1950E**

SIGNATURES: Kathryn O'Hay Granahan, Henry H. Fowler

SERIAL NUMBERS		NOTES PRINTED	CU
		NEW YORK	
B16 920 001K	B54 700 000K	12,600,000	35.00
B42 120 001★	B44 741 000★	2,621,000	60.00

		CHICAGO	
G46 080 001H		65,080,000	30.00
	G11 160 000I		30.00
G28 800 001★	G33 120 000★	4,320,000	50.00
		SAN FRANCISCO	
L31 680 001D	L048 960 000D	17,280,000	35.00
L15 840 001★	L16 560 000★	720,000	80.00

SERIES **1963**

SERIAL NUMBERS: All serial numbers both regular and star notes begin with 00 000 001.

PLATE SERIALS: Face and back check begin with 1. Motto IN GOD WE TRUST added to back.

SIGNATURES: Kathryn O'Hay Granahan, C. Douglas Dillon

SERIAL NUMBERS	NOTES PRINTED	CU
	BOSTON	
A-A	5,760,000	$20.00
A-★	640,000	30.00
	NEW YORK	
B-A	24,960,000	20.00
B-★	1,920,000	30.00
	PHILADELPHIA	
C-A	6,400,000	20.00
C-★	1,280,000	30.00
	CLEVELAND	
D-A	7,040,000	20.00
D-★	640,000	30.00
	RICHMOND	
E-A	4,480,000	20.00
E-★	640,000	30.00
	ATLANTA	
F-A	10,880,000	20.00
F-★	1,280,000	30.00

CHICAGO

G-A	35,200,000	20.00
G-★	2,560,000	30.00

ST. LOUIS

H-A	13,440,000	20.00
H-★	1,280,000	30.00

MINNEAPOLIS

I not issued

KANSAS CITY

J-A	3,840,000	20.00
J-★	640,000	30.00

DALLAS

K-A	5,120,000	20.00
K-★	640,000	30.00

SAN FRANCISCO

L-A	14,080,000	20.00
L-★	1,280,000	30.00

SERIES 1963A

SERIAL NUMBERS: All districts continue sequence from previous series.

SIGNATURES: Kathryn O'Hay Granahan, Henry H. Fowler

SERIAL NUMBERS		NOTES PRINTED	CU
BOSTON			
A05 760 001A	A99 999 999A	94,240,000	20.00
A00 000 001B	A37 120 000B	37,120,000	20.00
A00 640 001★	A07 040 000★	6,400,000	30.00

NEW YORK

B24 960 001**A**		75,040,000	20.00
B-B		99,999,999	20.00
	B24 320 000**C**	24,320,000	20.00
B01 920 000★	B11 520 000★	9,600,000	30.00

PHILADELPHIA

C06 400 001**A**		93,600,000	20.00
	C06 400 000**B**	6,400,000	20.00
C01 280 001★	C05 760 000★	4,480,000	30.00

CLEVELAND

D07 040 001**A**	D80 000 000**A**	72,960,000	20.00
D00 064 001★	D04 480 000★	3,840,000	30.00

RICHMOND

E04 480 001**A**		95,520,000	20.00
	E19 200 000**B**	14,720,000	20.00
E00 640 001★	E05 760 000★	5,120,000	30.00

ATLANTA

F10 880 001**A**	F90 880 000**A**	80,000,000	20.00
F01 280 001★	F05 120 000★	3,840,000	30.00

CHICAGO

G35 200 001**A**		64,800,000	20.00
G-B		99,999,999	20.00
	G37 200 000**C**	37,200,000	20.00
G02 560 001★	G12 160 000★	9,600,000	30.00

ST. LOUIS

H13 440 001**A**	H56 960 000**A**	43,520,000	20.00
H01 280 001★	H03 200 000★	1,920,000	30.00

MINNEAPOLIS

I00 000 001**A**	I16 640 000	16,640,000	20.00
I00 000 001★	I00 650 000★	640,000	30.00

KANSAS CITY

J03 840 001**A**	J35 200 000**A**	31,260,000	20.00
J00 640 001★	J02 560 000★	1,920,000	30.00

DALLAS

K05 120 001**A**	K56 320 000**A**	51,200,000	20.00
K00 640 001★	K02 560 000★	1,920,000	30.00

SAN FRANCISCO

L14 080 001**A**		87,200,000	20.00
	L01 280 000**B**		22.00
L01 280 001★	L06 400 000★	5,120,000	30.00

SERIES 1969

SERIAL NUMBERS: All serial numbers both regular and star notes begin with 00 000 001.
SIGNATURES: Dorothy Andrews Elston, David M. Kennedy

SERIAL NUMBERS	NOTES PRINTED	CU
BOSTON		
A-A	74,880,000	$20.00
A-★	2,560,000	30.00
NEW YORK		
B-A	99,999,999	20.00
B-B	99,999,999	20.00
B-C	47,360,000	20.00
B-★	10,240,000	25.00
PHILADELPHIA		
C-A	56,960,000	20.00
C-★	2,560,000	30.00
CLEVELAND		
D-A	57,600,000	20.00
D-★	2,560,000	30.00
RICHMOND		
E-A	56,960,000	20.00
E-★	2,560,000	30.00
ATLANTA		
F-A	53,760,000	20.00
F-★	2,560,000	30.00
CHICAGO		
G-A	99,999,999	20.00
G-B	42,240,000	20.00
G-★	6,400,000	25.00
ST. LOUIS		
H-A	22,400,000	20.00
H-★	640,000	30.00

	NOTES PRINTED	CU
MINNEAPOLIS		
I-A	12,800,000	20.00
I-★	1,280,000	30.00
KANSAS CITY		
J-A	31,360,000	20.00
J-★	1,280,000	30.00
DALLAS		
K-A	30,080,000	20.00
K-★	1,280,000	30.00

SAN FRANCISCO

L-A	56,320,000	20.00
L-★	3,185,000	25.00

SERIES 1969A

SERIAL NUMBERS: All districts continue sequence from previous series.
SIGNATURES: Dorothy Andrews Kabis, John B. Connally

SERIAL NUMBERS		NOTES PRINTED	CU
		BOSTON	
A74 880 001**A**		27,120,000	$20.00
A16 000 000**B**		16,000,000	20.00
A02 560 001★	A04 480 000★	1,920,000	25.00

	NEW YORK	
B47 360 001**C**	52,240,000	20.00
B59 520 000**D**	59,520,000	20.00
B10 240 001★ B14 080 000★	3,840,000	25.00
PHILADELPHIA		
C56 960 001**A** C81 280 000**A**	24,320,000	20.00
C01 920 001★ C03 840 000★	1,920,000	25.00
CLEVELAND		
D57 600 001**A** D81 280 000**A**	23,680,000	20.00
D02 560 001★ D03 836 000★	1,276,000	25.00
RICHMOND		
E56 960 001**A** E82 560 000**A**	25,600,000	20.00
E02 560 001★ E03 200 000★	640,000	30.00
ATLANTA		
F53 760 001**A** F74 240 000**A**	20,480,000	20.00
F02 56 0 000★ F03 200 000★	640,000	30.00
CHICAGO		
G42 240 001**B**	47,760,000	20.00
G22 400 000**C**	22,400,000	20.00
G06 400 001★ G08 960 000★	3,560,000	25.00
ST. LOUIS		
H22 400 001**A** H37 760 000**A**	15,360,000	20.00
H00 640 001★ H01 280 000★	640,000	30.00
MINNEAPOLIS		
I12 800 001**A** I21 120 000**A**	8,320,000	25.00
none printed		
KANSAS CITY		
J31 360 001**A** J42 240 000**A**	10,880,000	20.00
none printed		

DALLAS

K30 080 001A	K50 560 000A	20,480,000	20.00
K01 280 001★	K01 920 000★	640,000	30.00

SAN FRANCISCO

L56 320 001A	L83 840 000A	27,520,000	20.00
L03 200 001★	L04 480 000★	1,280,000	25.00

SERIES **1969B**

SERIAL NUMBERS: All districts continue sequence from previous series.
SIGNATURES: Romana Acosta Banuelos, John B. Connally

SERIAL NUMBERS		NOTES PRINTED	CU
BOSTON			
A16 000 001B	A32 640 000B	16,640,000	$30.00
		None printed	
NEW YORK			
B59 520 001D		60,320,000	$25.00
	B19 840 000E		25.00
B14 080 001★	B16 000 000★	1,920,000	40.00
PHILADELPHIA			
C81 280 001A	C93 080 000A	12,800,000	30.00
		None printed	
CLEVELAND			
D81 280 001A	D94 080 000A	12,800,000	30.00
		None printed	
RICHMOND			
E82 560 001A	E94 720 000A	12,160,000	30.00
E03 200 001★	E03 840 000★	640,000	50.00
ATLANTA			
F74 240 001A	F87 680 000A	13,440,000	30.00
F03 200 001★	F03 840 000★	640,000	50.00
CHICAGO			
G22 400 001C	G55 040 000C	32,640,000	25.00
G08 960 001★	G10 000 000★	1,040,000	40.00
ST. LOUIS			
H37 760 001A	H46 720 000A	8,960,000	30.00
H01 280 001★	H02 560 000★	1,280,000	40.00
MINNEAPOLIS			
I21 120 001A	I24 320 000A	3,200,000	35.00
		None printed	
KANSAS CITY			
J42 240 001A	J47 360 000A	5,120,000	35.00
J01 280 001★	J01 920 000★	640,000	50.00

DALLAS

K50 560 001**A**	K56 320 000**A**	5,760,000	35.00
		None printed	

SAN FRANCISCO

L83 840 001**A**		23,840,000	30.00
	L07 680 000**B**		25.00
L04 000 001	L05 120 000★	640,000	50.00

SERIES 1969C

SERIAL NUMBERS: All districts continue sequence from previous series.

SIGNATURES: Romana Acosta Banuelos, George P. Shultz

SERIAL NUMBERS		NOTES PRINTED	CU
		BOSTON	
A32 650 001**B**	A77 440 000**B**	44,800,000	$18.00
A04 480 001★	A05 120 000★	640,000	30.00
		NEW YORK	
B19 840 001**E**		18,160,000	18.00
B-F		99,999,999	18.00
	B23 040 000**G**	23,040,000	18.00
B16 000 001★	B23 040 000★	7,040,000	25.00
		PHILADELPHIA	
C97 280 000**A**		2,720,000	25.00
	C67 200 000**B**	67,200,000	18.00
C03 840 001★	C05 120 000★	1,280,000	30.00
		CLEVELAND	
D94 080 0001**A**		5,920,000	20.00
	D40 960 000**B**	40,960,000	18.00
D04 000 001★	D06 400 000★	2,400,000	25.00
		RICHMOND	
E94 720 001**A**		5, 280,000	20.00
	E40 320 000**B**	40,320,000	18.00
E04 000 001**A**	E05 120 000★	1,120,000	30.00

ATLANTA

F87 680 001**A**		12,320,000	18.00
	F33 920 000**B**	33,920,000	18.00
F03 840 001★	F05 760 000★	1,920,000	30.00

CHICAGO

G55 040 001**C**		44,960,000	18.00
	G10 240 000**D**	10,240,000	18.00
G10 000 001★	G10 880 000★	880,000	30.00

ST. LOUIS

H46 720 001A	H76 520 000A	29,800,000	18.00
H02 560 001★	H03 840 000★	1,280,000	30.00

MINNEAPOLIS

I24 320 001A	I35 840 000A	11,520,000	20.00
I01 280 001★	I01 920 000★	640,000	30.00

KANSAS CITY

J47 360 001A	J70 400 000A	23,040,000	18.00
J01 920 001★	J02 560 000★	640,000	30.00

DALLAS

K56 320 001A	K81 280 000A	24,960,000	18.00
K01 920 000★	K02 560 000★	640,000	30.00

SAN FRANCISCO

L07 680 001B	L65 650 000B	56,960,000	18.00
L05 120 001★	L05 760 000★	640,000	35.00

SERIES 1974

SIGNATURES: Francine I. Neff, William E. Simon
SERIAL NUMBERS: Continued from previous series.

SERIAL NUMBER		NOTES PRINTED	CU
BOSTON			
A77 440 001B	A99 999 999B	22,559,999	$17.00
A00 000 001C	A81 920 000C	81,920,000	17.00
A05 120 001★	A07 680 000★	2,048,000	25.00
NEW YORK			
B23 040 001G	B99 999 999G	76,960,000	17.00
B-H		99,999,999	17.00
B00 000 000I	B62 080 000I	62,080,000	17.00
B23 040 001★	B27 520 000★	3,712,000	20.00
PHILADELPHIA			
C67 200 001B	C99 999 999B	32,799,999	17.00
C00 000 001C	C36 480 000C	36,480,000	17.00
C05 120 001★	C07 680 000★	2,560,000	25.00
CLEVELAND			
D40 960 001B	D99 999 999B	59,039,999	17.00
D00 000 001C	D23 040 000C	23,040,000	17.00
D06 400 001★	D07 040 000★	640,000	30.00
RICHMOND			
E40 320 001B	E99 999 999B	59,680,000	17.00
E00 000 001C	E46 080 000C	46,080,000	17.00
E05 120 001★	E07 040 00★	1,920,000	25.00
ATLANTA			
F33 920 001B	F99 840 000B	65,920,000	17.00
F00 000 001C	F09 600 000C	9,600,000	17.00
F05 760 001★	F08 960 000★	3,200,000	20.00
CHICAGO			
G10 240 001D	G99 840 000D	89,600,000	17.00
G00 000 001E	G14 720 000E	14,720,000	17.00
G10 880 001★	G15 360 000★	4,096,000	20.00
ST. LOUIS			
H76 520 001A	H99 999 999A	23,480,000	17.00
H00 000 001B	H21 760 000B	21,760,000	17.00
H03 840 001★	H05 120 000★	1,280,000	25.00
MINNEAPOLIS			
I35 840 001A	I61 440 000A	25,600,000	17.00
I01 920 000★	I03 840 000★	896,000	30.00

KANSAS CITY

J70 400 001**A**	J94 720 000**A**	24,320,000	17.00
J02 560 001★	J03 200 000★	640,000	25.00

DALLAS

K81 280 001**A**	K99 999 999**A**	18,720,000	17.00
K00 000 001**B**	K21 120 000**B**	21,120,000	17.00
K02 560 001★	K04 480 000★	1,920,000	25.00

SAN FRANCISCO

L64 640 001**B**	L99 999 999**B**	35,360,000	17.00
L00 000 001**C**	L35 200 000**C**	35,200,000	17.00
L05 760 001★	L07 680 000★	1,920,000	25.00

SERIES 1977

SIGNATURES: Azie Taylor Morton, W. Michael Blumenthal

SERIAL NUMBERS: All districts started regular notes with 00 000 001.

PLATE SERIALS: Continue from previous series.

SERIAL NUMBERS		NOTES PRINTED	CU
BOSTON			
A00 000 001**A**	A96 640 000**A**	96,640,000	$17.00
A00 012 001★	A03 840 000★	2,698,000	25.00

NEW YORK

B00 000 001A		99,840,000	17.00
B-B		99,840,000	17.00
	B77 440 000C	77,440,000	17.00
B00 016 001★	B08 960 000★	7,168,000	25.00

PHILADELPHIA

C00 000 001A	C83 200 000A	83,200,000	17.00
C00 000 001★	C01 280 000★	896,000	25.00

CLEVELAND

D00 000 001A	D83 200 000A	83,200,000	17.00
D00 016 001★	D01 280 000★	768,000	25.00

RICHMOND

E00 000 001A	E71 040 000A	71,040,000	17.00
E00 000 001★	E02 560 000★	1,920,000	25.00

ATLANTA

F00 000 001A	F88 960 000A	88,960,000	17.00
F00 000 001★	F01 920 000★	1,536,000	25.00

CHICAGO

G00 000 001A	G99 840 000A	99,840,000	17.00
G00 000 001B	G74 880 000B	74,880,000	17.00
G00 016 001★	G06 400 000★	3,968,000	20.00

ST. LOUIS

H00 000 001A	H46 720 000A	46,720,000	17.00
H00 012 001★	H01 280 000★	896,000	25.00

MINNEAPOLIS

I00 000 001A	I10 240 000A	10,240,000	20.00
I00 012 001★	I00 740 000★	256,000	30.00

KANSAS CITY

J00 000 001A	J50 560 000A	50,560,000	17.00
J00 012 001★	J01 456 086★	896,000	25.00

DALLAS

K00 000 001A	K53 760 000A	53,760,000	17.00
K00 000 001★	K00 640 000★	640,000	25.00

SAN FRANCISCO

L00 000 001A	L73 600 000A	73,600,000	17.00
L00 012 001★	L02 560 000★	1,792,000	20.00

SERIES 1977A

SIGNATURES: Azie Taylor Morton, G. William Miller

SERIAL NUMBERS: Continued from previous series.

PLATE SERIALS: Continued from previous series.

SERIAL NUMBERS		NOTES PRINTED	CU
		BOSTON	
A96 640 000A	A99 840 000A	3,200,000	$20.00
A00 000 001B	A80 640 000B	80,640,000	16.00
A03 848 001★	A06 400 000★	1,664,000	25.00
		NEW YORK	
B77 440 001C	B99 840 000C	22,400,000	16.00
B-D		99,840,000	16.00
B-E		99,840,000	16.00
	B37 200 000F	37,200,000	16.00
B08 960 001★	B16 000 000★	5,248,000	20.00
		PHILADELPHIA	
C83 200 001A	C99 840 000A	16,640,000	16.00
C00 000 001B	C79 360 000B	79,360,000	16.00
C01 296 001★	C03 840 000★	2,048,000	20.00

CLEVELAND

D83 200 001A	D99 840 000A	16,640,000	16.00
D00 000 001B	D28 160 000B	28,160,000	16.00
D01 288 001★	D04 480 000★	2,048,000	20.00

RICHMOND

E71 040 001A	E99 840 000A	28,800,000	16.00
E00 000 001B	E75 520 000B	75,520,000	16.00
E02 576 001★	E07 040 000★	3,072,000	20.00

ATLANTA

F88 960 001A	F99 840 000A	10,880,000	16.00
F00 000 001B	F23 040 000B	23,040,000	16.00
F01 920 001★	F02 560 000★	640,000	25.00

CHICAGO

G74 880 001B	G99 840 000B	24,960,000	16.00
G00 000 001C	G83 200 000C	83,200,000	16.00
G06 400 001★	G10 240 000★	3,200,000	20.00

ST. LOUIS

H46 720 001A	H74 240 000A	27,520,000	16.00
H01 292 001★	H02 560 000★	640,000	25.00

MINNEAPOLIS

I10 240 001A	I14 920 000A	7,680,000	16.00
I00 656 001★	I01 280 000★	128,000	50.00

KANSAS CITY

J50 560 001A	J90 880 000A	4,032,000	20.00
J01 296 001★	J05 760 000★	2,136,000	20.00

DALLAS

K53 760 001A	K99 840 000A	46,080,000	16.00
K00 000 001B	K14 080 000B	14,080,000	16.00
K00 640 001★	K05 760 000★	4,224,000	20.00

SAN FRANCISCO

L73 600 001A	L99 840 000A	26,240,000	16.00
L00 000 001B	L33 280 000B	33,280,000	16.00
L02 572 001★	L05 760 000★	1,792,000	20.00

SERIES 1981

SIGNATURES: Angela M. Buchanan, Donald T. Regan
SERIAL NUMBERS: Both regular and stars start with 00 000 001.

SERIAL NUMBERS		NOTES PRINTED	CU
BOSTON			
A-A		99,840,000	$15.00
A-B		80,000,000	15.00
A-★	A00 567 703★	1,280,000	30.00

		NEW YORK	
B-A		99,840,000	15.00
B-B		99,840,000	15.00
B-C		99,840,000	15.00
B-D		99,200,000	15.00
B-E		35,200,000	15.00
B-★		1,920,000	30.00
		PHILADELPHIA	
C-A		99,840,000	15.00
C-B		32,000,000	15.00
C-★		632,000	35.00
		CLEVELAND	
D-A		99,840,000	15.00
D-B		22,400,000	15.00
D-★		1,268,000	30.00
		RICHMOND	
E-A		99,840,000	15.00
E-B		32,000,000	15.00
E-★	E03 200 000★	2,576,000	30.00
		ATLANTA	
F-A		99,840,000	15.00
F-B		32,000,000	15.00
F00 009 114★		1,908,000	30.00
		CHICAGO	
G-A		99,840,000	15.00
G-B		99,840,000	15.00
G-C		54,400,000	15.00
G00 584 048★		1,280,000	30.00
		ST. LOUIS	
H-A		33,280,000	15.00
H-B		22,000,000	15.00
		MINNEAPOLIS	
I-A		7,680,000	15.00
I-B		16,000,000	15.00
I-★		628,000	35.00

KANSAS CITY

J-A	43,520,000	15.00
J-B	9,600,000	15.00

DALLAS

K-A	21,760,000	15.00
K-B	28,800,000	15.00

SAN FRANCISCO

L-A	96,000,000	15.00
L-B	48,000,000	15.00
L00 739 777★	1,280,000	30.00

SERIES 1981A

SIGNATURES: Katherine Davalos Ortega, Donald T. Regan
SERIAL NUMBERS: Both regular and stars start with 00 000 001.

SERIAL NUMBERS		NOTES PRINTED	CU
BOSTON			
A-A		99,200,000	$15.00
A-B		12,800,000	15.00
NEW YORK			
B-A,B-C		259,000,000	15.00
B01 094 518★	B03 200 000★		30.00
PHILADELPHIA			
C-A		48,000,000	15.00
CLEVELAND			
D-A		80,000,000	15.00
RICHMOND			
E-A		92,800,000	15.00
E51 816 885★	E03 200 000★	3,200,000	30.00
ATLANTA			
F-A		83,200,000	15.00
F01 708 698A	F06 400 000A	4,736,000	30.00

CHICAGO

G-A	99,200,000	15.00
G-B	84,400,000	15.00

ST. LOUIS

H-A	25,600,000	15.00

MINNEAPOLIS

I-A	19,200,000	15.00

KANSAS CITY

J-A	48,000,000	15.00

DALLAS

K-A	48,000,000	15.00

SAN FRANCISCO

L-A	99,200,000	15.00
L-B	16,000,000	15.00

SERIES 1985

SIGNATURES: Katherine Davalos Ortega, James A. Baker III
SERIAL NUMBERS: Both regular and star notes begin with 00 000 001.

SERIAL NUMBERS		NOTES PRINTED	CU
BOSTON			
A-A		99,200,000	$15.00
A-B		99,200,000	15.00
A-C		99,200,000	15.00
A-D		83,200,000	15.00
A-★	A09 600 000★	7,296,000	20.00
NEW YORK			
B-A		99,200,000	15.00
B-B		99,200,000	15.00
B-C		99,200,000	15.00
B-D		99,200,000	15.00
B-E		99,200,000	15.00
B-F		99,200,000	15.00
B-G		99,200,000	15.00
B-H		99,200,000	15.00
B-I		99,200,000	15.00
B-J		96,400,000	15.00
B-K		38,400,000	15.00
B-★	B03 200 000★	2,560,000	25.00
PHILADELPHIA			
C-A		99,200,000	15.00
C-B		64,000,000	15.00
CLEVELAND			
D-A		99,200,000	15.00
D-B		99,200,000	15.00
D-C		99,200,000	15.00
D-D		6,400,000	20.00
D-★	D03 200 000★	2,688,000	25.00
RICHMOND			
E-A		99,200,000	15.00
E-B		99,200,000	15.00
E-C		12,800,000	17.50
ATLANTA			
F-A		99,200,0000	15.00
F-B		99,200,000	15.00
F-C		99,200,000	15.00
F-★	F03 200 000★	384,000	30.00

CHICAGO

G-A		99,200,000	15.00
G-B		99,200,000	15.00
G-C		99,200,000	15.00
G-D		60,800,000	15.00

ST. LOUIS

H-A		99,200,000	15.00
H-B		32,000,000	15.00
H-★	H03 200 000★	3,200,000	25.00

MINNEAPOLIS

I-A		64,000,000	15.00

KANSAS CITY

J-A		86,400,000	15.00

DALLAS

K-A		99,200,000	15.00
K-B		16,000,000	17.50
K-★	K06 400 000★	3,136,000	25.00

SAN FRANCISCO

L-A		99,200,000	15.00
L-B		99,200,000	15.00
L-C		99,200,000	15.00
L-D		3,200,000	20.00
L-★	L03 200 000★	2,688,000	25.00

SERIES 1988

None printed.

SERIES 1988A

SIGNATURES: Catalina Vasquez Villalpando, Nicholas F. Brady
PLATE SERIALS: Both face and back check numbers begin at #1, with some early muling from previous series on backs.
SERIAL NUMBERS: Both regular and star notes begin at 00 000 001.

SERIAL NUMBER		NOTES PRINTED	VG/F	CU
		BOSTON		
A-A		96,000,000		$15.00
A-B		96,000,000		15.00
A-C		6,400,000		20.00
A-★	A06 400 000★	6,400,000		25.00

		NEW YORK	
B-A through **B-D**		339,200,000	15.00
B-★	B03 200 000★	2,680,000	25.00
		PHILADELPHIA	
C-A		57,600,000	15.00
		CLEVELAND	
D-A through **D-B**		128,000,000	15.00
D-★	D03 200 000★		25.00
		RICHMOND	
E-A		96,000,000	15.00
E02 153 473**B**		9,600,000	15.00
		ATLANTA	
F-A through **F-C**		236,800,000	15.00
		CHICAGO	
G-A through **G-C**		192,000,000	15.00
		ST. LOUIS	
H-A		70,400,000	15.00
		MINNEAPOLIS	
I-A		19,200,000	15.00
		KANSAS CITY	
J-A		51,200,000	15.00
		DALLAS	
K-A		96,000,000	15.00
K-B		19,200,000	20.00
		SAN FRANCISCO	
L-A through **L-C**		192,000,000	15.00
L-★	L03 200 000★	3,200,000	25.00

SERIES 1990

SIGNATURES: Catalina Vasquez Villalpando, Nicholas F. Brady

PLATE SERIALS: Face check numbers begin at #1. Back check numbers continue sequence from previous series.

SERIAL NUMBERS: Both regular and star notes begin at 00 000 001.

(Series 1990 introduced the anti-counterfeiting security thread and the micro size printing around the portrait.)

SERIAL NUMBERS	NOTES PRINTED	CU
	BOSTON	
A-A	96,000,000	$15.00
A-B	32,000,000	15.00

NEW YORK

B-A		96,000,000	15.00
B-B		96,000,000	15.00
B-C		96,000,000	15.00
B-D		96,000,000	15.00
B-E		96,000,000	15.00
B-F		96,000,000	15.00
B-G		96,000,000	15.00
B-H		70,400,000	15.00
B-★	B19 200,000★	16,784,000	20.00

PHILADELPHIA

C-A		19,200,000	15.00
C-★	C03 200 000★	2,560,000	20.00

CLEVELAND

D-A		89,000,000	15.00

RICHMOND

E-A		96,000,000	15.00
E-B		9,600,000	20.00

ATLANTA

F-A		96,000,000	15.00
F-B		64,000,000	15.00

CHICAGO

G-A		96,000,000	15.00
G-B		96,000,000	15.00
G-C		96,000,000	15.00
G-D		19,200,000	15.00
G-★	G03 200 000★	2,560,000	25.00

ST. LOUIS

H-A		70,400,000	15.00
H-★	H03 200 000★	1,920,000	25.00

MINNEAPOLIS

I-A		12,800,000	17.50

KANSAS CITY

J-A		70,400,000	15.00

DALLAS

K-A		57,600,000	15.00

SAN FRANCISCO

L-A		83,200,000	15.00

SERIES **1993**

SIGNATURES: Mary Ellen Withrow, Lloyd Bentsen
PLATE SERIALS: Face check numbers begin at #1. Back check numbers continue from previous series, creating mules, then start at #1 in mid-series.
SERIAL NUMBERS: Both regular and star notes begin at 00 000 001.

SERIAL NUMBERS		NOTES PRINTED	CU
A-B,A-B	A51 200 000B	121,600,000	15.00
		NEW YORK	
B-A through **B-E**	B76 800 000E	564,000,000	15.00
B-★	B03 200 000★	3,200,000	25.00
		PHILADELPHIA	
C-A,C-B	C19 200 000B	115,200,000	15.00
C-★	C01 920 000★	1,920,000	25.00
		CLEVELAND	
D-A, D-B	D44 800 000B	140,800,000	15.00
		ATLANTA	
F-A, F-B	F25 600 000B	121,600,000	15.00
		CHICAGO	
G-A, G-B	G32 000 000B	128,000,000	15.00
G-★	G03 200 000★	2,560,000	20.00
		ST. LOUIS	
H-A	H38 400 000A	38,400,000	15.00
		KANSAS CITY	
J-A	J19 200 000A	19,200,000	15.00
		SAN FRANCISCO	
L-A	L76, 800 000A	76,800,000	15.00

SERIES **1995**

SIGNATURES: Mary Ellen Withrow, Robert E. Rubin
PLATE SERIALS: Both face and back check numbers begin at #1.
SERIAL NUMBERS: Both regular and star notes begin at 000 000 001.

SERIAL NUMBERS			NOTES PRINTED	CU
			BOSTON	
A-A	W		6,400,000	$20.00
			CLEVELAND	
D-★	FW	D01 920 000★	1,920,000	25.00
			RICHMOND	
E-A	FW		89,600,000	15.00
			ATLANTA	
F-A, F-B	FW		185,600,000	15.00
			CHICAGO	
G-A, G-B	FW		192,000,000	15.00
			ST. LOUIS	
H-A	FW		51,200,000	15.00
			MINNEAPOLIS	
I-A	FW		70,400,000	15.00
			KANSAS CITY	
J-A	FW		32,000,000	15.00
			DALLAS	
K-A	FW		44,800,000	15.00
			SAN FRANCISCO	
L-A	FW		96,000,000	15.00
L-★	FW	L03 200 000★	3,200,000	20.00

Series 1995 remains in production at press time.

TWENTY DOLLAR NATIONAL BANK NOTES

Brown Seal

Type I has black serial numbers on the ends of the note. The left reading horizontally, the right reading vertically. Type II is similar, but the brown serial number is succeeded or preceded by the charter number also. All notes have facsimile signatures of E. E. Jones and W. O. Woods at the top. Signatures of the officers of the local bank appear at the bottom.

See listing under Five Dollar denomination for detailed information as to rarity and value.

TWENTY DOLLAR NOTES
LEGAL TENDER
Red Seal
SERIES 1928

SERIAL NUMBERS: No Bureau record of printing.
PLATE SERIALS: Face and back check number 1.
SIGNATURES: Walter O. Woods, W.H. Woodin.
One specimen of this note was printed and displayed at the Chicago World's Fair in 1933.
No notes were ever printed for issue.

GOLD CERTIFICATE
Gold Seal
SERIES 1928

PLATE SERIALS: Face check #1 through #174.
SIGNATURES: Walter O. Woods, Andrew W. Mellon.

LOW	HIGH	NOTES PRINTED	VG/F	CU
SERIAL NUMBERS				
A00 000 001A	A66 204 000A	66,204,000	$50.00	$200.00
★00 000 001A	★00 488 307A	488,307	75.00	500.00
★00 000 365A				

SERIES 1928A
SIGNATURES: Walter O. Woods, Ogden L. Mills.
Notes were printed but were never issued.

FEDERAL RESERVE BANK NOTE
Brown Seal
SERIES 1929

SERIAL NUMBERS: Both regular and star notes start with 00 000 001.
PLATE SERIALS: Face check numbers begin with #1.
SIGNATURES: Same as $5.00 FRBN.

LOW	HIGH	NOTES PRINTED	VF	CU
SERIAL NUMBERS				
BOSTON				
A00 120 465A	A00 972 000A	972,000	$40.00	$200.00
A00 006 899★	A00 007 260★	24,000	150.00	1200.00
NEW YORK				
B00 003 049A	B02 568 000A	2,568,000	35.00	90.00
B00 000 913★	B00 019 404★	24,000	75.00	1200.00
PHILADELPHIA				
C00 000 816A	C01 008 000A	1,008,000	45.00	15.00
C00 001 382★	C00 015 349★	24,000	75.00	1200.00
CLEVELAND				
D00 000 696A	D01 020 000A	1,020,000	35.00	120.00
D00 000 899★	D00 005 823★	24,000	200.00	1200.00
RICHMOND				
E00 192 997A	E01 632 000A	1,632,000	35.00	120.00
E00 001 153★	E00 011 748★	24,000	150.00	1200.00

		ATLANTA		
F00 400 209A	F00 960 000A	960,000	35.00	120.00
F00 001 066★	F00 007 648★	8,000	200.00	2000.00
CHICAGO				
G00 000 013A	G02 028 000A	2,028,000	32.00	120.00
G00 000 013★	G00 003 990★	12,000	150.00	2000.00
ST. LOUIS				
H00 049 375A	H00 444 000A	444,000	40.00	120.00
H00 001 501★	H00 029 267★	24,000	75.00	700.00
MINNEAPOLIS				
I00 126 110A	I00 864 000A	864,000	35.00	120.00
I00 000 029★	I00 003 963★	12,000	200.00	1500.00
KANSAS CITY				
J00 015 745A	J00 612 000A	612,000	37.50	120.00
J00 001 159★	J00 005 686★	24,000	150.00	700.00

DALLAS

K00 098 193A	K00 468 000A	468,000	37.50	300.00
K00 000 455★		24,000	750.00	2500.00

SAN FRANCISCO

L00 330 866A	L00 888 000A	888,000	35.00	125.00
L00 005 691★		24,000	750.00	2000.00

FEDERAL RESERVE NOTE
Green Seal
SERIES 1928

SERIAL NUMBERS: All serial numbers both regular and star notes begin with 00 000 001A.

PLATE SERIALS: Face and back check numbers begin with number 1.

SIGNATURES: H.T. Tate, A.W. Mellon.

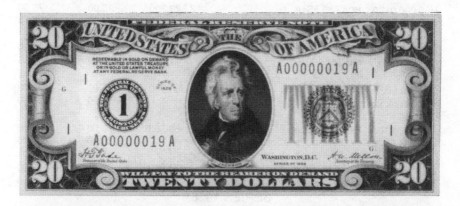

LOW	HIGH	NOTES		
SERIAL NUMBERS		PRINTED	VG/F	CU
BOSTON				
A00 000 019A	A00 763278A	3,790,880	$25.00	$125.00
A00 014 230A	A00 068 561★		150.00	500.00
NEW YORK				
B00 366 977A	B12 007 726A	12,797,200	25.00	125.00
B00 006 020★	B00 135 310★		75.00	400.00

PHILADELPHIA

C00 073 516A	C03 721 622A	3,797,200	25.00	100.00
C00 010 620★	C00 054 671★		150.00	500.00

CLEVELAND

D00 000 055A	D10 862 368A	10,626,900	9000	125.00
D00 025 405★	D00 146 506★		75.00	400.00

RICHMOND

E00 618 588A	E03 361 556A	4,119,600	75.00	125.00
	E00 047 239★		250.00	1000.00

ATLANTA

F00 093 466A	F03 833 076A	3,842,388	25.00	100.00
F00 009 408★	F00 076 000★ Official high		75.00	500.00

CHICAGO

G00 000 126A	G11 909 779A	10,891,740	25.00	75.00
G00 009 189★	G00 155 280★		75.00	400.00

ST. LOUIS

H00 000 012A	H04 485 554A	2,523,300	25.00	75.00
H00 009 985★	H00 026 811★		150.00	400.00

MINNEAPOLIS

I00 000 066A	I03 383 699A	2,633,100	25.00	75.00
I00 008 791★	I00 044 160★		150.00	500.00

KANSAS CITY

J00 000 080A	J02 602 170A	2,584,500	25.00	100.00
J00 021 825★	J00 044 737★		150.00	500.00

DALLAS

K00 000 010A	K01 354 612A	1,568,500	25.00	100.00
K00 014 063★	K00 072 000★Official high		250.00	1500.00

SAN FRANCISCO

L00 696593A	L07 376 739A	8,404,800	25.00	75.00
L00 060 471★	L00 072 361★		150.00	500.00

SERIES 1928A

SERIAL NUMBERS: All districts continued sequence from previous series.

PLATE SERIES: Face check numbers begin with #1. Back check numbers continue from previous series.

SIGNATURES: Walter O. Woods, A.W. Mellon.

LOW	HIGH	NOTES		
SERIAL NUMBERS		PRINTED	VG/F	CU
BOSTON				
A04 424 994A	A05 222 537A	1,293,900	$40.00	$85.00
A-★			400.00	1100.00
NEW YORK				
B11 562 434A	B12 004 673A	1,055,800	40.00	85.00
B00 118 389★			400.00	1100.00
PHILADELPHIA				
C03 826 055A	C05 496 678A	1,717,200	40.00	75.00
C-★			400.00	1100.00
CLEVELAND				
D10 445 886A	D10 801 854A	625,200	40.00	100.00
D-★			400.00	1100.00
RICHMOND				
E03 274 876A	E06 413 199A	1,534,500	40.00	75.00
E00 050 002★	E00 063 147★		400.00	1100.00
ATLANTA				
F03 825 719A	F04 892 700A	1,442,400	40.00	75.00
F-★			400.00	1100.00

CHICAGO

G09 545 579**A**	G13 654 684**A**	822,000	47.50	75.00
G-★			400.00	1100.00

ST. LOUIS

H02 031 755**A**	H02 733 838**A**	573,300	47.50	100.00
H-★			400.00	1100.00

KANSAS CITY

J02 393 151**A**	J02 708 315**A**	113,900	30.00	150.00
J-★			400.00	1000.00

DALLAS

K01 522 525**A**	K02 211 622**A**	1,032,000	30.00	75.00
K-★			400.00	1000.00

Dark Green Seals
SERIES 1928B

SERIAL NUMBERS: All districts continued from previous series.
SIGNATURES: Walter O. Woods, A.W. Mellon.

LOW SERIAL	HIGH NUMBERS	NOTES PRINTED	VG/F	CU
BOSTON				
A03 925 587**A**	A08 272 736**A**	7,749,636	$30.00	$100.00
A-★			100.00	400.00
NEW YORK				
B12 696 773**A**	B20 272 235**A**	19,448,436	30.00	90.00
B00 196 360★	B01 492 276★		100.00	400.00
PHILADELPHIA				
C05 732 443**A**	C10 620 164**A**	8,095,548	30.00	100.00
C-★			100.00	400.00
CLEVELAND				
D11 847 190**A**	D16 341 689**A**	11,684,548	30.00	100.00
D-★			100.00	400.00
RICHMOND				
E05 410 008**A**	E09 501 081**A**	4,413,900	30.00	120.00
E-★			100.00	400.00
ATLANTA				
F04 450 179**A**	F05 557 667**A**	2,390,240	30.00	150.00
F-★			100.00	400.00
CHICAGO				
G13 257 456★	G18 444 922**A**	17,220,276	30.00	100.00
G00 136 196★	G00 170 621★		100.00	400.00

ST. LOUIS

H03 003 293**A**	H04 796 286**A**	3,834,600	35.00	120.00
H-★			100.00	400.00

MINNEAPOLIS

I02 752 467**A**	I02 945 293**A**	3,298,920	35.00	120.00
I-★			100.00	400.00

KANSAS CITY

J02 758 206**A**	J04 788 668**A**	4,941,252	30.00	120.00
J-★			100.00	400.00

DALLAS

K02 643 964**A**		2,406,060	35.00	150.00
K-★			100.00	400.00

SAN FRANCISCO

L09 106 860**A**	L11 934 354**A**	9,689,124	30.00	120.00
L-★			100.00	400.00

Light Green Seal
SERIES 1928B

SERIAL NUMBERS: All districts continue sequence from 1028B Dark Green seal variety.
High official star serial numbers are listed in the high observed star serial numbers column.

LOW	HIGH	NOTES PRINTED	VG/F	CU
SERIAL NUMBERS				
BOSTON				
A08 674 262**A**	A09 183 361**A**	Included above	$30.00	$65.00
A00 086 912★	A00 144 000★		100.00	500.00
NEW YORK				
B24 212 797**A**	B30 238 010**A**	Included above	30.00	65.00
	B00 276 000★			
PHILADELPHIA				
C08 000 640**A**	C10 740 129**A**	Included above	30.00	65.00
	C00 120 000★			
CLEVELAND				
D12 375 176**A**	D17 005 964**A**	Included above	30.00	65.00
	D00 216 000★			
RICHMOND				
E09 413 116**A**	E09 428 654**A**	Included above	32.50	70.00
	E00 096 000★			

CHICAGO

G13 045 239**A**	G25 194 159**A**	Included above	30.00	65.00
	G00 264 000★			

ST. LOUIS

H05 143 648**A**	H06 348 822**A**	Included above	32.50	70.00
H00 073 005★	H00 096 000★		100.00	500.00

MINNEAPOLIS

I03 125 342**A**	I04 073 463**A**	Included above	32.50	75.00
	I00 072 000★			

KANSAS CITY

J04 854 465**A**	J06 023 572**A**	Included above	30.00	60.00
	J00 084 000★			

SAN FRANCISCO

L12 991 538**A**	L16 013 701**A**	Included above	30.00	65.00
L00 146 938★	L00 204 000★		100.00	500.00

SERIES **1928C**

SERIAL NUMBERS: All districts continued sequence from previous series.

SIGNATURES: Walter O. Woods, Ogden L. Mills.

LOW	HIGH	NOTES		
SERIAL NUMBERS		**PRINTED**	**VG/F**	**CU**
CHICAGO				
G23 425 134**A**	G25 181 247**A**	3,363,300	$100.00	$500.00
SAN FRANCISCO				
L15 631 459**A**	L16 434 325**A**	1,420,200	100.00	600.00

Light Green Seal

SERIES **1934**

SERIAL NUMBERS: Both regular and star notes begin at 00 000 001.

PLATE SERIALS: Face check numbers begin with #1. Back check numbers continue from previous series.

SIGNATURES: W. A. Julian, Henry Morgenthau, Jr.

Total 1934 quantities printed are listed under Dark Green seal Series 1934.

LOW	HIGH	NOTES		
SERIAL NUMBERS		**PRINTED**	**VG/F**	**CU**
BOSTON				
A01 957 256**A**	A03 795 125 **A**	Included below	$25.00	$40.00
A00 020 337★	A00 070 514★		40.00	300.00

NEW YORK				
B00 000 004A	B22 729 948A		25.00	40.00
B00 000 002★	B00 123 819★		40.00	300.00
PHILADELPHIA				
C00 050 443A			25.00	40.00
C00 022 502★	C00 050 443★		40.00	300.00
CLEVELAND				
D00 000 100A			25.00	40.00
D00 005 029★	D00 034 317★		40.00	300.00
RICHMOND				
E00 000 003A	E10 801 410A		25.00	40.00
E00 003 138★	E00 037 768★		40.00	300.00
ATLANTA				
F01 340 538A	F38 061 182A		25.00	40.00
F-★			40.00	300.00
CHICAGO				
G00 832 638A	G03 779 300A		25.00	40.00
G00 027 278★			40.00	300.00
ST. LOUIS				
H00 500 182A			25.00	40.00
H★			40.00	300.00
MINNEAPOLIS				
I00 076 074A	I01 556 744A		25.00	40.00
I00 002 603★	I00 033 655★		40.00	300.00
KANSAS CITY				
J00 146 655A	J03 014 419A		25.00	40.00
J00 008 961★			40.00	300.00
DALLAS				
K00 540 625A	K01 317 205A		25.00	40.00
K00 000 001★	K00 011 988★		40.00	300.00
SAN FRANCISCO				
L00 502 985A	L03 054 730A		25.00	40.00
L00 037 342★	L00 065 413★		40.00	300.00

Dark Green Seal
SERIES 1934

SERIAL NUMBERS: All districts continue sequence from 1934 Light Green seal variety.

PLATE SERIALS: Face check numbers and back check numbers continue from previous series, up to 317.

SIGNATURES: W.A. Julian, Henry Morgenthau, Jr.

LOW SERIAL	HIGH NUMBERS	NOTES PRINTED	VG/F	CU
BOSTON				
A09 181 041A	A14 367 757A	37,673,068	$25.00	$40.00
A00 141 571★	A00 213 662★		40.00	300.00
NEW YORK				
B16 712 592A	B23 945 422A	27,573,264	25.00	40.00
	B00 162 434★		40.00	300.00
PHILADELPHIA				
C08 515 738A	C70 548 540A	53,209,968	25.00	40.00
C00 132 242★			40.00	300.00
CLEVELAND				
D21 367 432A	D52 931 743A	48,301,416	25.00	40.00
D00 213 039★	D00 248 698★		40.00	300.00
RICHMOND				
E15 596 982A	E18 390 497A	36,259,224	25.00	40.00
E-★			40.00	300.00
ATLANTA				
F06 169 531A	F40 500 918A	41,547,660	25.00	40.00
F-★			40.00	300.00
CHICAGO				
G18 182 418A	G27 321 818A	20,777,832	25.00	40.00
G00 147 747★	G00 283 317★		40.00	300.00
ST. LOUIS				
H01 314 162A	H08 490 809A	27,174,552	25.00	40.00
H00 024 405★	H00 216 162★		40.00	300.00
MINNEAPOLIS				
I04 634 398A		16,795,116	25.00	40.00
I00 036 265★	I00 065 211★		40.00	300.00
KANSAS CITY				
J06 426 406A	J06 759 338A	28,865,304	25.00	40.00
J00 041 176★	J00 129 787★		40.00	300.00
DALLAS				
K04 170 661A		20,852,160	25.00	40.00
			40.00	300.00
SAN FRANCISCO				
L00 303 021A	L12 816 206A	32,203,956	25.00	40.00
			40.00	300.00

Dark Green Seal Mule
SERIES 1934

PLATE SERIALS: Back check #318 or higher.

LOW SERIAL	HIGH NUMBERS	NOTES PRINTED	VG/F	CU
BOSTON				
A14 861 928A	A39 229 242A	Included above	$25.00	$50.00
A00 303 992★	A00 367 445★		40.00	300.00
NEW YORK				
B10 745 706A	Low observed		40.00	60.00
PHILADELPHIA				
C17 025 718A	C46 581 327A	Included above	25.00	40.00
C00 039 610★	C00 464 657★		40.00	300.00
CLEVELAND				
D31 686 002A	D65 310 934A	Included above	25.00	40.00
D00 506 559★	D00 509 908★		70.00	300.00

RICHMOND

E40 639 850A	E66 199 889A	Included above	25.00	37.50
E00 337 214★			40.00	300.00

ATLANTA

F13 985 788A	F42 167 541A	Included above	25.00	40.00
F00 305 772★	F00 467 620★		40.00	300.00

ST. LOUIS

H12 283 123A	H29 004 060A	Included above	25.00	40.00
H00 115 780★	H00 269 679★		40.00	300.00

MINNEAPOLIS

I07 925 554A	I16 386 397A	Included above	25.00	40.00
I00 105 300★	I00 193 808★		40.00	300.00

KANSAS CITY

J08 858 537A	J29 785 870A	Included above	25.00	40.00
J00 167 229★	J00 251 124★		40.00	300.00

DALLAS

K02 533 586A	K18 398 887A	Included above	25.00	40.00
K00 040 468★	K00 177 211★		40.00	300.00

SAN FRANCISCO

L36 957 265A	L98 839 050A	Included above	25.00	40.00
	L00 856 878B		75.00	150.00
L01 057 275★	L01 157 528★		40.00	300.00

HAWAII NOTES

Official Print Runs - All Varieties Included

LOW	HIGH	NOTES
SERIAL NUMBERS		PRINTED
L30 540 001A	L31 090 000A	550,000
L31 632 001A	L32 032 000A	400,000
L33 420 001A	L34 220 000A	800,000
L56 412 001A	L56 912 000A	500,000
L60 588 001A	L61 592 000A	1,004,000
L67 984 001A	L69 976 000A	1,992,000
L76 980 001A	L78 480 000A	1,500,000
L85 536 001A	L90 036 000A	4,500,000
L00 360 001★	L00 378000★	8,000
L00 372 001★	L00 376 000★	4,000
L00 432 001★	L00 444 000★	12,000
L00 852 001★	L00 876 000★	24,000
L00 972 001★	L00 976 000★	4,000

Brown Seal
Hawaii

SERIES 1934

PLATE SERIALS: Back check numbers 317 or lower.

SIGNATURES: W.A. Julian, Henry Morgenthau, Jr.

LOW	HIGH	NOTES		
SERIAL NUMBERS		PRINTED	VG/F	CU
L33 991 746A	L34 007 351A		$500.00	$2500.00

SERIES 1934 MULE-HAWAII
Brown Seal

PLATE SERIALS: Back check number 318 and higher.

LOW	HIGH		
SERIAL NUMBERS		**VG/F**	**CU**
L30 551 637A	L89 614 996A	$95.00	$500.00
L00 361137★	L00 874 734★	500.00	2000.00

SERIES 1934 LATE FINISHED BACK #204
Green Seal

PLATE SERIAL: Back check 204.

TOTAL QUANTITY PRINTED: 3,328,728 (Includes both 1934 and 1934A green seal and Hawaii brown seal.)

LOW	HIGH	NOTES PRINTED	VG/F	CU
SERIAL NUMBERS				
CLEVELAND				
D62 357 648A	D67 074 936A	Included above	$50.00	$100.00
RICHMOND				
E48 287 195A	E57 805 065A	Included above	50.00	100.00
ATLANTA				
F34 119 489A		Included above	50.00	100.00
ST. LOUIS				
H20 309 291A	H27 244 074A	Included above	60.00	125.00
KANSAS CITY				
J19 436 527A	J21 209 759A	Included above	60.00	125.00

DALLAS

K19 684 093**A**		60.00	125.00

SERIES1934 - HAWAII
LATE FINISHED BACK #204
Brown Seal

PLATE SERIALS: Face check #24. Back check #204.

LOW	HIGH	NOTES		
SERIAL NUMBERS		**PRINTED**	**VG/F**	**CU**
	SAN FRANCISCO			
L85 583 901**A**	L89 374 858**A**		$350.00	$1000.00

SERIES 1934A MULE
Green Seal

SERIAL NUMBERS: All districts continued sequence from previous series.

PLATE SERIALS: Back check number 317 and lower.

SIGNARURES: W. A. Julian, Henry Morgenthau, Jr.

LOW	HIGH	NOTES		
SERIAL NUMBERS		**PRINTED**	**VG/F**	**CU**
	NEW YORK			
B23 138 408**A**	B56 384 416**A**	See below	$25.00	$40.00
B00 330 215★			75.00	250.00
	CLEVELAND			
D20 000 748**A**	D29 656 473**A**		25.00	40.00
	RICHMOND			
E18 705 311**A**	E31 617 341**A**		25.00	40.00
	CHICAGO			
G19 150 006**A**	G54 117 798**A**		25.00	40.00
G00 248 825★	G00 433 517★		65.00	200.00
	ST. LOUIS			
H11 841 224**A**				
	MINNEAPOLIS			
I09 054 582**A**	I09 689 683**A**		35.00	50.00
	KANSAS CITY			
J10 824 605**A**			35.00	50.00
	DALLAS			
K05 540 674**A**			35.00	50.00
	SAN FRANCISCO			
L18 235 793**A**	L24 952 726**A**		25.00	40.00
L00 176 920★	L00 221 644★		75.00	250.00

Green Seal
SERIES 1934A

SERIAL NUMBERS: All districts continued sequence from previous series.

PLATE SERIALS: Back check numbers begin at 318.

SIGNATURES: W.A. Julian, Henry Morgenthau, Jr.

Quantities include all variations.

LOW	HIGH	NOTES		
SERIAL NUMBERS		**PRINTED**	**VG/F**	**CU**
	BOSTON			
A19 373 046**A**	A27 563 839**A**	3,202,416	$30.00	$40.00
A00 197 111★	A00 245 112★		50.00	175.00

NEW YORK

B39 636 227A		102,555,538	25.00	40.00
	B31 418 413B		25.00	40.00
B00 468 332★	B01 362 303★		30.00	110.00

PHILADELPHIA

C21 827 204A	C50 540 853A	3,371,316	25.00	40.00
C00 220 996★	C00 405 883★		35.00	125.00

CLEVELAND

D29 825 865A	D60 532 980A	23,475,108	25.00	40.00
D00 213 039★	D00 511 916★		30.00	125.00

RICHMOND

E29 409 588A	E76 376 415A	46,816,224	25.00	40.00
E00 342 217★	E00 662 275★		35.00	125.00

ATLANTA

F27 620 753A	F47 661 653A	6,756,816	27.50	40.00
F00 342 217★	F00 498 974★		32.50	125.00

CHICAGO

G01 034 925A	G90 226 915A	91,141,452	25.00	40.00
	G07 815 480B		30.00	50.00
G00 383 825★	G01 108 953★		30.00	110.00

ST. LOUIS

H11 841 224A	H35 769 437A	3,701,568	30.00	40.00
H00 202 908★	H00 276 961★		35.00	125.00

MINNEAPOLIS

I08 927 359A	I10 333 924A	1,162,500	35.00	60.00
I-★			50.00	175.00

KANSAS CITY

J12 541 711A	J13 376 427A	3,221,184	30.00	40.00
J00 151 021★	J00 302 164★		35.00	125.00

DALLAS

K18 964 817A	K20 963 164A	2,531,700	30.00	40.00
K-★			50.00	175.00

SAN FRANCISCO

L17 570 455A		94,454,112	25.00	40.00
	L35 359 756B		25.00	40.00
L00 564 087★	L01 215 376★		30.00	125.00

SERIES **1934A MULE HAWAII**
(Brown Seal)

PLATE SERIALS: Back check numbers 317 or lower.

SIGNATURES: Same as Series 1934.

LOW	HIGH		
SERIAL NUMBERS		VG/F	CU
SAN FRANCISCO			
L30 567 214A	L34 174 516A	$150.00	$750.00
L00 361 329★	L00 441 242★	500.00	2500.00

SERIES **1934A HAWAII**
(Brown Seal)

PLATE SERIALS: Back check numbers 318 or higher.

SIGNATURES: Same as Series 1934 Hawaii Above.

LOW	HIGH		
SERIAL NUMBERS		VG/F	CU
SAN FRANCISCO			
L30 703 634A	L90 023 796A	$35.00	$500.00
L00 360 472★	L00 973 523★	75.00	2000.00

SERIES 1934A LATE FINISHED BACK 204 HAWAII
(Brown Seal)

PLATE SERIAL: Back check #204.

LOW	HIGH		
SERIAL NUMBERS		VG/F	CU
L85 718 843A	L89 660 095A	$60.00	$500.00

SERIES 1934A LATE FINISHED BACK 204
(Green Seal)

PLATE SERIAL: Back check #204.

LOW	HIGH		
SERIAL NUMBERS		VG/F	CU
NEW YORK			
B84 513 659A		$50.00	$100.00
	B14 661 059B		100.00
B01 073 369★			500.00
PHILADELPHIA			
C40 361 306A		50.00	100.00
RICHMOND			
E52 293 180A	E76 690 574A	50.00	100.00
E00 530 871★			500.00
ST. LOUIS			
H22 077 287A		50.00	100.00

SERIES 1934B LATE FINISHED BACK 204

PLATE SERIAL:Back check #204.

LOW	HIGH	NOTES PRINTED	VG/F	CU
NEW YORK				
B33 433 725B	B33 682 903B		$75.00	$200.00
B01 496 889★			150.00	500.00
ST. LOUIS				
H31 794 426A	H34 362 055A		75.00	200.00
DALLAS				
K24 964 183A			75.00	200.00

SERIES 1934B

SERIAL NUMBERS: All districts continued sequence from previous series.

PLATE SERIAL: Back check #381 and higher.

SIGNATURES; W. A. Julian, Fred M. Vinson.

LOW	HIGH	NOTES PRINTED	VG/F	CU
BOSTON				
A38 628 970A	A42 242 548A	3,904,800	$30.00	$40.00
A00 398 858★	A00 423 466★		45.00	400.00
NEW YORK				
B17 408 148B	B39 373 235B	14,876,436	27.50	40.00
B01 318 080★	B01 492 277★		45.00	400.00

		PHILADELPHIA			
C46 212 262A	C52 312 048A	3,271,452	30.00	40.00
C00 469 975★	C00 521 662★		45.00	400.00
		CLEVELAND			
D17 450 524A	D71 450 524A	2,814,600	30.00	50.00
D00 682 766★	D00 695 683★		45.00	400.00
		RICHMOND			
E72 879 805A	E82 979 964A	9,451,632	27.50	40.00
E00 758 543★	E00 868 014★		45.00	400.00
		ATLANTA			
F46 830 144A	F53 664 202A	6,887,640	30.00	40.00
F00 529 409★	F00 560 062★		45.00	400.00
		CHICAGO			
G07 015 107B	G16 105 041B	9,084,600	27.50	40.00
G01 124 759★	G01 245 500★		30.00	300.00
		ST. LOUIS			
H29 653 091A	H35 012 276A	5,817,300	30.00	40.00
H00 297 011★	H00 366 854★		45.00	400.00
		MINNEAPOLIS			
I17 021 710A	I19 150 206A	2,304,800	30.00	50.00
I00 189 973★	I00 216 073★		45.00	400.00
		KANSAS CITY			
J30 057 079A	J32 770 825A	3,524,244	30.00	40.00
J00 316 929★	J00 337 184★		35.00	300.00
		DALLAS			
K22 526 344A	K25 495 160A	2,807,388	30.00	50.00
K00 243 500★			45.00	400.00
		SAN FRANCISCO			
L08 554 084B	L22 243 980A	5,289,540	30.00	40.00
L01 245 495★	L01 268 198★		45.00	400.00

Although none are known it is quite possible mules (back check below 317) exist in this series.

SERIES **1934C**

(Old Back)

The early design has small shrubbery, no balcony, and titled "White House." The later (new) design has a balcony added to the White House with taller shrubbery, and titled "The White House."

SERIAL NUMBERS: All districts continued sequence from previous series.

PLATE SERIALS: Back check numbers up to 587.

SIGNATURES: W.A. Julian, John W. Snyder
Quantities include notes printed with both back varieties.

LOW SERIAL NUMBERS	HIGH SERIAL NUMBERS	NOTES PRINTED	VG/F	CU
BOSTON				
A42 295 063A	A46 373 548A	7,397,352	$22.50	$40.00
A00 470 557★			30.00	100.00
NEW YORK				
B38 676 412B	B50 152 113B	18,668,148	22.50	40.00
B01 547 128★			25.00	150.00
PHILADELPHIA				
C50 572 816A	C55 761 440A	11,590,752	22.50	40.00
C00 586 136★	C00 591 991★		25.00	100.00
CLEVELAND				
D71 615 392A	D78 721 934A	17,912,424	22.50	40.00
D00 733 432★			25.00	100.00
RICHMOND				
E82 463 253A		22,526,568	22.50	40.00
	E01 832 138B		30.00	50.00
E00 784 409★	E00 986 454★		25.00	100.00
ATLANTA				
F55 358 468A	F60 531 129A	18,858,876	22.50	40.00
F00 642 722★	F00 662 748★		25.00	100.00

CHICAGO

G16 185 385B	G25 570 747B	26,031,660	22.50	40.00
G01 263 515★	G01 455 294★		25.00	100.00

ST. LOUIS

H35 217 223A	H40 740 793A	13,276,984	22.50	40.00
H00 385 330★	H00 429 572★		25.00	100.00

MINNEAPOLIS

I19 499 949A	I20 772 004A	3,490,200	30.00	40.00
			35.00	100.00

KANSAS CITY

J34 199 254A	J35 100 540A	4,211,904	22.50	40.00
J00 380 206★			22.50	100.00

DALLAS

K25 346 457A	K27 911 670A	3,707,364	22.50	40.00
K00 304 910★			25.00	100.00

SAN FRANCISCO

L22 220 528B	L29 732 364B	12,015,228	22.50	40.00
L01 340 697★			25.00	100.00

SERIES 1934C
(New Back)

New design has balcony added to the White House, with taller shrubbery, and titled "The White House."

PLATE SERIALS: Back check numbers 588 and higher.

LOW	HIGH	NOTES		
SERIAL NUMBERS		**PRINTED**	**VG/F**	**CU**
BOSTON				
A46 733 962A	A52 528 286A		$22.50	$35.00
A00 515 662★			40.00	75.00
NEW YORK				
B50 380 463B	B55 063 435B		22.50	35.00
B01 707 067★	B01 740 308★		40.00	75.00
PHILADELPHIA				
C54 515 243A	C66 038 494A		22.50	35.00
C00 591 991★	C00 670 473★		40.00	75.00
CLEVELAND				
D79 037 088A			22.50	35.00
	D44 300 344B		22.50	35.00
D00 805 999★	D00 935 597★		50.00	90.00
RICHMOND				
E92 872 408A	E96 940 743A		22.50	35.00
E01 142 664★			35.00	75.00

ATLANTA

F61 618 982A	F73 332 888A	22.50	35.00
F-★		50.00	95.00

CHICAGO

G26 178 543B	G40 414 253B	22.50	35.00
G01 327 744★	G01 557 975★	40.00	75.00

ST. LOUIS

H41 535 478A	H48 706 748A	22.50	35.00
H00 459 889★	H00 467 580★	40.00	75.00

MINNEAPOLIS

I20 837 220A	I22 286 317A	30.00	50.00
I00 229 419★	I00 260 338A	50.00	90.00

KANSAS CITY

J36 196 825A	J41 600 887A	22.50	35.00
J00 430 491★		40.00	75.00

DALLAS

K31 042 702A	K34 625 505A	22.50	35.00
K00 354 202★	K00 367 773★	40.00	80.00

SAN FRANCISCO

L31 288 124B	L43 266 556B	22.50	35.00
L01 503 904★	L01 530 980★	40.00	80.00

SERIES 1934D

SERIAL NUMBERS: All districts continued sequence from previous series.

SIGNATURES: Georgia Neese Clark, John W. Snyder

LOW SERIAL	HIGH NUMBERS	NOTES PRINTED	VG/F	CU
BOSTON				
A41 971 456A	A53 896 892A	4,520,000		$35.00
A-★			$40.00	125.00
NEW YORK				
B55 961 199B	B69 083 642B	27,894,260		35.00
B01 750 367★	B01 808 695★		30.00	80.00
PHILADELPHIA				
C62 289 525A	C67 670 832A	6,022,428		35.00
C00660 092★	C00 725 518★		30.00	80.00
CLEVELAND				
D89 321 411A	D97 018 984A	8,981,688		35.00
D00 996 177★			30.00	80.00
RICHMOND				
E04 865 511B	E18 131 889B	14,055,984		35.00
E00 784 409★			30.00	80.00
ATLANTA				
F72 717 188A	F79 492 323A	7,495,440		35.00
F00 824 781★			30.00	80.00

CHICAGO

G41 576 352**B**	G53 814 518**B**	15,187,596		35.00
G01 574 917★	G01 760 204★		30.00	80.00

ST. LOUIS

H34 055 557**A**	H54 772 944**A**	5,923,248		35.00
H00 614 812★	H00 625 590★		30.00	80.00

MINNEAPOLIS

I22 721 807**A**	I24 318 690**A**	2,422,416	25.00	40.00
I-★			40.00	125.00

KANSAS CITY

J42 375 267**A**	J45 899 488**A**	4,211,904		35.00
J-★			40.00	125.00

DALLAS

K35 095 524**A**	K38 559 440**A**	3,707,364		35.00
K-★			40.00	125.00

SAN FRANCISCO

L43 679 344**B**	L54 995 012**B**	12,015,228		35.00
L01 692 683★			40.00	125.00

SERIES 1950

SERIAL NUMBERS: All serial numbers both regular and star notes begin with 00 000 001.

SIGNATURES: Georgia Neese Clark, John W. Snyder

LOW OFFICIAL	HIGH SERIAL NUMBERS	NOTES PRINTED	VF	CU
		BOSTON		
	A23 184 000**A**	23,184,000		$50.00
A-★			40.00	200.00
		NEW YORK		
	B80 064 000**A**	80,064,000		50.00
B00 927 711★			35.00	200.00
		PHILADELPHIA		
C16 156 648**A**	C29 520 000**A**	29,520,000		50.00
C-★			40.00	200.00
		CLEVELAND		
	D51 120 000**A**	51,120,000		50.00
D00 043 082★	D00 645 343★		35.00	200.00
		RICHMOND		
E52 379 248**A**	E67 536 000**A**	67,536,000		50.00
E00 443 052★	E00 685 052★		35.00	175.00

ATLANTA

F14 687 070**A**	**F**39 312 000**A**		39,312,000	50.00
F-★			40.00	175.00

CHICAGO

	G70 464 000**A**	70,464,000		50.00
G00 000 042★			40.00	175.00

ST. LOUIS

	H27 352 000**A**	27,352,000		50.00
	H00 291 160★		40.00	175.00

MINNEAPOLIS

I00 068 822**A**	**I**09 216 000**A**	9,216,000		50.00
I00 001 796★			40.00	275.00

KANSAS CITY

J22 455 589**A**	**J**22 752 000**A**	22,752,000		50.00
	J00 146 247★		40.00	275.00

DALLAS

	K22 656 000**A**	22,656,000		50.00
	K00 239 426★		40.00	275.00

SAN FRANCISCO

	L70 272 000**A**	70,272,000		50.00
	L00 609 911★		35.00	175.00

Serial nos. G70 464 001A thru G70 560 000A, H27 352 001A thru H27 360 000A and K22 656 001A thru K22 752 000A were assigned for Chicago, St. Louis and Dallas respectively, but were never used.

SERIES **1950A**

SIGNATURES: Ivy Baker Priest, George M. Humphrey

LOW	HIGH	NOTES	
OFFICIAL SERIAL NUMBERS		**PRINTED**	**CU**

BOSTON

A23 184 001**A**	**A**42 840 000**A**	19,656,000	$40.00
A00 488 035★	**A**01 686 306★		75.00

NEW YORK

B80 064 001A		82,568,000	40.00
	B62 640 000B		40.00
B-★			75.00

PHILADELPHIA

C29 520 001A	C46 080 000A	16,560,000	40.00
C00 491 484★	C01 158 511★		75.00

CLEVELAND

D51 120 001A		50,320,000	40.00
	D01 440 000B		50.00
D00 891 137★	D03 550 848★		75.00

RICHMOND

E67 536 001A		69,544,000	40.00
	E37 080 000B		40.00
E02 006 676★	E04 717 304★		70.00

ATLANTA

F39 312 001A	F66 960 000A	27,648,000	40.00
F00 886 404★	F02 032 622★		75.00

CHICAGO

G70 560 001A			40.00
	G44 280 000B	73,720,000	40.00
G02 044 082★	G03 590 704★		75.00

ST. LOUIS

H27 360 001A	H50 040 000A	22,680,000	40.00
H00 499 568★	H00 990 857★		75.00

MINNEAPOLIS

I09 216 001A	I14 760 000A	5,544,000	45.00
I00 506 617★	I00 570 430★		75.00

KANSAS CITY

J22 752 001A	J45 720 000A	22,968,000	40.00
J00 720 588★	J02 106 985★		75.00

DALLAS

K22 752 001A	K33 480 000A	10,728,000	40.00
K00 605 026★	K00 941 803★		75.00

SAN FRANCISCO

L70 272 001A			40.00
	L55 800 000B	85,528,000	40.00
L03 780 045★	L04 108 378★		75.00

(1) B90 236 001A to B90 240 000A and B90 252 001A to B90 256 000A were reported missing because of theft. When recovered they were destroyed.

SERIES **1950B**

SIGNATURES: Ivy Baker Priest, Robert B. Anderson

LOW OFFICIAL SERIAL NUMBERS	HIGH	NOTES PRINTED	CU

BOSTON

| A42 840 001A | A47 880 000A | 5,040,000 | $40.00 |
| | | | 100.00 |

NEW YORK

B62 640 001B			40.00
	B12 600 000C	49,960,000	50.00
B07 044 666★	B07 437 779★		75.00

PHILADELPHIA

| C46 080 001A | C54 000 000A | 7,920,000 | 40.00 |
| C-★ | | | 100.00 |

CLEVELAND

| D01 440 001B | D39 600 000B | 38,160,000 | 40.00 |
| D03 818 415★ | D07 072 453★ | | 75.00 |

RICHMOND

| E37 080 001B | E79 200 000B | 42,120,000 | 40.00 |
| E02 006 676★ | E05 817 251★ | | 75.00 |

ATLANTA

| F66 960 001A | F84 852 562A | 40,240,000 | 40.00 |
| | F00 049 866★ | | 75.00 |

CHICAGO

G44 280 001B			40.00
	G24 840 000C	80,560,000	40.00
G05 973 993★	G08 731 107★		75.00

ST. LOUIS

| H50 040 001A | H69 480 001A | 19,440,000 | 40.00 |
| | H02 126 650★ | | 100.00 |

MINNEAPOLIS

| I14 760 001A | I27 000 000A | 12,240,000 | 40.00 |
| I00 705 885★ | I01 022 288★ | | 75.00 |

KANSAS CITY

| J45 720 001A | J74 160 000A | 28,440,000 | 40.00 |
| J02 298 930★ | J02 562 256★ | | 100.00 |

DALLAS

| K33 480 001A | K45 360 000A | 11,880,000 | 40.00 |
| K01 578 478★ | | | 75.00 |

SAN FRANCISCO

L55 800 001B			40.00
	L06 840 000C	51,040,000	40.00
L08 202 036★	L08 946 721★		75.00

SERIES **1950C**

SIGNATURES: Elizabeth Rudel Smith, C. Douglas Dillon

LOW SERIAL	HIGH NUMBERS	NOTES PRINTED	VF	CU
BOSTON				
A47 880 001A	A55 080 000A	7,200,000		$50.00
	A02 087 540★			100.00
NEW YORK				
B12 600 001C	B55 800 000C	43,200,000		40.00
B09 254 383★	B09 629 397★			100.00
PHILADELPHIA				
C54 000 001A	C61 560 000A	7,560,000		50.00
C02 273 270★	C02 273 270★		100.00	400.00
CLEVELAND				
D39 600 001B	D68 040 000B	28,440,000		40.00
RICHMOND				
E79 200 001B				40.00
	E16 200 000C	37,000,000		40.00
E06 559 116★				100.00
ATLANTA				
F07 200 001B	F26 280 000B	19,080,000		40.00
F-★				100.00
CHICAGO				
G24 840 001C	G54 000 000C	29,160,000		40.00
G09 770 435★	G09 770 455★			100.00
ST. LOUIS				
H69 480 001A	H82 440 000A	12,960,000		40.00
H02 551 551★				100.00
MINNEAPOLIS				
I27 000 001A	I33 480 000A	6,480,000		40.00
I01 120 182★	I01 433 220★			100.00
KANSAS CITY				
J74 160 001A	J92 520 000A	18,360,000		40.00
J04 114 718★	J04 596 837★			100.00

LOW SERIAL	HIGH NUMBERS	NOTES PRINTED	VF	CU
DALLAS				
K45 360 001A	K54 360 000A	9,000,000		50.00
K01 971 414★	K02 010 051★			100.00
SAN FRANCISCO				
L06 840 001C	L52 200 000C	45,360,000		40.00
L-★				100.00

SERIES **1950D**

SIGNATURES: Kathryn O'Hay Granahan, C. Douglas Dillon

LOW	HIGH	NOTES	CU
SERIAL NUMBERS		**PRINTED**	
BOSTON			
A55 080 001A	A64 440 000A	9,360,000	$40.00
A02 463 553★			80.00
NEW YORK			
B55 800 001C	B99 999 999C	44,200,000	40.00
B00 000 001D	B10 080 000D	10,080,000	40.00
B-★			80.00
PHILADELPHIA			
C61 560 001A	C66 960 000A	5,400,000	40.00
C02 572 171★	C02 869 202★		80.00
CLEVELAND			
D68 040 001B	D91 800 000B	23,760,000	40.00
D06 050 490★	D06 080 609★		80.00
RICHMOND			
E16 200 001C	E46 440 000C	30,240,000	40.00
E09 159 574★			80.00
ATLANTA			
F26 280 001B	F48 960 000B	22,680,000	40.00
F04 739 303★	F04 940 203★		80.00
CHICAGO			
G54 000 001C	G99 999 999C	46,000,000	40.00
G00 000 000D	G21 960 001D	21,960,000	40.00
G11 285 075★	G12 567 741★		80.00
ST. LOUIS			
H82 440 001A	H88 560 000A	6,120,000	40.00
H03 224 717★			80.00
MINNEAPOLIS			
I33 480 001A	I36 720 000A	3,240,000	40.00
I-★			80.00

KANSAS CITY			
J92 520 001A		7,480,000	40.00
	J00 720 000B	720,000	60.00
J05 007 683★	J05 010 110★		80.00
DALLAS			
K54 360 001A	K60 840 000A	6,480,000	40.00
K02 393 123★	K02 415 583★		80.00

SAN FRANCISCO

L52 200 001C	L99 999 999C	47,800,000	40.00
L00 000 001D	L21 600 000D	21,600,000	40.00
L12 895 027★	L13 508 413★		80.00

SERIES 1950E

SIGNATURES: Kathryn O'Hay Granahan, Henry H. Fowler

LOW SERIAL NUMBERS	HIGH	NOTES PRINTED	CU

NEW YORK

B10 080 001D	B18 720 000D	8,640,000	$60.00
B12 389 340★	B13 025 214★	640,000 est.	175.00

CHICAGO

G21 960 001D	G31 320 000D	9,360,000	60.00
G12 706 343★	G12 765 186★	640,000 est.	250.00

SAN FRANCISCO

L21 600 001D	L30 240 000D	8,640,000	60.00
L14 198 992★	L14 739 549★	576,000 est.	200.00

FEDERAL RESERVE NOTES

Green Seal

SERIES 1963

SERIAL NUMBERS: All serial numbers both regular and star notes begin with 00 000 001.

PLATE SERIALS: Face and back check begin with Motto IN GOD WE TRUST added to back.

SIGNATURES: Kathryn O'Hay Granahan, C. Douglas Dillon

SERIAL NUMBER	NOTES PRINTED	CU

BOSTON

A-A	2,560,000	$40.00
A-★	640,000	50.00

		NEW YORK	
B-A		16,640,000	35.00
B-★		1,920,00	40.00
		CLEVELAND	
D-A		7,680,000	40.00
D-★		1,280,000	45.00
		RICHMOND	
E-A		4,480,000	40.00
E-★		640,000	50.00
		ATLANTA	
F-A		12,240,000	40.00
F-★		1,280,000	50.00
		CHICAGO	
G-A		2,560,00	40.00
G-★		640,000	60.00
		ST. LOUIS	
H-A		3,200,000	40.00
H-★	H00 031 779★	640,000	60.00
		KANSAS CITY	
J-A		3,840,000	40.00
J-★		640,000	50.00
		DALLAS	
K-A		2,560,000	40.00
K-★		640,000	50.00
		SAN FRANCISCO	
L-A		7,040,000	40.00
L-★		1,280,000	60.00

SERIES **1963A**

SIGNATURES: Kathryn O'Hay Granahan, Henry H. Fowler

SERIAL NUMBER		NOTES PRINTED	CU
		BOSTON	
A02 560 001A	A26 240 000A	23,680,000	$30.00
A00 640 001★	A01 920 000★		40.00
		NEW YORK	
B16 640 001A		93,600,000	30.00
	B10 240 000B		30.00
B01 920 001★		3,840,000	40.00
		PHILADELPHIA	
C00 000 001A	C17 920 000A	17,920,000	30.00
C00 000 001★	C00 640 000★	640,000	40.00

CLEVELAND

D07 690 001**A**	D76 160 000**A**	68,470,000	30.00
D01 280 001★	D03 840 000★	2,560,000	45.00

RICHMOND

E04 480 001**A**		128,800,000	30.00
	E33 280 000**B**		30.00
E00 640 001★	E06 400 000★	5,760,000	40.00

ATLANTA

F10 240 001**A**	F53 120 000**A**	43,880,000	30.00
F01 280 001★	F03 200 000★	1,920,000	40.00

CHICAGO

G02 560 001**A**		156,320,000	30.00
	G58 880 000**B**		30.00
G00 640 001★	G07 680 000★	7,040,000	40.00

ST. LOUIS

H03 200 001**A**	H37 760 000**A**	34,560,000	30.00
H00 640 001★	H02 560 000★	1,920,000	40.00

MINNEAPOLIS

I00 000 001**A**	I10 240 000**A**	10,240,000	30.00
★00 000 001★	I00 640 000★	640,000	40.00

KANSAS CITY

J00 000 001**A**	J40 960 000**A**	37,120,000	30.00
J00 640 001★	J02 560 000★	1,920,000	40.00

DALLAS

K02 560 001**A**	K40 960 000**A**	38,400,000	30.00
K00 640 001★	K01 920 000★	1,280,000	40.00

SAN FRANCISCO

L07 040 001**A**		92,960,000	30.00
	L76 160 000**B**	76,160,000	30.00
L01 280 001★	L09 600 000★	8,320,000	40.00

SERIES 1969

SERIAL NUMBERS: Both regular and star notes begin with 00 000 001.

SIGNATURES: Dorothy Andrews Elston, David M. Kennedy

SERIAL NUMBER	NOTES PRINTED	CU
BOSTON		
A-A	19,200,000	$30.00
A-★	1,280,000	50.00

NEW YORK

B-A	99,999,999	30.00
B-B	6,400,000	35.00
B-★	5,106,000	40.00

PHILADELPHIA

C-A	10,880,000	35.00
C-★	1,280,000	50.00

CLEVELAND

D-A	60,160,000	30.00
D-★	2,560,000	50.00

RICHMOND

E-A	66,560,000	30.00
E-★	2,560,000	45.00

ATLANTA

F-A	36,480,000	30.00
F-★	1,280,000	50.00

CHICAGO

G-A	99,999,999	30.00
G-B	7,680,000	30.00
G-★	3,200,000	45.00

ST. LOUIS

H-A	19,200,000	30.00
H-★	640,000	50.00

MINNEAPOLIS

I-A	12,160,000	35.00
I-★	640,000	50.00

KANSAS CITY

J-A	39,040,000	30.00
J-★	1,280,000	50.00

DALLAS

K-A	25,600,000	30.00
K-★	1,280,000	50.00

SAN FRANCISCO

L-A	99,999,999	30.00
L-B	3,840,000	35.00
L-★	5,120,000	45.00

SERIES **1969A**

SIGNATURES: Dorothy Andrews Kabis, John B. Connally

SERIAL NUMBER		NOTES PRINTED	CU
BOSTON			
A19 200 001**A**	**A**32 640 000**A**	13,440,000	$35.00
NEW YORK			
B06 400 001**B**	**B**76 160 000**B**	69,760,000	30.00
B05 120 001★	**B**07 680 000★	2,560,000	50.00
PHILADELPHIA			
C10 880 001**A**	**C**24 320 000**A**	13,440,000	35.00
CLEVELAND			
D60 160 001**A**	**D**89 600 000**A**	29,440,000	30.00
D02 560 001★	**D**03 200 000★	640,000	60.00
RICHMOND			
E66 560 001**A**		33,440,000	30.00
	E08 960 000**B**	8,960,000	30.00
E02 560 001★	**E**04 480 000★	1,920,000	50.00
ATLANTA			
F36 480 001**A**	**F**49 920 000**A**	13,440,000	35.00

		CHICAGO	
G07 680 001**B**	**G**88 320 000**B**	80,640,000	30.00
G06 320 000★	**G**05 280 000★	1,920,000	50.00
		ST. LOUIS	
H19 200 001**A**	**H**33 280 000**A**	14,080,000	35.00
H00 640 001★	**H**01 280 000★	640,000	50.00
		MINNEAPOLIS	
I12 160 001**A**	**I**19 200 000**A**	7,040,000	35.00
		KANSAS CITY	
J39 040 001**A**	**J**55 680 000**A**	16,640,000	30.00
		DALLAS	
K25 600 001**A**	**K**40 320 000**A**	14,720,000	30.00
K00 640 001★	**K**01 280 000★	640,000	50.00
		SAN FRANCISCO	
L03 840 001**B**	**L**54 400 000**B**	50,560,000	30.00
L05 120 001★	**L**06 400 000★	1,280,000	60.00

SERIES **1969B**

SIGNATURES: Romana A. Banuelos, John B. Connally

SERIAL NUMBER		NOTES PRINTED	CU
		NEW YORK	
B76 160 001B		25,040,000	$40.00
	B16 360 000C	15,360,000	40.00
B07 200 001★	B07 680 000★	480,000	75.00
		CLEVELAND	
D80 600 001A	D96 000 000A	6,400,000	45.00
		RICHMOND	
E08 960 001B	E36 480 000B	27,520,000	40.00
		ATLANTA	
F49 920 001A	F64 000 000A	14,080,000	40.00
F01 280 001★	F01 920 000★	640,000	75.00
		CHICAGO	
G88 320 001B		11,680,000	40.00
	G02 560 000C	2,560,000	40.00
G05 280 001★	G06 392 000★	1,112,000	65.00
		ST. LOUIS	
H33 280 001A	H38 400 000A	5,120,000	45.00
		MINNEAPOLIS	
I19 200 001A	I21 760 000A	2,560,000	50.00
		KANSAS CITY	
J55 680 001A	J59 520 000A	3,840,000	45.00
J01 280 001★	J01 920 000★	640,000	75.00
		DALLAS	
K40 320 001A	K52 480 000A	12,160,000	40.00
		SAN FRANCISCO	
L54 400 001B	L80 640 000B	26,240,000	40.00
L06 400 001★	L07 040 000★	640,000	75.00

SERIES **1969C**

SIGNATURES: Romana Acosta Banuelos, William E. Simon
PLATE SERIALS: All districts continue from previous series.

SERIAL NUMBERS: All districts continue from previous series.

SERIAL NUMBER		NOTES PRINTED	CU
		BOSTON	
A32 640 001A	A49 920 000A	17,280,000	$35.00
A01 280 001★	A01 920 000★	640,000	50.00

NEW YORK

B15 360 001C		84,640,000	30.00
	B50 560 000D	50,560,000	30.00
B07 320 001★	B08 906 000★	1,640,000	45.00

PHILADELPHIA

C24 320 001A	C65 280 000A	40,960,000	30.00
C01 280 001★	C01 920 000★	640,000	50.00

CLEVELAND

D96 000 001A		4,000,000	40.00
	D53 760 000B	53,760,000	30.00
D03 360 001★	D03 840 000★	480,000	50.00

RICHMOND

E36 480 001B		80,160,000	30.00
	E16 640 000C		30.00
E04 480 001★	E06 400 000★	1,920,000	45.00

ATLANTA

F64 000 001A	F99 840 000A	35,840,000	30.00
F01 024 001★	F02 560 000★	896,000	50.00

CHICAGO

G02 560 001C	G81 280 000C	78,720,000	30.00
G06 400 001★	G07 040 000★	640,000	50.00

ST. LOUIS

H32 320 000A	H38 400 001A	33,920,000	30.00
H01 280 001★	H01 920 000★	640,000	50.00

MINNEAPOLIS

I21 760 001A	I35 840 000A	14,080,000	35.00
I00 640 001★	I01 280 000★	640,000	50.00

KANSAS CITY

J59 520 001A	J91 520 000A	32,000,000	30.00
J01 920 001★	J02 560 000★	640,000	50.00

DALLAS

K52 480 001A	K83 840 000A	32,000,000	30.00
K01 280 001★	K03 200 000★	1,920,000	45.00

SAN FRANCISCO

L80 640 001B		19,360,000	30.00
	L62 720 000C	62,720,000	40.00
L07 200 001★	L08 320 000★	1,120,000	50.00

SERIES 1974

SIGNATURES: Francine I. Neff, William E. Simon
SERIAL NUMBERS: Continue from previous series.
PLATE SERIALS: Continue from previous series.

SERIAL NUMBER		NOTES PRINTED	CU
BOSTON			
A49 920 001A		57,120,000	$30.00
	A07 040 000B		35.00
A01 920 001★	A03 200 000★	768,000	40.00
NEW YORK			
B50 560 001D		296,900,000	30.00
B-E			30.00
B-F			30.00
	B47 360 000G		30.00
B08 960 001★	B17 280 000★	6,976,000	35.00
PHILADELPHIA			
C65 280 001A		59,680,000	30.00
	C24 960 000B		30.00
C01 920 001★	C03 840 000★	1,920,000	40.00
CLEVELAND			
D53 760 001B		148,160,000	30.00
	D99 840 000C		30.00
D03 840 001★	D08 320 000★	4,296,000	40.00
RICHMOND			
E16 640 001C		149,920,000	30.00
	E66 560 000D		30.00
E06 400 001★	E11 520 000★	3,040,000	40.00
ATLANTA			
F99 840 001A		53,200,000	50.00
	F53 120 000B		30.00
F02 560 001★	F03 480 000★	1,120,000	45.00
CHICAGO			
G81 280 001C		250,080,000	30.00
G-D			30.00
G-E			30.00
	G31 360 000F		30.00
G07 200 001★	G14 080 000★	4,928,000	40.00
ST. LOUIS			
H72 320 001A		73,120,000	30.00
	H45 440 000B		30.00
H01 920 001★	H03 200 000★	1,120,000	45.00
MINNEAPOLIS			
I35 840 001A	I71 680 000A	39,040,000	30.00
I01 280 001★	I02 560 000★	1,280,000	45.00
KANSAS CITY			
J91 520 001A		74,400,000	30.00
	J65 920 000B		30.00
J02 720 001★	J04 480 000★	736,000	45.00

DALLAS

K83 840 001**A**		68,640,000	30.00
	K52 480 000**B**		30.00
K03 360 001★	**K**04 480 000★	608,000	45.00

SAN FRANCISCO

L62 720 001**C**		128,800,000	30.00
	L90 880 000**D**		30.00
L08 320 001★	**L**14 080 000★	4,320,000	40.00

SERIES **1977**

SIGNATURES: Azie Taylor Morton, W. Michael Blumenthal

SERIAL NUMBERS: Both regular and star notes begin with 00 000 001.

PLATE SERIALS: Both face and back check continue from previous series.

SERIAL NUMBER		NOTES PRINTED	CU
		BOSTON	
A-A		94,720,000	$30.00
A00 008 001★	**A**03 840 000★	2,688,000	40.00
		NEW YORK	
B-A through **B-F**		569,600,000	30.00
B00 000 001★	**B**13 440 000★	4,736,000	40.00
		PHILADELPHIA	
C-A,C-B		117,320,000	30.00
C00 012 001★	**C**04 480 000★	2,816,000	40.00
		CLEVELAND	
D-A,D-B		189,440,000	30,00
D00 016 001★	**D**07 680 000★	5,632,000	40.00
		RICHMOND	
E-A, through **E-C**		258,660,000	30.00
E00 000 001★	**E**07 040 000★	6,272,000	40.00
		ATLANTA	
F-A		70,400,000	30.00
F00 000 001★	**F**03 840 000★	2,688,000	40.00

CHICAGO

G-A, through **G-D**	358,400,000	30.00
G00 012 001★ **G**10 240 000★	7,552,000	40.00

ST. LOUIS

H-A	98,560,000	30.00
H00 012 001★ **H**03 200 000★	1,792,000	40.00

MINNEAPOLIS

I-A	15,360,000	35.00
I00 000 001★ **I**01 280 000★	512,000	50.00

KANSAS CITY

J-A, J-B	148,480,000	30.00
J00 008 001★ **J**06 400 000★	4,736,000	40.00

DALLAS

K-A, K-B	163,840,000	30.00
K00 008 001★ **K**08 960 000★	3,456,000	40.00

SAN FRANCISCO

L-A through **L-C**	263,680,000	30.00
L00 012 001★ **L**09 600 000★	6,528,000	40.00

SERIES **1981**

SIGNATURES: Angela M. Buchanan, Donald T. Regan

SERIAL NUMBER	**NOTES PRINTED**	**CU**
BOSTON		
A-A, through **A-C**	191,360,000	$30.00
A00 008 001★ **A**01 280 000★	1,272,000	40.00
NEW YORK		
B-A, through **B-F**	592,000,000	30.00
B00 000 001★ **B**06 400 000★	2,544,000	40.00
PHILADELPHIA		
C-A, C-B	101,760,000	30.00
C00 008 001★ **C**00 640 000★	632,000	50.00
CLEVELAND		
D-A, D-B	147,840,000	30.00
D00 000 001★ **D**01 280 000★	1,280,000	40.00
RICHMOND		
E-A, through **E-D**	296,320,000	30.00
E00 000 001★ **E**01 280 000★	1,280,000	40.00
ATLANTA		
F-A, F-B	16,384,000	30.00
F00 000 001★ **F**03 200 000★	3,200,000	40.00

CHICAGO

G-A through **G-D**	361,600,000	30.00
G00 000 001★ G02 560 000★	1,920,000	40.00

ST. LOUIS

H-A, H-B	128,640,000	30.00
H00 012 001★ H01 920 000★	1,908,000	40.00

MINNEAPOLIS

I-A	9,840,000	35.00
I-B	12,800,000	30.00
I00 000 001★ I00 640 000★	640,000	50.00

KANSAS CITY

J-A	99,840,000	30.00
J-B	19,200,000	35.00
J-C	12,800,000	35.00
J00 000 001★ J01 280 000★	1,280,000	40.00

DALLAS

K-A, K-B	95,360,000	30.00
K00 000 001★ K01 280 000★	1,268,000	40.00

SAN FRANCISCO

L-A through **L-E**	404,480,000	30.00
L00 000 001★ L01 920 000★	1,904,000	40.00

SERIES **1981A**

SIGNATURES: Katherine Davalos Ortega, Donald T. Regan

SERIAL NUMBER	NOTES PRINTED	CU

BOSTON

A-A, A-B	156,860,000	$30.00

NEW YORK

B-A through **B-C**	297,600,000	30.00
B-D	55,400,000	30.00

PHILADELPHIA

C-A	57,600,000	30.00
C-★	3,840,000	40.00

CLEVELAND

D-A	99,200,000	30.00
D-B	60,800,000	30.00
D-★	3,840,000	40.00

RICHMOND

E-A, E-B	198,400,000	30.00
E-C	16,000,000	30.00

ATLANTA

F-A	99,200,000	30.00
F-B	41,600,000	30.00
F-★	3,200,000	40.00

CHICAGO

G-A, through **G-B**	198,400,000	30.00
G-C	12,800,000	35.00

ST. LOUIS

H-A	73,600,000	30.00

KANSAS CITY

J-A	86,400,000	30.00

DALLAS

K-A	99,200,000	30.00

SAN FRANCISCO

L-A through **L-E**	396,800,000	30.00
L-★	6,400,000	50.00

SERIES 1985

SIGNATURES: Katherine Davalos Ortega, James A. Baker III

SERIAL NUMBER	NOTES PRINTED	CU
BOSTON		
A-A through **A-E**	496,000,000	$30.00
A-★	3,200,000	40.00
NEW YORK		
B-A through **B-S**	1,587,200,000	30.00
B-★	5,760,000	40.00
PHILADELPHIA		
C-A through **C-C**	198,400,000	30.00
C-★	6,400,000	40.00
CLEVELAND		
D-A through **D-F**	684,800,000	30.00
D-★	6,400,000	40.00
RICHMOND		
E-A through **E-I**	864,000,000	30.00
E-★	6,400,000	40.00
ATLANTA		
F-A through **F-C**	310,400,000	30.00
F-D	12,800,000	35.00

	CHICAGO		
G-A through **G-H**	726,400,000	30.00
G-★	5,760,000	40.00
ST. LOUIS		
H-A through **H-C**	230,400,000	30.00
MINNEAPOLIS		
I-A,I-B	112,000,000	30.00
KANSAS CITY		
J-A through **J-C**	204,800 000	30.00
J-★	3,200,000	40.00
DALLAS		
K-A, **K-B**	192,000,000	30.00
K-★	3,200,000	40.00
SAN FRANCISCO		
L-A through **L-L**	1,136,000,000	30.00
L-★	3,200,000	40.00

SERIES **1988**

None Printed

SERIES **1988A**

SIGNATURES: Catalina Vasquez Villalpando, Nicholas F. Brady

PLATE SERIALS: Both face and back check numbers begin at #1, with extensive muling from previous series on backs.

SERIAL NUMBERS: Both regular and star notes begin at 00 000 001.

LOW	HIGH	NOTES	
SERIAL NUMBERS		**PRINTED**	**CU**
BOSTON			
A-A through **A-D**		313,600,000	$30.00
NEW YORK			
B-A through **B-K**		934,400,000	30.00
B-★	B12 800 000★	6,560,000	35.00
PHILADELPHIA			
C-A		96,000,000	30.00
C-★	C03 200 000★	80,000	45.00
CLEVELAND			
D-A through **D-D**		283,200,000	30.00
RICHMOND			
E-A through **E-C**		281,600,000	30.00
ATLANTA			
F-A through **F-C**		288,000,000	30.00
F-★	F03 200 000★	3,200,000	40.00
CHICAGO			
G-A through **G-F**		563,200,000	30.00
G-★	G03 200 000★	3,200,000	40.00

ST. LOUIS			
H-A, H-B		108,800,000	30.00
MINNEAPOLIS			
I-A		25,600,000	30.00
KANSAS CITY			
J-A, J-B		137,600,000	30.00
DALLAS			
K-A		51,200,000	30.00
K-★	K03 200 000★	3,200,000	40.00
SAN FRANCISCO			
L-A through **L-H**		729,600,000	30.00

SERIES **1990**

SIGNATURES: Catalina Vasquez Villalpando, Nicholas F. Brady
PLATE SERIALS: Face check numbers begin at #1. Back check numbers continue sequence from previous series.
SERIAL NUMBERS: Both regular and star notes begin at 00 000 001.
(Series 1990 introduced the anti-counterfeiting security thread and the microsize printing around the portrait.)

LOW SERIAL NUMBERS	HIGH	NOTES PRINTED	CU
BOSTON			
A-A through **A-C**		345,600,000	$30.00
A-★	A03 200 000★	2,560,000	40.00
NEW YORK			
B-A through **B-P**		1,536,000,000	30.00
B-Q		6,400,000	35.00
B-★	B19 200 000★	16,640,000	40.00
PHILADELPHIA			
C-A		96,000,000	30.00
CLEVELAND			
D-A, through **D-C**		279,600,000	30.00
D-★	D03 200 000★	3,200,000	40.00
RICHMOND			
E-A through **E-D**		288,000,000	30.00
E-★	E03 200 000★	3,200,000	40.00
ATLANTA			
F-A through **F-E**		537,600,000	30.00
F★	FW F00 965 189★ F02 695 240★	1,280,000	40.00

CHICAGO			
G-A through **G-G**		652,800,000	30.00
G-★ FW	G16 000 000★	13,440,000	40.00
ST. LOUIS			
H-A, H-B		172,800,000	30.00
H★	H00 320 000★	320,000	50.00
MINNEAPOLIS			
I-A		70,400,000	30.00
I-★ FW	I06 400 000★	5,120,000	40.00
KANSAS CITY			
J-A		83,200,000	30.00
DALLAS			
K-A		25,600,000	30.00

SAN FRANCISCO

L-A through **L-E** **W/FW**   416,000,000   30.00

SERIES **1993**

SIGNATURES: Mary Ellen Withrow, Lloyd Bentsen
PLATE SERIALS: Face check numbers begin at #1. Back check numbers both continue from previous series, creating mules, and start also with #1, simultaneously.
SERIAL NUMBERS: Both regular and star notes begin at 00 000 001.

LOW SERIAL NUMBERS		HIGH	NOTES PRINTED	CU
BOSTON				
A-A,A-C		A96 000 000C	288,000,000	30.00
A-★		A03 840 000★	2,560,000	40.00
NEW YORK				
B-A,B-C		B19 200 000G	595,200,000	30.00
B-★		B07 680 000★	5,120,000	35.00
PHILADELPHIA				
C-A		C76 800 000A	76,800,000	30.00
CLEVELAND				
D-A,D-C		D64 000 000C	256,000,000	30.00
D-★		D01 920 000★	1,920,000	40.00
RICHMOND				
E-A,E-G		E70 400 000G	646,400,000	30.00
E-★		E03 840 000★	2,560,000	40.00
ATLANTA				
F-A ,F-C	W		288,000,000	30.00
F-D	W/FW	F64 000 000D	64,000,000	30.00
CHICAGO				
G-A,G-C	FW		288,000,000	30.00
G-D	FW	G38 400 000D	38,400,000	30.00
ST. LOUIS				
H-A,H-B	W/FW	H89 600 000B	185,600,000	30.00
KANSAS CITY				
J-A	FW		96,000,000	30.00
J-B	FW		6,400,000	35.00
DALLAS				
K-A,K-B		K89 600 000B	185,600,000	30.00
SAN FRANCISCO				
L-A,L-I	FW	L38 400 000I	806,400,000	30.00
L-★	FW	L09 600 000★	7,680,000	35.00

SERIES **1995**

SIGNATURES: Mary Ellen Withrow, Robert F. Rubin
PLATE SERIALS: Face check numbers begin at #1. Back check numbers continue from previous series with the Fort Worth issues.
SERIAL NUMBERS: Both regular and star notes begin at 00 000 001.

LOW SERIAL NUMBERS		HIGH	NOTES PRINTED	CU
NEW YORK				
B-A			192,000,000	30.00
B-★		B01 920 000★	1,920,000	40.00
PHILADELPHIA				
C-A	W		51,200,000	30.00
ATLANTA				
F-A	FW		96,000,000	30.00

F-B	FW		76,800,000	30.00

CHICAGO

G-A,G-E	FW	G19 200 000C	403,200,000	30.00

ST. LOUIS

H-A	FW		96,000,000	30.00
H-B	FW		6,400,000	35.00

KANSAS CITY

J-A	FW		51,200,000	30.00

DALLAS

K-A	FW		96,000,000	30.00
K-B	FW		6,400,000	35.00

SAN FRANCISCO

L-A,L-E	FW	L83 220 000F	563,200,000	30.00

Series 1995 remain in production at press time.

FIFTY DOLLAR NATIONAL BANK NOTES

Brown Seal

Type I has black serial numbers on the ends of the note. The left reading horizontally, the right reading vertically. Type II is similar, but the brown serial number is succeeded or preceded by the charter number also. All notes have facsimile signatures of E. E. Jones and W. O. Woods at the top. Signatures of the officers of the local bank appear at the bottom.
See listings under Five Dollar denomination for detailed information as to rarity and value.

FIFTY DOLLAR NOTES
GOLD CERTIFICATE
Gold Seal
SERIES 1928

PLATE SERIALS: Face check #1 through #41.

SIGNATURES: Walter O. Woods, Andrew W. Mellon

LOW	HIGH	NOTES		
SERIAL	NUMBERS	PRINTED	VG/F	CU
A00 000 001A	A05 520 000A	5,520,000	$125.00	$750.00
★00 000 211A	★00 028 165A		750.00	4000.00

FEDERAL RESERVE BANK NOTES
Brown Seal
SERIES 1929

SERIAL NUMBERS: Both regular and star notes start with 00 000 001.

PLATE SERIALS: Face check numbers begin with #1.

SIGNATURES: Same as $5.00 FRBN.

LOW	HIGH	NOTES		
SERIAL	NUMBERS	PRINTED	VG/F	CU
NEW YORK				
B00 032 657A	B00 636 000A	636,000	$65.00	$175.00
B00 001 578★	B00 015 571★	24,000	100.00	600.00
CLEVELAND				
D00 346 569A	D00 684 000A	684,000	65.00	175.00
D00 000 204★	D00 006 440★	12,000	100.00	600.00
CHICAGO				
G00 038 051A	G00 300 000A	300,000	65.00	150.00
G-★	G00 003 305★	4,000	225.00	900.00
MINNEAPOLIS				
I00 022 469A	I00 276 000A	276,000	75.00	175.00
I00 001 914★		12,000	225.00	1000.00

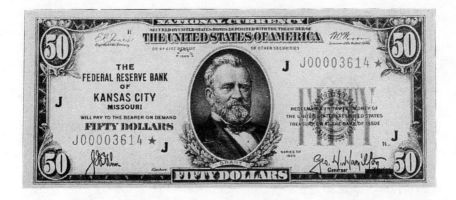

KANSAS CITY

J00 207 066A	J00 276 000A	276,000	75.00	150.00
J00 000 055★	J00 003 735★	12,000	135.00	500.00

DALLAS

K00 145 505A	K00 168 000A	168,000	85.00	200.00
K-★		12,000	450.00	1500.00

SAN FRANCISCO

L00 233 295A	L00 576 000A	576,000	85.00	300.00
L00 002 435★		12,000	200.00	1500.00

FEDERAL RESERVE NOTES

Green Seal

SERIES 1928

SERIAL NUMBERS: All serial numbers both regular and star notes begin with 00 000 001.

High official star serial numbers are listed under the High Star serial number column.

PLATE SERIALS: Both face and back checks start with number 1.

SIGNATURES: Walter O. Woods, A.W. Mellon

LOW	HIGH	NOTES		
SERIAL NUMBERS		PRINTED	VG/F	CU
BOSTON				
A-A		265,200	$75.00	$200.00
A00 000 058★	A00 010 558★		90.00	800.00
NEW YORK				
B00 576 777A	B01 199 158A	1,351,800	60.00	200.00
B00 019 980★		76,000	85.00	600.00
PHILADELPHIA				
C00 573 650A	C00 792 468A	997,056	60.00	200.00
C-★		48,000	85.00	600.00
CLEVELAND				
D00 263 927A	D01 730 714A	1,161,900	60.00	200.00
D00 004 252★	D00 010 276★	48,000	85.00	600.00
RICHMOND				
E00 167 065A		539,400	65.00	120.00
E00 001 985★	E00 002 000★	24,000	90.00	500.00

ATLANTA

F00 096 218A	F00 412 976A	538,800	65.00	200.00
F00 006 494★			90.00	600.00
	F00 024 000★			

CHICAGO

G00 257 419A	G02 662 453A	1,348,620	60.00	200.00
G00 000 177★	G00 023 615★	84,000	85.00	600.00

ST. LOUIS

H00 152 967A	H00 315 651A	627,300	65.00	200.00
H00 000 761★	H00 002 366★	24,000	90.00	600.00

MINNEAPOLIS

I00 013 488A	I00 099 867A	106,200	100.00	200.00
I00 000 069★		24,000	150.00	800.00

KANSAS CITY

J00 070 582A	J00 164 328A	252, 600	75.00	200.00
J00 000 254★	J00 006 850★	24,000	90.00	600.00

DALLAS

K00 081 870A	109,920	100.00	200.00
K00 003 342★	12,000	150.00	800.00

SAN FRANCISCO

L00 078 169A	L00 366 666A	447,600	65.00	200.00
L00 000 732★		24,000	90.00	750.00

SERIES 1928A

Dark Green Seal

DESIGN CHANGE: District numeral in seal replaced by letter. Face check begins with 1.

SIGNATURES: Walter O. Woods, A.W. Mellon

LOW SERIAL NUMBERS	HIGH	NOTES PRINTED	VG/F	CU
BOSTON				
A00 276 314A	A00 711 856A	1,834,989	$60.00	$150.00
NEW YORK				
B01 392 109A	B01 758 494A	3,392,328	60.00	150.00
PHILADELPHIA				
C00 875 752A	C01 516 053A	3,078,944	60.00	150.00
CLEVELAND				
D01 207 831A	D01 798 304A	2,453,364	60.00	150.00

RICHMOND				
E00 488 679A	E00 614 252A	1,516,500	60.00	150.00
ATLANTA				
F00 455 764A	F00 543 233A	338,400	80.00	175.00
CHICAGO				
G01 209 292A	G03 750 686A	5,263,956	60.00	150.00
ST. LOUIS				
H00 280 205A	H00 626 709A	880,500	67.50	175.00
MINNEAPOLIS				
I00 102 228A	I00 948 807A	780,240	67.50	175.00
KANSAS CITY				
J-A		791,604	67.50	175.00
DALLAS				
K00 133 819A		701,496	55.00	175.00
SAN FRANCISCO				
L00 744 400A	L01 078 735A	1,522,620	60.00	150.00

SERIES 1928A

Light Green Seal

SERIAL NUMBERS: Continue in sequence from 1028A Dark Green Seal variety.

LOW	HIGH	NOTES		
SERIAL NUMBERS		**PRINTED**	**VG/F**	**CU**
KANSAS CITY				
J00 267 258A	J00 536 632A	Included Above	$75.00	$200.00
SAN FRANCISCO				
L01 261 965A		ncluded Above	75.00	200.00

SERIES 1934

Light Green Seal

SERIAL NUMBERS: Both regular and stars begin with 00 000 007.

PLATE SERIALS: Face check numbers start with #1. Back check numbers continue in sequence from series 1928A.

LOW	HIGH	NOTES		
SERIAL NUMBERS		**PRINTED**	**VG/F**	**CU**
BOSTON				
A00 200 420A	A00 649 183A	2,729,400	$55.00	$200.00
A00 000 043★	A00 009 960★		75.00	400.00

NEW YORK

B00 000 890A	B01 015 540A	17,894,676	55.00	200.00
B00 000 057★	B00 001 207★		75.00	400.00

PHILADELPHIA

C00 189 154A	5,833,000	55.00	200.00
C-★		75.00	400.00

CLEVELAND

D00 007 988A	D00 307 324A	8,817,720	55.00	200.00
D-★			75.00	400.00

RICHMOND

E00 373 055A	4,826,628	55.00	100.00
E-★		75.00	400.00

ATLANTA

F00 029 498A	F00 038 278A	3,069,348	55.00	160.00
F-★			100.00	600.00

CHICAGO

G00 141 106A	G00 596 674A	8,675,940	55.00	100.00
G00 002 591★			100.00	600.00

ST. LOUIS

H00 038 085A	H00 194 410A	1,497,144	55.00	100.00
H-★			100.00	600.00

MINNEAPOLIS

I00 009 898A	I00 081 186A	539,700	55.00	100.00
I-★			100.00	600.00

KANSAS CITY

J00 046 468A	1,133,520	55.00	100.00
J-★		100.00	600.00

DALLAS

K00 011 067A	K00 128 533A	1,194,876	55.00	100.00
K00 000 797★			100.00	600.00

SAN FRANCISCO

L00 042 653A	8,101,200	55.00	160.00
L-★		100.00	600.00

Dark Green Seal
SERIES 1934

SERIAL NUMBERS: All serial numbers both regular and star continue in sequence from 1934 Light Seal variety.

PLATE SERIALS: Back check number up to 162.

SIGNATURES: W.A. Julian, Henry Morgenthau, Jr.

Quantities included in Light Green Seal above.

LOW	HIGH	NOTES		
SERIAL NUMBERS		PRINTED	VG/F	CU
BOSTON				
A00 992 807A A01 304 972A			$55.00	$160.00
A00 012 537★			70.00	450.00
NEW YORK				
B01 978 294A B16 128 828A			55.00	160.00
B00 009 593★ B00 132 401★			70.00	450.00
PHILADELPHIA				
C01 026 815A C05 377 316A			55.00	160.00
C00 013 679★ C00 049 617★			70.00	450.00
CLEVELAND				
D02 165 562A D09 374 113A			55.00	160.00
D00 022 997★ D00 042 147★			70.00	450.00
RICHMOND				
E01 080 887A E06 647 594A			55.00	160.00
E00 010 289★			70.00	550.00
ATLANTA				
F01 486 452A F03 528 759A			55.00	160.00
F00 005 876★			70.00	450.00
CHICAGO				
G02 282 601A G08 288 483A			55.00	160.00
G00 015 281★ G00 046 310★			70.00	450.00
ST. LOUIS				
H00 938 598A H01 656 284A			57.50	160.00
H-★			75.00	550.00
MINNEAPOLIS				
I00 151 503A I00 673 439A			57.50	160.00
I00 006 851★			75.00	550.00
KANSAS CITY				
J00 538 925A J01 148 956A			57.50	160.00
J00 006 055★ J00 022 425★			75.00	400.00
DALLAS				
K00 613 277A K01 172 484A			57.50	160.00
K00 009 695★			75.00	400.00
SAN FRANCISCO				
L00 523 023A L07 568 656A			55.00	140.00
L00 076 580★ L00 082 750★			75.00	400.00

Dark Green Seal
SERIES 1934 MULE

PLATE SERIALS: Back check number begins with 163.

Quantities included in Light Green Seal above.

LOW	HIGH	NOTES		
SERIAL NUMBERS		PRINTED	VG/F	CU
BOSTON				
A00 821 285A			$55.00	$140.00
A-★			75.00	400.00
NEW YORK				
B19 028 213A			55.00	140.00
B-★			75.00	400.00
PHILADELPHIA				
C03 030 503A			55.00	140.00
C-★			75.00	400.00
CLEVELAND				
D03 122 704A			55.00	140.00
D-★			75.00	400.00

RICHMOND

E-A	55.00	140.00
E-★	75.00	400.00

ATLANTA

F-A	75.00	140.00
F-★	75.00	400.00

CHICAGO

G06 657 429A	55.00	140.00
G-★	75.00	400.00

ST. LOUIS

H00 945 828A	55.00	140.00
H-★	75.00	400.00

MINNEAPOLIS

I-A	55.00	140.00
I-★	75.00	400.00

KANSAS CITY

J-A	55.00	140.00
J-★	75.00	400.00

DALLAS

K01 003 195A	55.00	140.00
K-★	75.00	400.00

SAN FRANCISCO

L14 696 723A	55.00	140.00
L-★	75.00	400.00

SERIES **1934A MULE**

Dark Green Seal

SIGNATURES: W.A. Julian, Henry Morgenthau, Jr.

PLATE SERIALS: Back check numbers 162 and lower (micro size).

SERIAL NUMBERS: All districts continue from previous series.

All observations and reported information indicate that all $50.00 Federal Reserve notes from 1934A through 1950 are MULES.

LOW SERIAL	HIGH NUMBERS	NOTES PRINTED	VF	CU
BOSTON				
A02 197 478A	A02 675 477A	406,200	$55.00	$160.00
A-★			75.00	450.00
NEW YORK				
B04 672 222A	B17 173 989A	4,710,648	55.00	160.00
B00 046 194★	B00 113 592★		75.00	450.00

CLEVELAND

D00 703 136A	D07 950 056A	864,168	55.00	160.00
D-★			75.00	450.00

RICHMOND

E03 219 261A	E04 649 831A	2,235,372	55.00	160.00
E-★			75.00	450.00

ATLANTA

F01 393 635A	F03 201 653A	416,100	55.00	160.00
F00 025 815★			75.00	450.00

CHICAGO

G04 411 186A	G08 972 632A	1,014,600	55.00	160.00
G-★			75.00	450.00

ST. LOUIS

H01 146 859A	H01 714 428A	361,944	55.00	160.00
H-★			75.00	450.00

MINNEAPOLIS

I00 334 835A	I00 533 635A	93,300	65.00	160.00
I-★			75.00	450.00

KANSAS CITY

J00 595 835A	J00 613 587A	189,300	55.00	160.00
J-★			75.00	450.00

DALLAS

K00 394 159A	K01 653 036A	266,700	55.00	160.00
K-★			75.00	400.00

SAN FRANCISCO

L00 414 384A	L02 871 431A		55.00	160.00
L-★		162,000	75.00	450.00

SERIES 1934B MULE

SIGNATURES: W.A. Julian, Fred M. Vinson

PLATE SERIALS: Back check number 162 and lower.

SERIAL NUMBERS: All districts continued from previous series.

LOW	HIGH	NOTES		
SERIAL NUMBERS		PRINTED	VF	CU
PHILADELPHIA				
C05 604 319A	C06 351 435A	509,100	$65.00	$125.00

CLEVELAND

D09 504 477A	D10 146 571A	359,100	65.00	125.00
D00 116 564★			550.00	2500.00

RICHMOND

E07 131 290A	E07 284 378A	596,700	65.00	125.00
E-★	E00 090 094★			

ATLANTA

F03 294 629A	F03 604 187A	416,720	65.00	125.00

CHICAGO

	G09 399 017A	306,000	65.00	125.00

ST. LOUIS

H01 745 970A	H01 869 658A	306,000	65.00	125.00

MINNEAPOLIS

I00 580 912A	I00 692 511A	120,000	75.00	200.00

KANSAS CITY

J01 253 391A	J01 495 360A	221,340	65.00	175.00
J00 034 838★			550.00	2500.00

DALLAS

K01 445 543A	K01 460 049A	120,108	75.00	200.00

SAN FRANCISCO

L07 831 530A	L08 019 470A	441,000	65.00	150.00

SERIES 1934C MULE

SIGNATURES: W.A. Julian, John W. Snyder
PLATE SERIALS: Back check number 162 and lower.

SERIAL NUMBERS: All districts continue from previous series.

LOW	HIGH	NOTES		
SERIAL NUMBERS		PRINTED	VG/F	CU

BOSTON

A03 048 570A	A03 156 674A	117,600	$75.00	$125.00

NEW YORK

B16 487 892A	B19 095 949A	1,556,400	55.00	85.00
B00 153 289★	B00 153 458★		300.00	1000.00

PHILADELPHIA

C05 888 759A	C07 683 555A	107,283	75.00	125.00

CLEVELAND

D09 466 522A	D11 973 634A	374,400	65.00	85.00
D00 117 789★	D00 145 476★		300.00	1000.00

RICHMOND

E07 527 278A	E08 786 836A	1,821,960	55.00	85.00
E00 097 595★			300.00	1000.00

LOW SERIAL NUMBERS	HIGH	District	NOTES PRINTED	VG/F	CU
F-A		**ATLANTA**	107,640	75.00	150.00
G09 166 774A	G09 623 069A	**CHICAGO**	294,432	55.00	85.00
H02 188 571A	H02 570 405A	**ST. LOUIS**	535,200	55.00	85.00
		MINNEAPOLIS	118,800	75.00	125.00
I00 010 437★				300.00	1000.00
J01 558 727A	J01 805 454A	**KANSAS CITY**	303,600	55.00	85.00
K01 560 306A		**DALLAS**	429,900	55.00	85.00
K00 025 502★				300.00	1000.00

SERIES 1934D MULE

SIGNATURES: Georgia Neese Clark, John W. Snyder
PLATE SERIALS: Back check number 162 and lower.

SERIAL NUMBERS: All districts continue from previous series. All high numbers are official endings.

LOW SERIAL NUMBERS	HIGH	District	NOTES PRINTED	VG/F	CU
A03 129 512A	A03 468 000A	**BOSTON**	279,600	$55.00	$150.00
A00 032 419★				750.00	2000.00
B18 147 152A	B19 248 000A	**NEW YORK**	898,776	55.00	100.00
B00 169 925A				750.00	2000.00
C07 371 807A	C08 004 000A	**PHILADELPHIA**	699,000	55.00	100.00
E09 200 267A	E09 216 000A	**RICHMOND**	156,000	90.00	250.00
	F04 020 000A	**ATLANTA**	216,000	90.00	250.00
F00 036 681★				750.00	2000.00
G07 479 216A	G10 188 000A	**CHICAGO**	494,016	55.00	100.00
G00 100 066★				750.00	2000.00
I00 750 686A		**MINNEAPOLIS**		250.00	—
K01 856 747A	K01 984 000A	**DALLAS**	103,200	65.00	200.00

SERIES 1950 MULE

SIGNATURES: Georgia Neese Clark, John W. Snyder
PLATE SERIALS: Back check number 162 and lower (micro size).

SERIAL NUMBERS. All districts begin with 00 000 001 both star and regular notes.

LOW SERIAL NUMBERS	HIGH	District	NOTES PRINTED	CU
A00 402 265A	A01 248 000A	**BOSTON**	1,248,000	$120.00
A-★				300.00
B01 380 093A	B10 236 000A	**NEW YORK**	10,236,000	120.00
B00 097 827★				300.00

PHILADELPHIA

C02 352 000A   2,352,000   120.00

C-★   300.00

CLEVELAND

D06 180 000A   6,180,000   120.00

D-★   D00 088 000★   300.00

RICHMOND

E05 064 000A   5,064,000   120.00

E-★   350.00

ATLANTA

F01 812 000A   1,812,000   120.00

F-★   350.00

CHICAGO

G04 212 000A   4,212,000   120.00

G-★   300.00

ST. LOUIS

H00 045 774A   H00 892 000A   892,000   120.00

H-★   350.00

MINNEAPOLIS

I00 384 000A   384,000   120.00

I-★   350.00

KANSAS CITY

J00 696 000A   696,000   120.00

J-★   350.00

DALLAS

K01 100 000A   1,100,000   120.00

K-★   K00 004 300★   300.00

SAN FRANCISCO

L00 661 366A   L03 996 000A   3,996,000   120.00

L-★   350.00

Higher serial numbers were assigned to this series but were not used.

SERIES 1950A

SERIAL NUMBERS: Continued sequence from previous series, with small gap.

SIGNATURES: Ivy Baker Priest, George M. Humphrey

LOW	HIGH	NOTES	VALUE
	SERIAL NUMBERS	PRINTED	CU

BOSTON

| A01 296 001A | A02 016 000A | 720,000 | $120.00 |
| A00 155 016★ | | | 300.00 |

NEW YORK

B10 368 001A	B16 848 000A	6,480,000	120.00
B-★			300.00

PHILADELPHIA

C02 448 001A	C04 176 000A	1,728,000	120.00
C-★			300.00

CLEVELAND

D06 192 001A	D08 064 000A	1,872,000	120.00
D00 183 149★			300.00

RICHMOND

E05 184 001A	E07 200 000A	2,016,000	120.00
E-★			300.00

ATLANTA

F01 872 000A	F02 160 000A	288,000	120.00
F00 280 895★			350.00

CHICAGO

G04 320 001A	G06 336 000A	2,016,000	120.00
G00 208 571★			300.00

ST. LOUIS

H01 008 001A	H01 584 000A	576,000	120.00
H00 248 918★			300.00

KANSAS CITY

J00 720 001A	J00 864 000A	144,000	120.00
J-★			350.00

DALLAS

K01 152 001A	K02 016 000A	864,000	120.00
K-★			300.00

SAN FRANCISCO

L04 032 001A	L04 608 000A	576,000	120.00
L-★			300.00

SERIES 1950B

SERIAL NUMBERS: Continued sequence from previous series.

SIGNATURES: Ivy Baker Priest, Robert B. Anderson

LOW	HIGH	NOTES	VALUE
SERIAL NUMBERS		PRINTED	CU

BOSTON

A02 016 001A	A02 880 000A	864,000	$120.00
A00 405 269★			300.00

NEW YORK

B16 848 001A	B25 200 000A	8,352,000	120.00
B-★			300.00

PHILADELPHIA

C04 176 001A	C06 768 000A	2,592,000	120.00
C00 068 221★	C00 502 437★		300.00

CLEVELAND

D08 064 001A	D09 792 000A	1,728,000	120.00
D-★			300.00

RICHMOND

E07 200 001A	E08 784 000A	1,584,000	120.00
E-★			300.00

CHICAGO

G06 336 001A	G10 656 000A	4,320,000	120.00
G-★			300.00

ST. LOUIS

H01 584 001A	H02 160 000A	576,000	120.00
H-★			300.00

KANSAS CITY

J00 864 001A	J01 872 000A	1,008,000	120.00
J-★	J00 362 687★		300.00

DALLAS

K02 016 001A	K03 024 000A	1,008,000	120.00
K-★	K00 445 855★		300.00

SAN FRANCISCO

L04 608 001A	L06 480 000A	1,872,000	120.00
L00 395 779★			300.00

SERIES 1950C

SERIAL NUMBERS: Continued sequence from previous series.

SIGNATURES: Elizabeth Rudel Smith, C. Douglas Dillon

LOW	HIGH	NOTES	VALUE
SERIAL NUMBERS		PRINTED	CU

BOSTON

A02 880 001A	A03 600 000A	720,000	$110.00
A-★			250.00

NEW YORK

B25 200 001A	B30 528 000A	5,328,000	110.00
B-★	B02 120 622★		200.00

PHILADELPHIA

| C06 768 001A | C08 064 000A | 1,296,000 | 110.00 |
| C00 820 981★ | | | 250.00 |

CLEVELAND

| D09 792 001A | D11 088 000A | 1,296,000 | 110.00 |
| D-★ | D00 784 714★ | | 300.00 |

RICHMOND

| E08 784 001A | E10 080 000A | 1,296,000 | 110.00 |
| E-★ | | | 300.00 |

CHICAGO

| G10 656 001A | G12 384 000A | 1,728,000 | 110.00 |
| G-★ | | | 300.00 |

ST. LOUIS

| H02 160 001A | H02 736 000A | 576,000 | 110.00 |
| H-★ | H00 664 170★ | | 300.00 |

MINNEAPOLIS

| I00 432 001A | I00 576 000A | 144,000 | 110.00 |
| I00 217 587★ | I00 248 473★ | | 300.00 |

KANSAS CITY

| J01 872 001A | J02 304 000A | 432,000 | 110.00 |
| J00 488 285★ | J00 489 436★ | | 300.00 |

DALLAS

| K03 024 001A | K03 744 000A | 720,000 | 110.00 |
| K-★ | | | 300.00 |

SAN FRANCISCO

L06 480 001A	L07 632 000A	1,152,000	110.00
L-★			300.00

SERIES 1950D

SERIAL NUMBERS: Continued sequence from previous series.
SIGNATURES: Kathryn O'Hay Granahan, C. Douglas Dillon

LOW	HIGH	NOTES	VALUE
SERIAL NUMBERS		PRINTED	CU

BOSTON

A03 600 001A	A05 328 000A	1,728,000	$150.00
A-★			400.00

NEW YORK

B30 528 001A	B37 728 000A	7,200,000	150.00
B02 413 559★	B02 421 193★		400.00

PHILADELPHIA

C08 064 000A	C10 800 000A	2,736,000	150.00
C00 920 045★			400.00

CLEVELAND

D11 088 001A	D13 968 000A	2,880,000	150.00
D01 057 317★			400.00

RICHMOND

E10 080 001A	E12 096 000A	2,016,000	150.00
E-★			400.00

ATLANTA

F02 160 001A	F02 736 000A	576,000	150.00
F-★			400.00

CHICAGO

G12 384 001A	G16 560 000A	4,176,000	150.00
G-★			400.00

ST. LOUIS

H02 736 001A	H04 176 000A	1,440,000	150.00
H00 787 337★	H00 848 570★		400.00

MINNEAPOLIS

I00 576 001A	I00 864 000A	288,000	150.00
I-★			400.00

KANSAS CITY

J02 304 001A	J03 024 000A	720,000	150.00
J-★			400.00

DALLAS

K03 744 001A	K05 040 000A	1,296,000	150.00
K-★			400.00

SAN FRANCISCO

L07 632 001**A** L09 792 000**A**		2,160,000	150.00
L-★			400.00

SERIES **1950E**

SERIAL NUMBERS: Districts printed continued sequence from previous series.

SIGNATURES: Kathryn O'Hay Granahan, Henry H. Fowler

LOW	HIGH	NOTES	VALUE
SERIAL NUMBERS		**PRINTED**	**CU**

NEW YORK

B37 728 001**A** B40 752 000**A**		3,024,000	$150.00
B02 657 448★ B02 847 457★			300.00

CHICAGO

G01 391 815**A** G17 568 000**A**		1,008,000	175.00
			400.00

SAN FRANCISCO

L09 792 001**A** L11 088 000**A**		1,296,000	175.00
L01 060 138★			400.00

Federal Reserve Notes

Green Seal

SERIES **1963**

None printed

SERIES **1963A**

SERIAL NUMBERS: All serial numbers both regular and star notes begin with 00 000 001.

PLATE SERIALS: Face and back check begin with 1. Motto IN GOD WE TRUST added on back.

SIGNATURES: Kathryn O'Hay Granahan, Henry H. Fowler.

SERIAL NUMBERS	NOTES PRINTED	CU

BOSTON

A-A		1,536,000	$100.00
A-★		320,000	200.00

NEW YORK

B-A		11,008,000	100.00
B-★	B01 397 635★	1,408,000	175.00

PHILADELPHIA

C-A		3,328,000	100.00
	C00 512 118★	704,000	175.00

CLEVELAND

D-A		3,584,000	100.00
D00 000 008★	D00 048 895★	256,000	175.00

RICHMOND

E-A	3,072,000	100.00
E-★	704,000	175.00

ATLANTA

F-A	768,000	100.00
F-★	384,000	175.00

CHICAGO

G-A	6,912,000	100.00
G-★	768,000	175.00

ST. LOUIS

H-A		512,000	120.00
H00 000 007★	H00 114 370★	128,000	200.00

MINNEAPOLIS

I00 199 768A	512,000	120.00
I00 025 975★	128,000	275.00

KANSAS CITY

J-A	512,000	100.00
J-★	64,000	200.00

DALLAS

K-A	1,536,000	100.00
K-★	128,000	200.00

SAN FRANCISCO

L-A	4,352,000	100.00
L-★	704,000	175.00

SERIES 1969

SERIAL NUMBERS: All serial numbers both regular and star notes begin with 00 000 001.

SIGNATURES: Dorothy Andrews Elston, David M. Kennedy

SERIAL NUMBERS	NOTES PRINTED	CU

BOSTON

A-A	2,048,000	$100.00

NEW YORK

B-A	12,032,000	100.00
B-★	384,000	150.00

PHILADELPHIA

C-A	3,584,000	100.00
C-★	128,000	150.00

CLEVELAND

D-A	3,584,000	100.00
D-★	192,000	150.00

RICHMOND

E-A	2,560,000	100.00
E00 016 678★	64,000	200.00

ATLANTA

F-A	256,000	150.00

CHICAGO

G-A	9,728,000	100.00
G-★	256,000	150.00

ST. LOUIS

H-A	256,000	100.00

MINNEAPOLIS

I-A	512,000	100.00

KANSAS CITY

J-A	1,280,000	100.00
J-★	64,000	200.00

DALLAS

K-A	1,536,000	100.00
K00 061 927★	64,000	175.00

SAN FRANCISCO

L-A	6,912,000	100.00
L-★	256,000	175.00

SERIES 1969A

SERIAL NUMBERS: Continued sequence from previous series.
SIGNATURES: Dorothy Andrews Kabis, John B. Connally

SERIAL NUMBERS		NOTES PRINTED	CU
BOSTON			
A02 048 001A	A03 584 000A	1,536,000	$100.00
A00 000 001★	A00 128 000★	128,000	140.00
NEW YORK			
B12 032 000A	B21 760 000A	9,728,000	90.00
B00 384 001★	B01 088 000★	704,000	120.00
PHILADELPHIA			
C03 584 001A	C06 144 000A	2,560,000	90.00

CLEVELAND

D03 584 001A	D06 400 000A	2,816,000	100.00

RICHMOND

E02 560 001A	E04 864 000A	2,304,000	100.00
E00 064 001★	E00 128 000★	64,000	200.00

ATLANTA

F00 256 001A	F00 512 000A	256,000	100.00
F00 002 330★	F00 064 000★	64,000	200.00

CHICAGO

G09 728 001A	G13 312 000A	3,584,000	100.00
G00 256 001★	G00 448 000★	192,000	150.00

ST. LOUIS

H00 256 001A	H00 512 000A	256,000	110.00

MINNEAPOLIS

I00 512 001A	I01 024 000A	512,000	100.00

KANSAS CITY

J01 280 001A	J01 536 000A	256,000	110.00

DALLAS

K01 536 001A	K02 560 000A	1,024,000	100.00
K00 064 001★	K00 128 000★	64,000	200.00

SAN FRANCISCO

L06 912 001A	L12 032 000A	5,120,000	90.00
L00 256 001★	L00 512 000★	256,000	120.00

SERIES 1969B

SERIAL NUMBERS: Continued sequence from previous series.

SIGNATURES: Romano Acosta Banuelos, John B. Connally

SERIAL NUMBERS		NOTES PRINTED	CU

BOSTON

A03 584 001A	A04 608 000A	1,024,000	$100.00

SERIAL NUMBERS		NOTES PRINTED	CU
	NEW YORK		
B21 760 001**A**	B24 320 000**A**	2,560,000	90.00
	RICHMOND		
E04 864 001**A**	E06 400 000**A**	1,536,000	100.00
	ATLANTA		
F00 512 001**A**	F01 024 000**A**	512,000	120.00
	CHICAGO		
G13 312 001**A**	G14 336 000**A**	1,024,000	100.00
	DALLAS		
K02 560 001**A**	K03 584 000**A**	1,024,000	100.00
K00 128 001★	K00 256 000★	128,000	1000.00

SERIES **1969C**

SERIAL NUMBERS: Continue sequence from previous series.
SIGNATURES: Romano Acosta Banuelos, George P. Shultz

SERIAL NUMBERS		NOTES PRINTED	CU
	BOSTON		
A04 608 001**A**	A06 400 000**A**	1,792,000	$100.00
A00 128 001★	A00 192 000★	64,000	300.00
	NEW YORK		
B24 320 001**A**	B31 360 000**A**	7,040,000	100.00
B01 088 001★	B01 280 000★	192,000	200.00
	PHILADELPHIA		
C06 144 001**A**	C09 728 000**A**	3,584,000	100.00
C00 128 001★	C00 327 405★	256,000	200.00

CLEVELAND

D06 400 001A	D11 520 000A	5,120,000	70.00
D00 192 001★	D00 384 000★	192,000	100.00

RICHMOND

E06 400 001A	E08 704 000A	2,304,000	70.00
E00 128 001★	E00 192 000★	64,000	300.00

ATLANTA

F01 024 001A	F01 280 000A	256,000	100.00
F00 064 001★	F00 128 000★	64,000	300.00

CHICAGO

G14 336 001A	G21 120 000A	6,784,000	70.00
G00 448 001★	G01 024 000★	576,000	85.00

ST. LOUIS

H00 512 001A	H03 200 000A	2,688,000	70.00
H00 000 001★	H00 064 000★	64,000	300.00

MINNEAPOLIS

I01 024 001A	I01 280 000A	256,000	100.00
I00 000 001★	I00 064 000★	64,000	300.00

KANSAS CITY

J01 536 001A	J02 816 000A	1,280,000	75.00
J00 064 001★	J00 192 000★	128,000	125.00

DALLAS

K03 584 001A	K07 040 000A	3,456,000	70.00
K00 256 001★	K00 320 000★	64,000	300.00

SAN FRANCISCO

L12 032 001A	L16 640 000A	4,608,000	70.00
L00 512 001★	L00 768 000★	256,000	100.00

SERIES 1974

SIGNATURES: Francine I. Neff, William E. Simon

PLATE SERIALS: Face & back check numbers continue from previous series.

SERIAL NUMBERS: All districts continue from previous series

SERIAL NUMBERS		NOTES PRINTED	CU
BOSTON			
A06 400 001A	A10 240 000A	3,840,000	$100.00
A00 192 001★	A00 448 000★	768,000	160.00
NEW YORK			
B31 360 001A	B69 760 000A	38,400,000	100.00
B01 280 001★	B02 048 000★	768,000	160.00
PHILADELPHIA			
C09 728 001A	C17 280 000A	7,040,000	100.00
C00 384 000★	C00 576 000★	192,000	160.00

SERIAL NUMBERS		District	NOTES PRINTED	CU
		CLEVELAND		
D11 520 001A	D32 640 000A		21,120,000	100.00
D00 384 001★	D01 024 000★		640,000	160.00
		RICHMOND		
E08 704 001A	E23 040 000A		14,080,000	100.00
E00 192 001★	E00 768 000★		576,000	160.00
		ATLANTA		
F01 280 001A	F01 920 000A		1,280,000	100.00
F00 128 001★	F00 768 000★		640,000	160.00
		CHICAGO		
G21 120 001A	G51 840 000A		30,720,000	100.00
G01 024 001★	G02 560 000★		1,536,000	160.00
		ST. LOUIS		
H03 200 001A	H05 120 000A		1,920,000	100.00
H00 064 001★	H00 192 000★		128,000	160.00
		MINNEAPOLIS		
I01 280 001A	I03 840 000A		3,200,000	100.00
I00 064 001★	I00 256 000★		192,000	160.00
		KANSAS CITY		
J02 816 001A	J07 680 000A		4,480,000	100.00
J00 192 001★	J00 284 000★		192,000	160.00
		DALLAS		
K07 040 001A	K15 260 000A		8,320,000	100.00
K00 320 001★	K00 448 000★		128,000	160.00
		SAN FRANCISCO		
L16 640 001A	L24 320 000A		7,680,000	100.00
L00 768 001★	L00 832 000★		64,000	160.00

SERIES 1977

SIGNATURES: Azie Taylor Morton, W. Michael Blumenthal

PLATE SERIALS: Both face and back check numbers continue from previous series.

SERIAL NUMBERS: All districts begin with 00 000 001.

SERIAL NUMBERS		NOTES PRINTED	CU
		BOSTON	
A-A		16,640,000	$95.00
A00 000 001★	A04 480 000★	1,088,000	125.00

NEW YORK

B-A		49,920,000	95.00
B00 000 001★	B12 900 000★	2,112,000	125.00

PHILADELPHIA

C-A		5,120,000	95.00
C00 016 001★	C00 640 000★	128,000	125.00

CLEVELAND

D-A		23,040,000	95.00
D00 000 001★	D09 600 000★	1,024,000	125.00

RICHMOND

E-A		19,200,000	95.00
E00 000 001★	E03 840 000★	640,000	125.00

ATLANTA

F-A		2,560,000	95.00
F00 000 001★	F00 640 000★	640,000	125.00

CHICAGO

G-A		47,360,000	95.00
G00 000 001★	G14 080 000★	1,152,000	125.00

ST. LOUIS

H-A		3,840,000	95.00
H00 016 001★	H01 920 000★	512,000	125.00

MINNEAPOLIS

I00 011 000A		3,840,000	95.00
I00 016 001★	I00 640 000★	128,000	125.00

KANSAS CITY

J-A		7,680,000	95.00
J00 000 001★	J01 920 000★	256,000	125.00

DALLAS

K-A		14,086,000	95.00
K00 000 001★	K03 200 000★	448,000	125.00

SAN FRANCISCO

L-A		19,200,000	95.00
L00 000 001★	L04 480 000★	768,000	125.00

SERIES 1981

SIGNATURES: Angela M. Buchanan, Donald T. Regan

PLATE SERIALS: Both face and back check numbers begin with #1.

SERIAL NUMBERS: Regular and star notes begin with 00 000 001, star notes begin as shown below. All B blocks resumed at 00 000 001 prior to completion of A blocks, making for an unusual two-tiered numbering pattern in each district.

SERIAL NUMBERS		NOTES PRINTED	CU
BOSTON			
A-A		8,960,000	$85.00
A-B		9,600,000	85.00
NEW YORK			
B-A		46,080,000	85.00
B-B		32,000,000	85.00
B00 004 001★	B01 280 000★	768,000	125.00
PHILADELPHIA			
C-A		1,280,000	85.00
CLEVELAND			
D-A		15,360,000	85.00
D-B		12,800,000	85.00
D00 012 001★	D00 640 000★	256,000	85.00

RICHMOND			
E-A		12,800,000	85.00
E-B		12,800,000	85.00
ATLANTA			
F-A		1,280,000	85.00
F-B		3,200,000	85.00
F00 640 001★	F01 920 000★	768,000	125.00
CHICAGO			
G-A		44,800,000	85.00
G-B	G03 385 327B	22,400,000	85.00
G00 016 001★	G00 640 000★	128,000	125.00
ST. LOUIS			
H-A		1,280,000	85.00
H-B		3,200,000	85.00
MINNEAPOLIS			
I-A		2,560,000	85.00
I-B		3,200,000	85.00
I00 016 001★	I00 640 000★	128,000	125.00

KANSAS CITY

		NOTES PRINTED	CU
J-A		8,960,000	85.00
J-B		9,600,000	85.00
J00 016 001★	J00 640 000★	128,000	125.00

DALLAS

	NOTES PRINTED	CU
K-A	10,240,000	85.00
K-B	9,600,000	85.00

SAN FRANCISCO

		NOTES PRINTED	CU
L-A		25,600,000	85.00
L-B		9,600,000	85.00
L00 012 001★	L00 640 000★	256,000	125.00

SERIES 1981A

SIGNATURES: Katherine Davalos Ortega, Donald T. Regan
SERIAL NUMBERS: Both regular and star notes begin 00 000 001.

SERIAL NUMBERS		NOTES PRINTED	CU
BOSTON			
A-A		9,600,000	$80.00
NEW YORK			
B-A		28,800,000	80.00
B-★	B03 200 000★	3,200,000	125.00
CLEVELAND			
D-A		12,800,000	80.00
RICHMOND			
E-A		12,800,000	80.00
E-★	E03 200 000★	704,000	125.00
ATLANTA			
F-A		3,200,000	80.00

		NOTES PRINTED	CU
CHICAGO			
G-A		28,800,000	80.00
ST. LOUIS			
H-A		3,200,000	80.00
MINNEAPOLIS			
I01 048 554A		3,200,000	80.00
DALLAS			
K-A		6,400,000	80.00
SAN FRANCISCO			
L-A		22,400,000	80.00
L-★	L00 640 000★	640,000	125.00

SERIES 1985

SIGNATURES: Katherine Davalos Ortega, James A. Baker III
SERIAL NUMBERS: Both regular and star notes begin with 00 000 001.

SERIAL NUMBERS		NOTES PRINTED	CU
BOSTON			
A-A		51,200,000	$75.00
A-★	A03 200 000★	64,000	110.00
NEW YORK			
B-A		99,200,000	75.00
B-B		83,200,000	75.00
B-★	B03 200 000★	1,408,000	110.00
PHILADELPHIA			
C-A		3,200,000	75.00
CLEVELAND			
D-A		57,600,000	75.00
D02 784 473★	D03 200 000★	64,000	110.00

		RICHMOND	
E-A		54,400,000	75.00
		ATLANTA	
F-A		9,600,000	75.00
		CHICAGO	
G-A		99,200,000	75.00
G-B		12,800,000	75.00
G-★	G06 400 000★	1,280,000	110.00
		ST. LOUIS	
H-A		9,600,000	75.00
		MINNEAPOLIS	
I01 388 038A		12,800,000	75.00
		KANSAS CITY	
J-A		12,800,000	75.00
		DALLAS	
K-A		25,600,000	75.00
		SAN FRANCISCO	
L-A		54,400,000	75.00

SERIES **1988**

SIGNATURES: Katherine Davalos Ortega, Nicholas F. Brady
SERIAL NUMBERS: Both regular and star notes begin with 00 000 001.

SERIAL NUMBERS	NOTES PRINTED	CU
BOSTON		
A-A	9,600,000	$65.00
NEW YORK		
B79 363 558**A**	214,400,000	70.00
B-C		65.00
B06 400 000★	1,408,000	100.00
CLEVELAND		
D-A	32,000,000	70.00
RICHMOND		
E-A	12,800,000	70.00

CHICAGO		
G-A	80,000,000	70.00
KANSAS CITY		
J-A	6,400,000	70.00
SAN FRANCISCO		
L-A	12,800,000	70.00

SERIES **1990**

SIGNATURES: Catalina Vasquez Villalpando, Nicholas F. Brady
PLATE SERIALS: Face check numbers begin at #1. Back check numbers continue sequence from previous series.
SERIAL NUMBERS: Both regular and star notes begin at 00 000 001.
(Series 1990 introduced the anti-counterfeiting security thread and the microsize printing around the portrait.)

SERIAL NUMBERS		NOTES PRINTED	CU
		BOSTON	
A-A		28,800,000	$65.00
		NEW YORK	
B-A – B-C		232,000,000	65.00
B-★	B06 400 000★	3,116,000	80.00
		PHILADELPHIA	
C-A		41,600,000	65.00
C-★	C03 200 000★	1,280,000	80.00
		CLEVELAND	
D-A		92,800,000	65.00
		RICHMOND	
E-A		76,800,000	65.00

		CHICAGO	
G-A – G-B		109,600,000	65.00
G-★	G03 200 000★	1,032,000	80.00
		ST. LOUIS	
H-A		16,000,000	65.00
		MINNEAPOLIS	
I02 051 214A		22,400,000	65.00
		KANSAS CITY	
J-A		35,200,000	65.00
J00 596 409★	J03 200 000★	640,000	80.00
		DALLAS	
K-A		16,000,000	65.00
		SAN FRANCISCO	
L-A – L-B		119,200,000	65.00

SERIES 1993

SIGNATURES: Mary Ellen Withrow, Lloyd Bentsen
PLATE SERIALS: Face check numbers begin at #1. Back check numbers continue
sequence from previous series. Near end of series, new back check numbers starting at #1
appear, and are very scarce.
SERIAL NUMBERS: Both regular and star notes begin at 00 000 001.

SERIAL NUMBERS		NOTES PRINTED	CU
		BOSTON	
A-A		41,600,000	$65.00
		NEW YORK	
B-A,-B-E	B32 000 000E	428,800,000	65.00
B-★	B07 680 000★	3,200,000	75.00
		CLEVELAND	
D-A		60,800,000	65.00
D-★	D05120 000★	1,280,000	75.00
		RICHMOND	
E-A		51,200,000	65.00
		CHICAGO	
G-A		96,000,000	65.00
G-B		44,800,000	65.00
G-★	G05 120 000★	1,280,000	75.00
		ST. LOUIS	
H-A		3,200,000	65.00
		KANSAS CITY	
J-A		12,800,000	65.00
		DALLAS	
K-A		9,600,000	65.00

Series 1993 remains in production at press time.

ONE HUNDRED DOLLAR NOTES

GOLD CERTIFICATE

Gold Seal

SERIES **1928**

PLATE SERIALS: Face check #1 through #24.
SIGNATURES: Walter O. Woods, Andrew W. Mellon

LOW	HIGH	NOTES		
SERIAL NUMBERS		PRINTED	VG/F	CU
A00 000 001A	A03 240 000A	3,240,000	$150.00	$1200.00
★00 000 001A	★00 011 566A	11,566	275.00	2750.00

SERIES **1934**

SIGNATURES: W. A. Julian, Henry Morgenthau Jr.

These notes had orange (not green) backs. Their text specified that the $100 was "in gold payable to the bearer on demand as authorized by law." These last four words had been added because the 1934 Gold Notes were for use only among banks and were not to be released into general circulation. The Bureau occasionally exhibits the uncut specimen sheet of these orange-back notes.

NATIONAL BANK NOTES

Brown Seal

Type I has black serial numbers on the ends of the note. The left reading horizontally, the right reading vertically. Type II is similar, but the brown serial number is succeeded or preceded by the charter number also. All notes have facsimile signatures of E. E. Jones and W. O. Woods at the top. Signatures of the officers of the local bank appear at the bottom.

See lisings under Five Dollar denomination for detailed information as to rarity and value.

FEDERAL RESERVE BANK NOTE

Brown Seal

SERIES 1929

SERIAL NUMBERS: Both regular and star notes begin with 00 000 001.

PLATE SERIALS: Face check numbers begin with #1.

SIGNATURES: Same as $5.00 FRBN.

LOW SERIAL NUMBERS	HIGH	NOTES PRINTED	VG/F	CU
NEW YORK				
B00 002 942A	B00 480 000A	480,000	$125.00	$300.00
B00 000 610★		12,000	300.00	2000.00
CLEVELAND				
D00 055 760A	D00 570 082A	276,000	135.00	250.00
D00 003 595★	D00 003 918★	12,000	150.00	1200.00
RICHMOND				
E00 002 056A	E00 192 000A	192,000	125.00	500.00
E00 006 700★		36,000	300.00	1200.00

		CHICAGO		
G00 085 204A	G00 384 000A	384,000	125.00	300.00
G00 000 011★	G00 003 689★	12,000	300.00	1500.00
		MINNEAPOLIS		
I00 002 489A	I00 144 000A	144,000	125.00	300.00
I00 003 107★		12,000	300.00	1750.00
		KANSAS CITY		
J00 027 566A	J00 096 000A	96,000	125.00	275.00
J00 008 026★	J00 011 891★	12,000	200.00	750.00
		DALLAS		
K00 004 288A	K00 036 000A	36,000	150.00	500.00
K-★		12,000	450.00	2200.00

Legal Tender

Red Seal

SERIES 1966

PLATE SERIALS: Face check numbers begin with 1.

SIGNATURES: Kathryn O'Hay Granahan, Henry H. Fowler.

Back design has INDEPENDENCE HALL, Philadelphia, Pa. with motto added.

LOW	HIGH	NOTES		
SERIAL NUMBERS		PRINTED	VF	CU
A00 000 001A	A00 768 000A	768,000		$300.00
★00 000 001A	★00 128 000A	128,000	$175.00	600.00

SERIES 1966A

SIGNATURES: Dorothy Andrews Elston, David M. Kennedy

LOW	HIGH	NOTES		
SERIAL NUMBERS		PRINTED	VF	CU
A00 768 001A	A01 280 000A	512,0000	$135.00	$750.00

No star noted printed

FEDERAL RESERVE NOTES
Green Seal
SERIES 1928

SERIAL NUMBERS: Both regular and star notes begin with 00 000 001. High official star serial numbers would be the same as notes printed.
PLATE SERIALS: Face and back check begin with 1.
SIGNATURES: Walter O. Woods, A.W. Mellon

LOW SERIAL	HIGH NUMBERS	NOTES PRINTED	VG/F	CU
BOSTON				
A00 283 490A	A00 337 097A	376,000	$125.00	$300.00
A-★	A00 024 000★	24,000	150.00	600.00
NEW YORK				
B00 038 919A	B00 582 809A	755,400	125.00	225.00
B00 001 414★	B00 006 749★	48,000	150.00	450.00
PHILADELPHIA				
C00 191 030A	C00 418 732A	389,100	125.00	250.00
C00 001 799★	C00 005 389★	24,000	150.00	500.00
CLEVELAND				
D00 006 665A	D00 383 761A	542,400	125.00	300.00
D00 001 824★		24,000	150.00	600.00
RICHMOND				
E00 041 310A	E00 198 174A	364,416	125.00	300.00
E-★		24,000	150.00	600.00
ATLANTA				
F00 285 015A	F00 314 340A	357,000	125.00	300.00
F-★		24,000	150.00	600.00
CHICAGO				
G00 048 733A	G01 309 026A	783,300	125.00	200.00
G00 000 010★	G00 022 719★	72,000	150.00	375.00

ST. LOUIS				
H00 049 870A	H00 187 252A	187,200	135.00	250.00
H00 003 551★			160.00	500.00
MINNEAPOLIS				
I10 014 321A	I00 083 910A	102,000	135.00	250.00
I00 007 129★	I00 007 606★	24,000	160.00	500.00
KANSAS CITY				
J00 000 042A	J00 167 767A	234,612	125.00	250.00

J00 003 341★		24,000	200.00	600.00

DALLAS

K00 048 748A	K00 067 002A	80,140	160.00	200.00
K00 002 208★		24,000	200.00	500.00

SAN FRANCISCO

L-A	L00 475 857A	486,000	125.00	200.00
L00 000 073★	L00 004 932★	40,000	150.00	450.00

SERIES 1928A

Dark Green Seal

SERIAL NUMBERS: All districts continued sequence from previous series.
DESIGN CHANGE: District lnumeral in seal replaced by letter. Face check begins with 1.
SIGNATURES: Walter O. Woods, A.W. Mellon

LOW SERIAL	HIGH NUMBERS	NOTES PRINTED	VG/F	CU
BOSTON				
A00 451 982A	A00 726 436A	980,400	$125.00	$275.00
NEW YORK				
B01 054 965A	B01 416 207A	2,938,176	125.00	200.00
PHILADELPHIA				
C00 378 456A	C00 636 371A	1,496,844	125.00	275.00
CLEVELAND				
D00 555 962A		992,436	125.00	250.00
RICHMOND				
E00 393 654A	E00 477 467A	621,364	125.00	350.00
ATLANTA				
F00 377 479A	F00 543 232A	371,400	125.00	300.00

CHICAGO				
G00 523 209A	G02 807 844A	4,010,424	125.00	200.00
ST. LOUIS				
H00 172 058A	H00 423 313A	749,544	125.00	250.00
H00 009 994★		24,000	500.00	2000.00
MINNEAPOLIS				
I00 091 450A	I00 159 436A	503,040	125.00	300.00
KANSAS CITY				
J00 271 521A		681,804	125.00	350.00
DALLAS				
K00 081 337A	K00113 037A	594,456	125.00	300.00

SAN FRANCISCO

L00 527 502**A**	L00 686 347**A**	1,228,032	125.00	250.00

SERIES **1928A**
Light Green Seal

SERIAL NUMBERS: Continue in sequence from 1928A Dark Green seal variety.

LOW SERIAL NUMBERS	HIGH	NOTES PRINTED	VG/F	CU
		NEW YORK		
B02 082 403**A**	B02 342 430**A**	Included above	$150.00	300.00
		ST. LOUIS		
H00 518 601**A**	H00 569 390**A**	Included above	150.00	300.00
		SAN FRANCISCO		
L00 947 243**A**	L01 098 462**A**	Included above	150.00	300.00

SERIES **1934**
Light Green Seal

SERIAL NUMBERS: Both regular and star notes begin with 00 000 001.

PLATE SERIALS: Face check numbers begin with #1. Back check numbers continue in sequence from series 1928A.

SIGNATURES: W.A. Julian, Henry Morgenthau, Jr.

LOW SERIAL NUMBERS	HIGH	NOTES PRINTED	VG/F	CU
		BOSTON		
A00 171 113**A**		3,710,000	$120.00	$250.00
A00 001 257★	A00 002 513★		135.00	325.00
		NEW YORK		
B00 216 498**A**		3,086,000	120.00	225.00
B00 002 885★			135.00	325.00
		PHILADELPHIA		
C00 020 739**A**	C00 022 498**A**	2,776,800	$120.00	225.00
C00 002 010★			135.00	325.00

		CLEVELAND		
D00 047 045**A**		3,447,108	120.00	225.00
D00 000 001★			135.00	325.00
		RICHMOND		
E00 093 889**A**		4,317,600	120.00	225.00
E-★			135.00	350.00

ATLANTA

F00 051 405A	F00 108 864A	3,264,420	120.00	275.00
F-★			135.00	375.00

CHICAGO

G00 001 081A	G00 076 989A	7,075,000	120.00	225.00
G00 002 665★	G00 009 410★		135.00	275.00

ST. LOUIS

H00 000 418A	H00 437 848A	2,106,192	120.00	225.00
H-★			135.00	370.00

MINNEAPOLIS

I00 027 358A	I00 119 453A	852,600	120.00	225.00
I00 003 032★	I00 006 697★		135.00	300.00

KANSAS CITY

J00 006 043A	J00 035 525A	1,932,900	120.00	225.00
J-★			135.00	350.00

DALLAS

K00 017 478A		1,506,516	120.00	275.00
K-★			135.00	375.00

SAN FRANCISCO

L00 019 304A	L00 384 679A	6,521,940	120.00	225.00
L00 000 001★			135.00	350.00

SERIES 1934 MULE

PLATE SERIALS: Back check 113 and higher.
Quantities included above.

LOW	HIGH	NOTES		
SERIAL NUMBERS		PRINTED	VG/F	CU
BOSTON				
A02 876 991A			$150.00	$250.00
PHILADELPHIA				
C02 973 508A			150.00	250.00
CHICAGO				
G08 548 213A			150.00	250.00
G00 088 061★			2500.00	500.00
KANSAS CITY				
J01 880 175A			150.00	250.00
SAN FRANCISCO				
L05 938 350A	L06 593 880A		150.00	250.00

SERIES 1934

Dark Green Seal

PLATE SERIALS: Back check number up to 112.
SIGNATURES: W.A. Julian, Henry Morgenthau, Jr.

LOW	HIGH	NOTES		
SERIAL NUMBERS		PRINTED	VG/F	CU
BOSTON				
A00 850 539A	A03 551 012A	See above	$120.00	$200.00
A00 009 254★	A00 038 278★		135.00	250.00
NEW YORK				
B01 590 412A	B03 962 686A	See above	120.00	200.00
B00 005 295★			135.00	250.00
PHILADELPHIA				
C00 646 932A	C03 565 041A	See above	120.00	200.00
C00 012 798★	C00 018 053★		135.00	275.00

CLEVELAND

D01 974 271A	D01 974 273A	See above	120.00	200.00
D-★			135.00	275.00

RICHMOND

E00 460 483A	E04 194 652A	See above	120.00	200.00
E-★			135.00	300.00

ATLANTA

F01 322 422A	F03 216 128A	See above	120.00	200.00
F00 009 499★	F00 033 942★		135.00	275.00

CHICAGO

G06 375 531A	G09 717 675A	See above	120.00	200.00
G00 013 795★	G00 078 888★		135.00	275.00

ST. LOUIS

H00 030 176A	H02 356 140A	See above	120.00	200.00
H00 014 404★	H00 021 836★		135.00	275.00

MINNEAPOLIS

I00 119 453A	I01 006 604A	See above	125.00	200.00
I00 011 219★	I00 013 169★		150.00	275.00

KANSAS CITY

J00 345 455A	J01 238 129A	See above	120.00	200.00
J00 011 139★	J00 035 525★		135.00	275.00

DALLAS

K00 159 585A	K01 267 294A	See above	120.00	200.00
K00 005 732★	K00 022 861★		135.00	275.00

SAN FRANCISCO

L00 986 517A	L07 358 167A	See above	120.00	200.00
L00 025 535★	L00 081 420★		135.00	275.00

SERIES 1934A

SERIAL NUMBERS: Continued sequence from previous series.
PLATE SERIALS: Back check number 113 and higher.
SIGNATURES: W.A. Julian, Henry Morgenthau, Jr.

LOW	HIGH	NOTES		
SERIAL NUMBERS		PRINTED	VG/F	CU

BOSTON

A-A		102,000	$125.00	$200.00
A00 026 689★			135.00	300.00

NEW YORK

B05 525 202A	B17 131 507A	15,278,892	115.00	200.00
B00 063 693★	B00 155 943★		200.00	300.00

PHILADELPHIA

C01 325 038A	C02 586 618A	588,000	115.00	200.00
C-★			125.00	275.00

CLEVELAND

D-A		645,300	115.00	200.00
D-★			125.00	275.00

RICHMOND

E-A		770,100	115.00	200.00
E-★			125.00	275.00

ATLANTA

F-A		589,896	115.00	200.00
F-★			125.00	275.00

CHICAGO

G00 226 618A	G09 657 601A	3,328,800	115.00	200.00
G-★			125.00	275.00

ST. LOUIS

H-A		434,208	115.00	200.00
H-★			125.00	275.00

MINNEAPOLIS

I00 816 356A		153,000	115.00	200.00
I-★			125.00	275.00

KANSAS CITY

J00 078 918A		455,100	115.00	200.00
J-★			125.00	275.00

DALLAS

K00 534 394A	K00 800 499A	226,164	115.00	200.00
K-★			125.00	275.00

SAN FRANCISCO

L-A	L03 787 578A	1,130,400	115.00	200.00
L-★			125.00	275.00

SERIES 1934A MULE

SERIAL NUMBERS: Continue sequence from previous series.
PLATE SERIALS: Back check 112 and lower.
SIGNATURES: W. A. Julian, Henry Morgenthau, Jr.
Quantities included below under series 1934A.

LOW	HIGH	NOTES		
SERIAL NUMBERS		PRINTED	VG/F	CU

BOSTON

A02 457 880A	A02 510 836A		$115.00	$200.00
A00 026 689★			125.00	250.00

NEW YORK

B03 830 832A	B18 147 245A		115.00	225.00
B00 054 456★	B00 108 827★		125.00	350.00

PHILADELPHIA

C01 647 445A	C02 842 098A		115.00	225.00

CLEVELAND

D01 861 704A	D02 783 238A		115.00	225.00

RICHMOND

E00 998 410A	E06 298 291A		115.00	225.00

ATLANTA

F01 332 433A	04 009 312A		115.00	225.00

CHICAGO

G02 038 907A	G09 735 335A		115.00	200.00
G00 050 063★	G00 067 416★		125.00	250.00

ST. LOUIS

H00 931 248**A**	H01 940 941**A**		115.00	200.00

MINNEAPOLIS

I00 349 938**A**	I00 667 506**A**		115.00	225.00

KANSAS CITY

J01 630 998**A**	J02 476 621**A**		115.00	225.00

DALLAS

K00 400 125**A**	K00 510 577**A**		115.00	200.00

SAN FRANCISCO

L03 787 578**A**	L05 350 891**A**		115.00	225.00
L00 033 148★			175.00	375.00

SERIES **1934B MULE**

PLATE SERIALS: Back check number up to 112.
Quantities included below under Series 1934B.

LOW	HIGH	NOTES		
SERIAL NUMBERS		**PRINTED**	**VG/F**	**CU**
		BOSTON		
A03 664 481**A**	A03 685 891**A**		$150.00	$225.00
		NEW YORK		
B13 971 535**A**			150.00	275.00
		PHILADELPHIA		
C03 691 382**A**	C03 773 271**A**		150.00	275.00
		CLEVELAND		
D03 846 692**A**			150.00	275.00
		RICHMOND		
E04 960 680**A**	E05 429 922**A**		150.00	275.00
		ATLANTA		
F03 905 459**A**			150.00	275.00
		CHICAGO		
G10 260 001**A**	G10 719 235**A**		150.00	275.00
		ST. LOUIS		
H02 625 516**A**	H03 287 190**A**		150.00	275.00
H00 049 053★			500.00	1500.00
		MINNEAPOLIS		
I00 967 190**A**	I01 238 696**A**		150.00	275.00
I00 019 318★			500.00	1500.00
		KANSAS CITY		
J02 378 551**A**	J02 886 775**A**		150.00	275.00
		DALLAS		
K01 636 156**A**	K02 075 431**A**		150.00	275.00
K00 028 713★	K00 029 974★		500.00	1500.00
		SAN FRANCISCO		
L07 891 808**A**			150.00	275.00

SERIES **1934B**

SERIAL NUMBERS: Continued sequence from previous series.
PLATE SERIALS: Back check number 113 and higher.
SIGNATURES: W.A. Julian, Fred M. Vinson

LOW	HIGH	NOTES		
SERIAL NUMBERS		**PRINTED**	**VG/F**	**CU**
		BOSTON		
A-A		41,400	$160.00	$250.00
		PHILADELPHIA		
C03 758 953**A**	C03 760 891**A**	39,600	160.00	250.00

		NOTES PRINTED	VG/F	CU
CLEVELAND				
D03 847 526**A**		61,200	160.00	250.00
RICHMOND				
E-A		977,400	135.00	250.00
E★			150.00	2000.00
ATLANTA				
F04 109 312**A**		645,000	125.00	250.00
F-★			150.00	2000.00
CHICAGO				
G10 663 300**A**		396,000	125.00	250.00
G-★			150.00	2000.00
ST. LOUIS				
H02 518 355**A** H02 916 928**A**		676,200	125.00	250.00
H-★			150.00	2000.00
MINNEAPOLIS				
I-A		377,000	125.00	250.00
I-★			150.00	2000.00
KANSAS CITY				
J02 476 621**A** J02 644 307**A**		364,500	125.00	250.00
J-★			150.00	2000.00
DALLAS				
K-A		392,700	125.00	250.00
K-★			150.00	2000.00

SERIES **1934C MULE**

Quantities included below. Back check numbers are 112 and lower.

LOW	HIGH	NOTES		
SERIAL NUMBERS		**PRINTED**	**VG/F**	**CU**
BOSTON				
A03 632 017**A**			$150.00	$200.00
PHILADELPHIA				
C03 719 564**A** C03 777 657**A**			150.00	200.00
CLEVELAND				
D03 867 222**A** D03 941 112**A**			150.00	200.00
RICHMOND				
E04 574 908**A** E06 724 336**A**			150.00	200.00
ATLANTA				
F03 663 561**A** F04 303 994**A**			150.00	200.00
F00 057 872★			500.00	2000.00
CHICAGO				
G10 906 938**A** G11 364 347**A**			150.00	200.00

ST. LOUIS

H02 938 155A	H04 196 861A	150.00	200.00
H00 049 795★	H00 060 718★	500.00	2000.00

MINNEAPOLIS

I01 097 949A	I01 503 778A	150.00	200.00

KANSAS CITY

J02 435 400A	J03 004 263A	150.00	200.00

DALLAS

K01 896 990A	K02 252 422A	150.00	200.00

SAN FRANCISCO

L07 253 484A	L07 717 988A	150.00	200.00

SERIES 1934C

SERIAL NUMBERS: Continued sequence from previous series.
PLATE SERIALS: Back check 113 and higher.
SIGNATURES: W.A. Julian, John W. Snyder

LOW	HIGH	NOTES		
SERIAL NUMBERS		PRINTED	VG/F	CU
BOSTON				
A-A		13,800	$160.00	$200.00
possibly none released				
NEW YORK				
B-A		1,556,400	160.00	275.00
PHILADELPHIA				
C-A		13,200	160.00	275.00
possibly none released				
CLEVELAND				
D-A		1,473,200	160.00	275.00
RICHMOND				
none				
ATLANTA				
F-A		493,900	160.00	275.00

CHICAGO				
G-A		612,000	160.00	275.00
ST. LOUIS				
H03 791 599A		957,000	160.00	275.00
MINNEAPOLIS				
I-A		392,904	160.00	275.00

KANSAS CITY			
J-A	401,100	160.00	275.00
DALLAS			
K02 179 536A	280,700	160.00	275.00
SAN FRANCISCO			
L-A	432,600	150.00	275.00

SERIES **1934D MULE**

PLATE SERIALS: Back check number 112 or lower.
Quantities included below under Series 1934D.

LOW	HIGH	NOTES		
SERIAL NUMBERS		PRINTED	VG/F	CU
PHILADELPHIA				
C03 486 749A	C03 686 627A		$125.00	$175.00
ATLANTA				
F04 704 434A			125.00	175.00
F00 063 147★			500.00	3500.00
CHICAGO				
G08 504 434A	G11 238 414A		125.00	175.00
G00 110 615★			1500.00	3500.00
ST. LOUIS				
H03 910 708A	H04 201 253A		125.00	175.00
DALLAS				
K02 346 085A			125.00	175.00

SERIES **1934D**

SERIAL NUMBERS: Continued sequence from previous series.
PLATE SERIALS: Back check 113 and higher.
SIGNATURES: Georgia Neese Clark, John W. Snyder.

LOW	HIGH	NOTES		
SERIAL NUMBERS		PRINTED	VG/F	CU
NEW YORK				
B-A		156	$1000.	$2500.

PHILADELPHIA			
C-A	308,400	125.00	225.00
ATLANTA			
F-A	260,400	125.00	225.00
CHICAGO			
G-A	78,000	125.00	225.00

H-A	**ST. LOUIS**	166,800	125.00	225.00
K02 334 983**A**	**DALLAS**	66,000	125.00	225.00

SERIES **1950 MULE**

SERIAL NUMBERS: All serial numbers both regular and star notes begin with 00 000 001.
PLATE SERIALS: Back check number 112 or lower.
Quantities included below.

LOW	HIGH	NOTES	VALUE
SERIAL NUMBERS		**PRINTED**	**CU**
		NEW YORK	
B00 122 127**A**	B02 751 837**A**		$225.00
		PHILADELPHIA	
C00 053 387**A**	C01 084 365**A**		225.00
		CLEVELAND	
D00 855 975**A**	D01 414 048**A**		225.00
D00 005 215★			400.00
		RICHMOND	
E02 541 614**A**	E02 641 908**A**		225.00
		ATLANTA	
F00 327 612**A**	F00 786 704**A**		225.00
		CHICAGO	
G00 014 163**A**	G04 256 957**A**		225.00
G00 001 506★	G00 020 411★		400.00
		ST. LOUIS	
H00 001 309★			500.00
		MINNEAPOLIS	
I00 017 557**A**	I00 059 476**A**		150.00
		KANSAS CITY	
J00 121 019**A**	J00 810 832**A**		225.00
		DALLAS	
K00 959 412**A**			225.00
		SAN FRANCISCO	
L00 516 976**A**	L01 509 796**A**		225.00
L00 009 491★			400.00

SERIES **1950**

PLATE SERIALS: Back check number 113 and higher.
SIGNATURES: Georgia Neese Clark, John W. Snyder

LOW	HIGH	NOTES	VALUE
SERIAL NUMBERS		**PRINTED**	**CU**
		BOSTON	
	A00 768 000**A**	768,000	$250.00
		NEW YORK	
B00 908 194**A**	B03 908 000**A**	3,908,000	250.00
		PHILADELPHIA	
	C01 332 000**A**	1,332,000	250.00
	C00 012 034★		500.00
		CLEVELAND	
	D01 632 000**A**	1,632,000	250.00
		RICHMOND	
	E04 076 000**A**	4,076,000	250.00
		ATLANTA	
F00 995 600**A**	F01 824 000**A**	1,824,000	250.00

CHICAGO

G01 750 559**A**　G04 428 000**A**　　　　　　　　4,428,000　　　　　　　　250.00

ST. LOUIS

H01 284 000**A**　　　　　　　　1,284,000　　　　　　　　250.00

MINNEAPOLIS

I00 564 000**A**　　　　　　　　564,000　　　　　　　　250.00

KANSAS CITY

J00 864 000**A**　　　　　　　　864,000　　　　　　　　250.00

DALLAS

K01 216 000**A**　　　　　　　　1,216,000　　　　　　　　250.00

SAN FRANCISCO

L01 925 392**A**　L02 524 000**A**　　　　　　　2,524,000　　　　　　　　250.00

SERIES 1950A

SERIAL NUMBERS: Continued sequence from previous series. Numbers between high serial number of Series 1950 and low serial number of this series were not used.

SIGNATURES: Ivy Baker Priest, George M. Humphrey

LOW SERIAL	HIGH NUMBERS	NOTES PRINTED	VALUE CU
BOSTON			
A00 864 001**A**	A01 872 000**A**	1,008,000	$175.00
NEW YORK			
B04 032 001**A**	B06 912 000**A**	2,880,000	175.00
B00 180 750★			300.00
PHILADELPHIA			
C01 440 001**A**	C02 016 000**A**	720,000	175.00
CLEVELAND			
D01 728 001**A**	D02 016 000**A**	288,000	175.00

RICHMOND

E04 176 001A	E06 336 000A	2,160,000	130.00

ATLANTA

F01 872 001A	F02 160 000A	288,000	175.00

CHICAGO

G04 464 001A	G05 328 000A	864,000	175.00

ST. LOUIS

H01 296 001A	H01 728 000A	432,000	175.00

MINNEAPOLIS

I00 576 001A	I00 720 000A	144,000	175.00

KANSAS CITY

J00 864 001A	J01 152 000A	288,000	175.00

DALLAS

K01 296 001A	K01 728 000A	432,000	175.00

SAN FRANCISCO

L02 592 001A	L03 312 000A	720,000	175.00

SERIES 1950B

SERIAL NUMBERS: Continued sequence from previous series.
SIGNATURES: Ivy Baker Priest, Robert B. Anderson

LOW SERIAL	HIGH NUMBERS	NOTES PRINTED	VALUE CU
		BOSTON	
A01 872 001A	A02 592 000A	720,000	$250.00
		NEW YORK	
B06 912 001A	B13 248 000A	6,336,000	250.00
B00 559 405★	B00 709 813★		375.00
		PHILADELPHIA	
C02 016 001A	C02 736 000A	720,000	250.00
C00 312 348★	C00 336 628★		375.00
		CLEVELAND	
D02 016 001A	D02 448 000A	432,000	250.00
		RICHMOND	
E06 336 001A	E07 344 000A	1,008,000	250.00
		ATLANTA	
F02 160 001A	F02 736 000A	576,000	250.00

CHICAGO

G05 328 001A	G07 920 000A	2,592,000	250.00
G00 401 346★	G00 411 346★		375.00

ST. LOUIS

H01 728 001A	H02 880 000A	1,152,000	250.00
H00 386 986★			375.00

MINNEAPOLIS

I00 720 001A	I01 008 000A	288,000	250.00
I00 321 672★			375.00

KANSAS CITY

J01 152 001A	J01 872 000A	720,000	250.00

DALLAS

K01 728 001A	K03 456 000A	1,728,000	250.00
K00 345 060★			375.00

SAN FRANCISCO

L03 312 001A	L06 192 000A	2,880,000	250.00

SERIES 1950C

SERIAL NUMBERS: Continued sequence from previous series.
SIGNATURES: Elizabeth Rudel Smith, C. Douglas Dillon.

LOW	HIGH	NOTES	VALUE
SERIAL NUMBERS		PRINTED	CU

BOSTON

A02 592 001A	A03 456 000A	864,000	$225.00
A00 304 758★	A00 329 199★		425.00

NEW YORK

B13 248 001A	B15 696 000A	2,448,000	225.00
B-★			425.00

PHILADELPHIA

C02 736 001A	C03 312 000A	576,000	225.00
C00 536 648A			425.00

CLEVELAND

D02 448 001A	D03 024 000A	576,000	225.00
			425.00

		RICHMOND		
E07 344 001**A**	E08 784 000**A**		1,440,000	225.00
E-★				425.00
		ATLANTA		
F02 736 001**A**	F04 032 000**A**		1,296,000	225.00
F-★				425.00
		CHICAGO		
G07 920 001**A**	G09 504 000**A**		1,584,000	225.00
G-★				425.00
		ST. LOUIS		
H02 880 001**A**	H03 600 000**A**		720,000	225.00
H00 456 335★				425.00
		MINNEAPOLIS		
I01 008 001**A**	I01 296 000**A**		288,000	225.00
I-★				425.00
		KANSAS CITY		
J01 872 001**A**	J02 304 000**A**		432,000	225.00
J-★				425.00
		DALLAS		
K03 456 001**A**	K04 176 000**A**		720,000	225.00
K-★				425.00
		SAN FRANCISCO		
L06 192 001**A**	L08 352 000**A**		2,160,000	225.00
L00 681 278★	L00 698 118★			425.00

SERIES **1950D**

SERIAL NUMBERS: Continued sequence from previous series.
SIGNATURES: Kathryn O'Hay Granahan, C. Douglas Dillon

LOW	HIGH	NOTES	VALUE
SERIAL NUMBERS		PRINTED	CU
BOSTON			
A03 456 001A	A05 328 000A	1,872,000	$250.00
A-★			400.00
NEW YORK			
B15 696 001A	B23 328 000A	7,632,000	250.00
B-★			400.00
PHILADELPHIA			
C03 312 001A	C05 184 000A	1,872,000	250.00
C00 688 567★			400.00

		CLEVELAND		
D03 024 001A	D04 608 000A	1,584,000		250.00
D00 630 903★				400.00
		RICHMOND		
E 08 784 001A	E11 664 000A	2,880,000		250.00
E00 492 556★	E00 558 910★			400.00
		ATLANTA		
F04 032 001A	F05 904 000A	1,872,000		250.00
F00 651 130★				400.00
		CHICAGO		
G09 504 001A	G14 112 000A	4,608,000		250.00
G00 456 013★				400.00
		ST. LOUIS		
H03 600 001A	H05 040 000A	1,440,000		250.00
				400.00
		MINNEAPOLIS		
I01 296 001A	I01 728 000A	432,000		250.00
				400.00
		KANSAS CITY		
J02 304 001A	J03 168 000A	864,000		250.00
				400.00
		DALLAS		
K04 176 001A	K05 904 000A	1,728,000		250.00
				400.00

SAN FRANCISCO

L08 352 001**A**	L11 664 000**A**	3,312,000	250.00
			400.00

SERIES **1950E**

SERIAL NUMBERS: Districts printed continued sequence from previous series.
SIGNATURES: Kathryn O'Hay Granahan, Henry H. Fowler

LOW	HIGH	NOTES	VALUE
SERIAL NUMBERS		PRINTED	CU
NEW YORK			
B23 328 001**A**	B26 352 000**A**	3,024,000	$250.00
B01 301 125★	B01 422 992★		1250.00
CHICAGO			
G14 112 001**A**	G14 688 000**A**	576,000	250.00
G-★			1250.00

SAN FRANCISCO

L11 664 001**A**	L14 400 000**A**	2,736,000	250.00
L01 020 680★	L01 098 184★		1250.00

SERIES **1963**

No $100.00 notes for Series 1963 were printed.

SERIES **1963A**

SERIAL NUMBERS: All serial numbers both regular and star notes begin with 00 000 001.
PLATE SERIALS: Both face and back check numbers begin with 1. Motto IN GOD WE TRUST added to back.
SIGNATURES: Kathryn O'Hay Granahan, Henry H. Fowler

SERIAL NUMBERS		NOTES PRINTED	CU
BOSTON			
A-A		1,536,000	$200.00
A-★		128,000	275.00
NEW YORK			
B-A		12,544,000	200.00
B-★		1,536,000	275.00
PHILADELPHIA			
C-A		1,792,000	200.00
C-★		192,000	275.00
CLEVELAND			
D-A		2,304,000	200.00
D-★	D00 146 656★	192,000	275.00

RICHMOND

E-A	2,816,000	200.00
E-★	192,000	275.00

ATLANTA

F-A	1,280,000	200.00
F-★	128,000	275.00

CHICAGO

G-A	4,352,000	200.00
G-★	512,000	275.00

ST. LOUIS

H-A	1,536,000	200.00
H-★	256,000	275.00

MINNEAPOLIS

I-A	512,000	200.00
I-★	128,000	275.00

KANSAS CITY

J-A	1,024,000	200.00
J00 063 304★	128,000	275.00

DALLAS

K-A	1,536,000	200.00
K-★	192,000	275.00

SAN FRANCISCO

L-A	6,400,000	200.00
L-★	832,000	275.00

SERIES 1969

SERIAL NUMBERS: All serial numbers both regular and star notes begin with 00 000 001.
SIGNATURES: Dorothy Andrews Elston, David M. Kennedy

SERIAL NUMBERS	NOTES PRINTED	CU
BOSTON		
A-A	2,048,000	$175.00
A-★	128,000	250.00
NEW YORK		
B-A	11,520,000	175.00
B-★	128,000	250.00
PHILADELPHIA		
C-A	2,560,000	175.00
C-★	128,000	250.00
CLEVELAND		
D-A	768,000	175.00
D-★	64,000	250.00

RICHMOND

E-A		2,560,000	175.00
E-★		192,000	250.00

ATLANTA

F-A		2,304,000	175.00
F-★	F00 076 915★	128,000	250.00

CHICAGO

G-A		5,880,000	175.00
G-★		256,000	250.00

ST. LOUIS

H-A		1,280,000	175.00
H-★		64,000	250.00

MINNEAPOLIS

I-A		512,000	175.00
I00 010 631★		64,000	250.00

KANSAS CITY

J-A		1,792,000	175.00
J-★		384,000	250.00

DALLAS

K-A		2,048,000	175.00
K-★		128,000	250.00

SAN FRANCISCO

L-A		7,168,000	175.00
L-★		320,000	250.00

SERIES 1969A

SERIAL NUMBERS: Continued sequence from previous series.
SIGNATURES: Dorothy Andrews Kabis, John B. Connally

SERIAL NUMBERS		NOTES PRIINTED	CU
BOSTON			
A02 048 001A	A03 328 000A	1,280,000	$175.00
A00 128 001★	A00 448 000★	320,000	275.00
NEW YORK			
B11 520 001A	B22 784 000A	11,264,000	175.00
B00 128 001★	B00 768 000★	640,000	275.00
PHILADELPHIA			
C02 560 001A	C05 120 000A	2,048,000	175.00
C00 128 001★	C00 576 000★	448,000	275.00

CLEVELAND

D00 768 001A	D03 584 000A	1,280,000	175.00
D00 064 001★	D00 256 000★	192,000	275.00

RICHMOND

E02 560 001**A**	E04 864 000**A**	2,304,000	175.00
E00 192 001★	E00 384 000★	192,000	275.00

ATLANTA

F02 304 001**A**	F04 608 000**A**	2,304,000	175.00
F00 128 001★	F00 192 000★	640,000	275.00

CHICAGO

G05 888 001**A**	G11 264 000**A**	5,376,000	175.00
G00 256 001★	G00 576 000★	320,000	275.00

ST. LOUIS

H01 280 001**A**	H02 304 000**A**	1,024,000	175.00
H00 064 001★	H00 128 000★	64,000	275.00

MINNEAPOLIS

I00 512 001**A**	I01 536 000**A**	1,024,000	175.00
none printed			

KANSAS CITY

J01 792 001**A**	J02 304 000**A**	512,000	175.00
none printed			

DALLAS

K02 048 001**A**	K05 376 000**A**	3,328,000	175.00
K00 128 001★	K00 256 000★	128,000	275.00

SAN FRANCISCO

L07 168 001**A**	L11 520 000**A**	4,352,000	175.00
L00 320 001★	L00 960 000★	640,000	275.00

SERIES 1969C

SIGNATURES: Romana Acosta Banuelos, George P. Schultz

SERIAL NUMBERS		NOTES PRINTED	CU

BOSTON

A03 328 001**A**	A05 376 000**A**	2,048,000	$150.00
A00 448 001★	A00 512 000★	64,000	350.00

NEW YORK

B22 784 001**A**	B38 400 000**A**	15,616,000	150.00
B00 768 001★	B01 024 000★	256,000	250.00

PHILADELPHIA

C05 120 001**A**	C07 936 000**A**	2,816,000	150.00
C00 576 001★	C00 640 000★	64,000	350.00

CLEVELAND

D03 584 001**A**	D07 040 000**A**	3,456,000	150.00
D00 256 001★	D00 320 000★	64,000	350.00

RICHMOND

E04 864 001**A**	E12 160 000**A**	7,296,000	150.00
E00 384 001★	E00 512 000★	128,000	300.00

ATLANTA

F04 608 001**A**	F07 040 000**A**	2,432,000	150.00
F00 192 001★	F00 256 000★	64,000	350.00

CHICAGO

G11 264 001**A**	G17 280 000**A**	6,016,000	150.00
G00 576 001★	G00 896 000★	320,000	250.00

ST. LOUIS

H02 304 001**A**	H07 680 000**A**	5,376,000	150.00
H00 128 001★	H00 192 000★	64,000	350.00

MINNEAPOLIS

I01 536 001**A**	I02 048 000**A**	512,000	150.00
I00 064 001★	I00 128 000★	64,000	350.00

KANSAS CITY

J02 304 001**A**	J07 040 000**A**	4,736,000	150.00
J00 384 001★	J00 576 000★	192,000	250.00

DALLAS

K05 376 001**A**	K08 320 000**A**	2,944,000	150.00
K00 256 001★	K00 320 000★	64,000	350.00

SAN FRANCISCO

L11 520 001**A**	L21 760 000**A**	10,240,000	150.00
L00 960 001★	L01 472 000★	512,000	250.00

SERIES 1974

SIGNATURES: Francine I. Neff, William E. Simon

PLATE SERIALS: Both face and back check numbers continue from previous series.

SERIAL NUMBERS: All districts continue from previous series.

SERIAL NUMBERS		NOTES PRINTED	CU
		BOSTON	
A05 376 001**A**	A17 280 000**A**	11,520,000	$150.00
A00 512 001★	A00 768 000★	256,000	250.00
		NEW YORK	
B32 400 001**A**		62,880,000	150.00
	B01 280 000**B**	1,280,000	150.00
B01 024 001★	B02 752 000★	1,728,000	200.00
		PHILADELPHIA	
C07 936 001**A**	C16 000 000**A**	7,680,000	150.00
C00 640 001★	C00 768 000★	128,000	250.00
		CLEVELAND	
D07 040 001**A**	D33 920 000**A**	26,880,000	150.00
D00 320 001★	D00 512 000★	192,000	250.00
		RICHMOND	
E12 160 001**A**	E23 680 000**A**	11,520,000	150.00
E00 512 001★	E00 640 000★	128,000	250.00
		ATLANTA	
F07 040 001**A**	F11 520 000**A**	4,480,000	150.00
F00 256 001★	F00 384 000★	128,000	250.00

CHICAGO

G17 280 001A	G44 160 000A	26,880,000	150.00
G00 896 001★	G02 112 000★	1,216,000	200.00

ST. LOUIS

H07 680 001A	H13 440 000A	5,760,000	150.00
H00 192 001★	H00 384 000★	192,000	250.00

MINNEAPOLIS

I02 048 001A	I07 040 000A	3,840,000	150.00
I00 128 001★	I00 384 000★	256,000	250.00

KANSAS CITY

J07 040 001A	J12 800 000A	5,760,000	150.00
J00 576 001★	J01 024 000★	448,000	250.00

DALLAS

K08 320 001A	K18 560 000A	10,240,000	150.00
K00 320 001★	K00 512 000★	192,000	250.00

SAN FRANCISCO

L21 760 001A	L51 200 000A	29,440,000	150.00
L01 472 001★	L02 304 000★	832,000	200.00

SERIES 1977

SIGNATURES: Azie Taylor Morton, W. Michael Blumenthal
PLATE SERIALS: Both face and back check numbers continue from previous series.
SERIAL NUMBERS: The regular notes in all districts start at 00 000 001.

SERIAL NUMBER		NOTES PRINTED	CU
		BOSTON	
A00 001 237A		19,200,000	$150.00
A00 014 001★	A01 300 000★	320,000	190.00

NEW YORK

B-A		99,840,000	150.00
B-B		53,760,000	150.00
B00 000 001★	B08 960 000★	1,664,000	180.00

PHILADELPHIA

C-A		5,120,000	150.00
C00 016 001★	C00 640 000★	128,000	190.00

CLEVELAND

D-A		14,080,000	150.00
D00 000 001★	D01 280 000★	192,000	180.00

RICHMOND

E-A		17,920,000	150.00
E00 000 001★	E01 920 000★	256,000	180.00

ATLANTA

F-A		3,840,000	150.00
F00 000 001★	F00 064 000★	64,000	225.00

CHICAGO

G-A	33,280,000	150.00
G00 000 001★	576,000	180.00

ST. LOUIS

H-A	15,360,000	150.00
H00 000 008★	448,000	180.00

MINNEAPOLIS

I-A	5,120,000	150.00
I00 000 001★	192,000	190.00

KANSAS CITY

J-A		20,480,000	150.00
J00 000 001★	J03 840 000★	512,000	180.00

DALLAS

K-A		38,400,000	150.00
K00 000 001★	K01 280 000★	512,000	180.00

SAN FRANCISCO

L-A		39,680,000	150.00
L00 000 001★	L03 200 000★	576,000	180.00

SERIES 1981

SIGNATURES: Angela M. Buchanan, Donald T. Regan

SERIAL NUMBERS: Both regular and star notes begin with 00 000 001. All B blocks resumed at 00 000 001, prior to completion of A blocks, making for an unusual two-tiered numbering pattern in each district.

SERIAL NUMBERS	NOTES PRINTED	CU
BOSTON		
A-A	2,560,000	$200.00
A-B	6,400,000	200.00
NEW YORK		
B-A	44,800,000	200.00
B-B	60,800,000	200.00
PHILADELPHIA		
C-A	6,400,000	200.00
C-B	6,400,000	200.00
CLEVELAND		
D-A	2,560,000	200.00
D-B	3,200,000	200.00

RICHMOND

E-A	7,680,000	200.00
E-B	16,000,000	200.00
E-★	640,000	375.00

ATLANTA

F-A	6,400,000	200.00

CHICAGO

G-A	20,480,000	200.00
G-B	12,800,000	200.00

ST. LOUIS

H-A	2,560,000	200.00
H-B	3,200,000	200.00

MINNEAPOLIS

I01 643 150A	3,200,000	200.00

KANSAS CITY

J-A	7,680,000	200.00
J-B	16,000,000	200.00

DALLAS

K-A	14,080,000	200.00
K-B	9,600,000	200.00

SAN FRANCISCO

L-A	15,360,000	200.00
L-B	9,600,000	200.00

SERIES 1981A

SIGNATURES: Katherine Davalos Ortega, Donald T. Regan
SERIAL NUMBERS: Both regular and star notes begin with 00 000 001.

SERIAL NUMBERS	NOTES PRINTED	CU
BOSTON		
A-A	16,000,000	$200.00
NEW YORK		
B-A	64,000,000	200.00
PHILADELPHIA		
C-A	3,200,000	200.00
CLEVELAND		
D-A	6,400,000	200.00
RICHMOND		
E-A	12,800,000	200.00
ATLANTA		
F-A	12,800,000	200.00

SERIAL NUMBER	NOTES PRINTED	CU
	CHICAGO	
G-A	22,400,000	200.00
	ST. LOUIS	
H-A	12,800,000	200.00
	MINNEAPOLIS	
I00 437 366**A**	3,200,000	200.00
	DALLAS	
K-A	3,200,000	200.00
	SAN FRANCISCO	
L-A	19,200,000	200.00
L-★	3,200,000	375.00

SERIES 1985

SIGNATURES: Katherine Davalos Ortega, James A. Baker III
SERIAL NUMBERS: Both regular and star notes begin with 00 000 001.

SERIAL NUMBER	NOTES PRINTED	CU
	BOSTON	
A-A	32,000,000	$175.00
	NEW YORK	
B-A	99,200,000	175.00
B-B	99,200,000	175.00
B-C	60,800,000	175.00
	PHILADELPHIA	
C-A	19,200,000	175.00

CLEVELAND

D-A		28,800,000	175.00
D-★	D03 200 000★	1,280,000	300.00

RICHMOND

E-A	54,400,000	175.00

ATLANTA

F-A	16,000,000	175.00

CHICAGO

G-A	64,000,000	175.00

ST. LOUIS

H-A	12,800,000	175.00

MINNEAPOLIS

I01 341 982A	12,800,000	175.00

KANSAS CITY

J-A		12,800,000	175.00
J-★	J03 200 000★	1,280,000	300.00

DALLAS

K-A		48,000,000	175.00
K-★	K03 200 000★	3,200,000	300.00

SAN FRANCISCO

L-A	38,400,000	175.00

SERIES 1988

PLATE SERIALS: Face check numbers begin with #1. Back check numbers continue from previous series.

SIGNATURES: Katherine Davalos Ortega, Nicholas F. Brady

SERIAL NUMBERS		NOTES PRINTED	CU

BOSTON

A-A	9,600,000	$150.00

NEW YORK

B-A -B-E	B48 000 000E	448,000,000	150.00
B00 934 984★	B06 400 000★	4,480,000	250.00

PHILADELPHIA

C-A	9,600,000	150.00

CLEVELAND

D00 820 000A	35,200,000	150.00

RICHMOND

E-A	19,200,000	150.00

CHICAGO

G-A	51,200,000	150.00

ST. LOUIS

H-A		9,600,000	150.00

KANSAS CITY

J-A		9,600,000	150.00

SAN FRANCISCO

L-A		19,200,000	150.00

SERIES 1990

SIGNATURES: Catalina Vasquez Villalpando, Nicholas F. Brady

PLATE SERIALS: Face check numbers begin at #1. Back check numbers continue sequence from previous series.

SERIAL NUMBERS: Both regular and star notes begin at 00 000 001.

(Series 1990 introduced the anti-counterfeiting security thread and the microsize printing around the portrait.)

SERIAL NUMBERS		NOTES PRINTED	CU
		BOSTON	
A-A		76,800,000	$125.00
		NEW YORK	
B-A – B-F	B99 200 000F	595,200,000	125.00
	B09 600 000★	1,880,000	145.00

		PHILADELPHIA	
C-A		99,200,000	125.00
C-B	C12 800 000B	12,800,000	125.00
	C03 200 000★	2,560,000	145.00
		CLEVELAND	
D-A		99,200 000	125.00
D-B	D16 000 000B	16,000,000	125.00
		RICHMOND	
E-A	E09 600 000B	99,200,000	125.00
E-B		9,600,000	125.00
		ATLANTA	
F-A		64,000,000	125.00
		CHICAGO	
G-A		99,200,000	125.00
G-B	G35 200 000B	35,200,000	125.00
G-★	G03 200 000★	640,000	145.00
		ST. LOUIS	
H-A		99,200 000	125.00
H-B	H22 400 000B	22,400,000	125.00
		MINNEAPOLIS	
I29 484 330A		48,000,000	125.00

		KANSAS CITY	
J-A		76,800,000	125.00
J01 884 704★	J03 200 000★	80,000	175.00

		DALLAS	
K-A		99,200,000	125.00
K-B	K67 200 000B	67,200,000	125.00
K-★	K03 200 000★	1,920,000	145.00

		SAN FRANCISCO	
L-A		99,200,000	125.00
L-B	L48 000 000B	48,000,000	125.00
L-★	L03 200 000★	3,200,000	145.00

SERIES 1993

SIGNATURES: Mary Ellen Withrow, Lloyd Bentsen

PLATE SERIALS: Back check numbers continue from previous series creating mules, until very near the end of the run, when new backs starting at #1 appear, and are quite scarce.

SERIAL NUMBERS: Both regular and star notes begin at 00 000 001.

SERIAL NUMBERS		NOTES PRINTED	CU
		BOSTON	
A-A	B25 600 000C	83,200,000	120.00
		NEW YORK	
B-A through B-C	B25 600 000C	224,000,000	120.00
B-★	B03 200 000★	1,280,000	130.00
		PHILADELPHIA	
C-A	(C43 142 207A obsvd.)	41,600,000	120.00
C-★	C01 280 000★	1,280,000	130.00
		CLEVELAND	
D-A		9,600,000	120.00
D-★	D03 200 000★	1,280,000	130.00
		RICHMOND	
E-A		64,000,000	120.00
		ATLANTA	
F-A		99,200,000	120.00
F-B		51,200,000	120.00
		CHICAGO	
G-A		44,800,000	120.00
		ST. LOUIS	
H-A		16,000,000	120.00
H-★	H03 200 000★	640,000	135.00
		MINNEAPOLIS	
I-A		9,600,000	120.00
		KANSAS CITY	
J-A		9,600,000	120.00
		DALLAS	
K-A		51,200,000	120.00
		SAN FRANCISCO	
L-A		19,200,000	120.00

SERIES 1996

SIGNATURES: Mary Ellen Withrow, Robert E. Rubin

PLATE SERIALS: Both face and back check numbers begin at #1.

SERIAL NUMBERS: Both regular and star notes begin at 00 000 001. Prefix letter A positioned before district letter.

See narrative in introduction, describing features of this design.

SERIAL NUMBERS		NOTES PRINTED	CU
BOSTON			
AA-A		51,200,000	115.00
AA-★	AA02 560 000★	2,560,000	125.00
NEW YORK			
AB-A—AB-G	AB19 200 000G	614,400,000	115.00
AB-★	AB10 240 000★	8,960,000	120.00
PHILADELPHIA			
AC-A		16,000,000	115.00
CLEVELAND			
AD-A—AD-B	AD03 200 000B	102,400,000	115.00
AD-★	AD00 160 000★	160,000	135.00
RICHMOND			
AE-A—AE-B	AE19 200 000B	118,400,000	115.00
ATLANTA			
AF-A		32,000,000	115.00
CHICAGO			
AG-A		70,400,000	115.00
ST. LOUIS			
AH-A		28,800,000	115.00
MINNEAPOLIS			
AI-A		9,600,000	125.00
KANSAS CITY			
AJ-A		19,200,000	115.00
DALLAS			
AK-A		83,200,000	115.00
SAN FRANCISCO			
AL-A—AL-D	AL44 480 000D	342,400,000	115.00
AL-★	AL02 560 000★	2,560,000	120.00

FIVE HUNDRED DOLLAR NOTES

GOLD CERTIFICATE

Gold Seal

SERIES 1928

PLATE SERIALS: Begin with 1 face and back check.
SIGNATURES: Walter O. Woods, A.W. Mellon

LOW	HIGH	NOTES		
SERIAL NUMBERS		PRINTED	VG/F	CU
A00 000 001A	A00 420 000A	420,000	$850.00	$3600.00

FEDERAL RESERVE NOTES
Green Seal
SERIES 1928

SERIAL NUMBERS: All serial numbers both regular and star notes begin with 00 000 001. High official star serial numbers are listed in the high observed star serial number column.

PLATE SERIALS: Face and back check begin with 1.

SIGNATURES: Walter O. Woods, A.W. Mellon

LOW SERIAL NUMBERS	HIGH	NOTES PRINTED	VF	CU
BOSTON				
A00 026 924A		69,120	$600.00	$850.00
A-★	A00 000 360★		800.00	1200.00
NEW YORK				
B00 000 005A	B00 137 067A	299,400	575.00	750.00
B-★	B00 002 160★		675.00	1000.00
PHILADELPHIA				
C00 003 745A	C00 016 382A	135,120	575.00	800.00
C00 001 080★	C00 016 382★		800.00	1200.00
CLEVELAND				
D00 016 530A	D00 030 771A	166,440	575.00	800.00
D-★	D00 001 080★		800.00	1200.00

LOW SERIAL NUMBERS	HIGH	NOTES PRINTED	VF	CU
RICHMOND				
E00 017 036A	E00 017 152A	84,720	600.00	850.00
E-★	E00 000 720★		800.00	1200.00
ATLANTA				
F00 000 085A	F00 010 569A	69,360	600.00	850.00
F-★	F00 000 360★		800.00	1200.00
CHICAGO				
G00 147 899A	G00 163 638A	573,600	575.00	750.00
G-★	G00 002 160★		650.00	1000.00
ST. LOUIS				
H00 000 202A	H00 027 310A	66,180	600.00	850.00
H-★	H00 000 720★		800.00	1200.00

MINNEAPOLIS

I00 000 158**A**	I00 005 041**A**	34,680	600.00	900.00
I-★	I00 000 360★		850.00	1300.00

KANSAS CITY

J00 011 191**A**	J00 011 631**A**	510,720	575.00	750.00
J-★	J00 001 080★		675.00	1000.00

DALLAS

K00 001 336**A**	K00 009 711**A**	70,560	600.00	850.00
K-★	K00 000 360★		800.00	1200.00

SAN FRANCISCO

L00 013 036**A**	L00 030 137**A**	64,080	600.00	850.00
L-★	L00 000 360★		800.00	1200.00

SERIES **1934**

Light Green Seal

SERIAL NUMBERS: Both regular and star notes begin with 00 000 001.

PLATE SERIALS: Face and back check begin with 1.

SIGNATURES: W.A. Julian, Henry Morgenthau, Jr.

LOW	HIGH	NOTES		
SERIAL NUMBERS		**PRINTED**	VF	CU

BOSTON

A00 000 054**A**	A00 041 818**A**	56,628	$650.00	$850.00
A-★			800.00	1250.00

NEW YORK

B00 002 193**A**	B00 073 286**A**	288,000	600.00	750.00
B-★			750.00	1250.00

PHILADELPHIA

C00 002 855**A**	C00 015 557**A**	31,200	650.00	850.00
C-★			800.00	1250.00

CLEVELAND

D00 003 665**A**	D00 004 775**A**	39,000	650.00	850.00
D00 001 944★			800.00	1250.00

RICHMOND

E00 002 909**A**		40,800	650.00	850.00
E-★	E00 002 209★		800.00	1250.00

ATLANTA

F00 001 043**A**	F00 009 481**A**	46,200	650.00	850.00
F-★			800.00	1250.00

CHICAGO				
G00 010 079**A**	G00 024 194**A**	212,400	600.00	800.00
G00 001 321★			800.00	1250.00
ST. LOUIS				
H00 005 659**A**	H00 017 999**A**	24,000	650.00	850.00
H-★			800.00	1250.00
MINNEAPOLIS				
I00 000 666**A**	I00 008 304**A**	24,000	650.00	850.00
I-★			800.00	1250.00
KANSAS CITY				
J00 000 793**A**	J00 006 930**A**	40,800	650.00	850.00
J-★			800.00	1250.00
DALLAS				
K00 000 063**A**	K00 047 368**A**	31,200	675.00	900.00
K-★			850.00	1350.00
SAN FRANCISCO				
L00 007 326**A**		83,400	625.00	850.00
L-★			800.00	1250.00

SERIES **1934**

Dark Green Seal

SERIAL NUMBERS: Continue sequence from 1934 Light Green Seal.

SIGNATURES: W. A. Julian, Henry Morgenthau, Jr.

LOW	HIGH	NOTES		
SERIAL NUMBERS		**PRINTED**	**VF**	**CU**
BOSTON				
A00 008 154**A**	A00 054 077**A**	Included Above	$575.00	$750.00
A-★			700.00	1200.00
NEW YORK				
B00 133 512**A**	B00 254 373**A**	Included Above	550.00	700.00
B-★			700.00	1200.00
PHILADELPHIA				
C00 023 541**A**		Included Above	575.00	750.00
C-★			700.00	1200.00
CLEVELAND				
D00 025 647**A**		Included Above	575.00	750.00
D00 001 094			700.00	1200.00
RICHMOND				
E00 021 673**A**	E00 063 581**A**	Included Above	575.00	750.00
E00 002 209★			700.00	1200.00
ATLANTA				
	F00 063 770**A**	Included Above	575.00	750.00
F00 00 204★	F00 002 799★		700.00	1200.00
CHICAGO				
G00 040 000**A**	G00 264 376**A**	Included Above	575.00	700.00
G00 000 206★	G00 003 503★		700.00	1200.00
ST. LOUIS				
H00 066 951**A**	H00 067 144**A**	Included Above	575.00	750.00
H-★			700.00	1200.00
MINNEAPOLIS				
I00 009 705**A**	I00 012 161**A**	Included Above	575.00	750.00
I00 000 800★			750.00	1250.00
KANSAS CITY				
	J00 067 164**A**	Included Above	575.00	750.00
J00 000 001★			750.00	1250.00

DALLAS

		Included Above	575.00	750.00
K00 028 863A	K00 047 368A			
K00 000 733★			750.00	1250.00

SAN FRANCISCO

		Included Above	575.00	700.00
	L00 153 444A			
L00 000 208★	L00 003 775★		700.00	1200.00

SERIES 1934A Mule

SERIAL NUMBERS: Continue sequence from previous series.

SIGNATURES: W.A. Julian, Henry Morgenthau, Jr.

LOW	HIGH	NOTES	VF	CU
SERIAL NUMBERS		PRINTED		
NEW YORK				
B00 268 014A	B00 426 371A	276,000	$600.00	$700.00
B00 003 959★				1000.00
PHILADELPHIA				
C00 025 038A	C00 310 675A	45,300	650.00	750.00
CLEVELAND				
D00 047 894A	D00 057 516A	23,800	650.00	750.00
RICHMOND				
E00 020 284A	E00 063 100A	36,000	650.00	750.00
E00 001 844★				1000.00
ATLANTA				
F00 037 292A	F00 102 055A		700.00	850.00

CHICAGO				
G00 177 659A	G00 383 045A	214,800	600.00	700.00
G00 002 211★				
ST. LOUIS				
	H00 064 036A	57,600	650.00	750.00
MINNEAPOLIS				
I00 013 989A	I00 023 481A	14,400	700.00	850.00
KANSAS CITY				
J00 026 293A	J00 078 168A	55,200	650.00	750.00
J00 000 202★				1000.00

DALLAS

K00 019 595**A**	K00 038 793**A**	34,800	650.00	750.00

SAN FRANCISCO

L00 066 726**A**	L00 153 909**A**	73,000	650.00	750.00
L00 003 991★				1000.00

SERIES **1934B**

SERIAL NUMBERS: Continued sequence from previous series.

SIGNATURES: W.A. Julian, Fred M. Vinson

LOW HIGH SERIAL NUMBERS	NOTES PRINTED	XF	CU
ATLANTA			
F-A	2,472	$3000.00	$5500.00

SERIES **1934C**

SERIAL NUMBERS: Continue sequence from previous series.

SIGNATURES: W.A. Julian, John W. Snyder

LOW HIGH SERIAL NUMBERS	NOTES PRINTED	XF	CU
BOSTON			
A-A	1,440	$3000.00	$5500.00
NEW YORK			
B-A	204	3000.00	5500.00

ONE THOUSAND DOLLAR NOTES
GOLD CERTIFICATE
Gold Seal
SERIES 1928

PLATE SERIALS: Face and back check numbers. Begin with 1.
SIGNATURES: Walter O. Woods, A.W. Mellon

LOW SERIAL NUMBERS	HIGH	NOTES PRINTED	VF	CU
A00 000 001A	A00 288 000A	288,000	$3000.00	$7000.00
A-★				

SERIES 1934

PLATE SERIALS: As above. Begin with 1.
SIGNATURES: W.A. Julian, Henry Morgenthau, Jr.

These 1934 notes had orange (not green) backs, and their text specified payment "in gold payable to the bearer on demand as authorized by law." Those last four words have been added because these 1934 gold notes were for use only among banks and were not to be released into public circulation.

The Bureau occasionally exhibits its specimen sheet of these orange-back notes.

LOW SERIAL NUMBERS	HIGH	NOTES PRINTED
A00 000 001A	A00 084 000A	84,000

FEDERAL RESERVE NOTES
Green Seal
SERIES 1928

SERIAL NUMBERS: All serial numbers both regular and star notes begin with 00 000 001. High official star serial numbers are listed in the high observed star serial number column.
PLATE SERIALS: Face and back check begin with 1.
SIGNATURES: Walter O. Woods, A.W. Mellon

LOW SERIAL NUMBERS	HIGH	NOTES PRINTED	VF	CU
BOSTON				
A-A		58,320	$1250.00	$1450.00
A-★	A00 000 360★		1500.00	2000.00
NEW YORK				
B00 027 606A	B00 089 961A	139,200	1200.00	1400.00
B-★	B00 002 160★		1450.00	1850.00
PHILADELPHIA				
C-A		96,708	1250.00	1450.00
C00 000 191★	C00 000 720★		1500.00	2000.00
CLEVELAND				
D00 014 869A	D00 019 879A	79,680	1250.00	1450.00
D00 000 102★	D00 001 080★		1500.00	2000.00
RICHMOND				
E00 000 720A	E00 018 183A	66,840	1250.00	1450.00
E-★	E00 000 360★		1500.00	2000.00
ATLANTA				
F-A		47,400	1250.00	1450.00
F-★	F00 000 240★		1500.00	2000.00
CHICAGO				
G00 019 152A	G00 141 890A	355,800	1200.00	1400.00
G00 000 589★	G00 001 800★		1450.00	1850.00
ST. LOUIS				
H00 002 806A	H00 035 826A	60,000	1250.00	1450.00
H00 000 189★	H00 000 360★		1500.00	2000.00
MINNEAPOLIS				
I-A		26,640	1300.00	1600.00
I-★	I00 000 360★		1500.00	2000.00
KANSAS CITY				
J00 003 914A	J00 004 024A	62,172	1250.00	1450.00
	J00 030 886A Light green seal		1350.00	1750.00
J-★	J00 000 750★		1500.00	2000.00
DALLAS				
K00 001 472A	K00 008 415A	42,960	1250.00	1450.00
K-★	K00 000 360★		1500.00	2000.00
SAN FRANCISCO				
L00 010 713A	L00 013 921A	67,920	1250.00	1450.00
L-★	L00 000 360★		1500.00	2000.00

SERIES 1934
Light Green Seal

SERIAL NUMBERS: All serial numbers both regular and star notes begin with 00 000 001.

PLATE SERIALS: Face and back check begin with 1.

SIGNATURES: W.A. Julian, Henry Morgenthau, Jr.

LOW SERIAL NUMBERS	HIGH	NOTES PRINTED	VF	CU

BOSTON

| A00 001 971A | A 00 036 565A | 46,200 | $1200.00 | $1400.00 |
| A-★ | | | 1400.00 | 1800.00 |

NEW YORK

| B00 012 261A | B00 304 019A | 332,784 | 1150.00 | 1350.00 |
| B-★ | | | 1350.00 | 1700.00 |

PHILADELPHIA

| C00 009 681A | C00 012 068A | 33,000 | 1200.00 | 1400.00 |
| C-★ | | | 1400.00 | 1800.00 |

CLEVELAND

| D00 000 497A | D00 009 871A | 35,400 | 1200.00 | 1400.00 |
| D00 000 497★ | D00 001 202★ | | 1300.00 | 1600.00 |

RICHMOND

| E00 000 013A | E00 008 414A | 19,560 | 1250.00 | 1650.00 |
| E-★ | | | 1400.00 | 2500.00 |

ATLANTA

| F00 013 438A | | 67,800 | 1200.00 | 1400.00 |
| F-★ | | | 1400.00 | 1800.00 |

CHICAGO

| G00 000 231A | G00 026 664A | 167,040 | 1150.00 | 1350.00 |
| G-★ | | | 1300.00 | 1600.00 |

ST. LOUIS

| H00 000 100A | H00 011 605A | 22,440 | 1200.00 | 1400.00 |
| H-★ | | | 1400.00 | 1800.00 |

MINNEAPOLIS

| I00 005 286A | | 12,000 | 1500.00 | 2500.00 |
| I-★ | | | 1600.00 | 2750.00 |

KANSAS CITY

| J00 006 280A | J00 015 642A | 51,840 | 1200.00 | 1400.00 |
| J-★ | | | 1400.00 | 1800.00 |

DALLAS

| K00 004 584A | K00 035 255A | 46,800 | 1200.00 | 1400.00 |
| K-★ | | | 1400.00 | 1800.00 |

SAN FRANCISCO

| L00 004 470A | L00 010 643A | 90,600 | 1200.00 | 1400.00 |
| L-★ | | | 1400.00 | 1800.00 |

SERIES 1934

Dark Green Seal

SERIAL NUMBERS: Continue sequence from 1934 Light Green seal.

SIGNATURES: W. A. Julian, Henry Morgenthau, Jr.

LOW	HIGH	NOTES		
SERIAL NUMBERS		**PRINTED**	**vF**	**CU**
BOSTON				
A00 020 887A	A00 033 781A	Included above	$1150.00	$1350.00
A-★			1350.00	1750.00
NEW YORK				
B00 290 594A	B00 304 019A	Included above	1100.00	1300.00
B-★			1300.00	1650.00
PHILADELPHIA				
C-A		Included above	1150.00	1350.00
C00 001 989★			1350.00	1750.00
CLEVELAND				
D00 026 980A		Included above	1150.00	1350.00
D-★			1300.00	1750.00
RICHMOND				
E00 025 927A		Included above	1200.00	1400.00
E-★			1350.00	1750.00
ATLANTA				
F00 022 533A	F00 119 866A	Included above	1150.00	1350.00
F00 003 317★			1350.00	1750.00
CHICAGO				
G00 082 940A	G00 126 595A	Included above	1100.00	1300.00
G00 001 234★	G00 003 509★		1250.00	1600.00
ST. LOUIS				
H-A		Included above	1150.00	1350.00
H00 001 094★			1350.00	1750.00
MINNEAPOLIS				
I00 008 795A	I00 015 289A	Included above	1200.00	1450.00
I-★			1350.00	1750.00
KANSAS CITY				
J00 057 596A		Included above	1200.00	1400.00
J-★			1350.00	1750.00
DALLAS				
K00 026 595A	K00 035 255A	Included above	1200.00	1400.00
K-★			1350.00	1750.00
SAN FRANCISCO				
L00 066 320A	L00 066 710A	Included above	1150.00	1350.00
L00 000 467★	L00 003 651★		1350.00	1750.00

SERIES 1934A Mule

SERIAL NUMBERS: Continue sequence from previous series.
SIGNATURES: W.A. Julian, Henry Morgenthau, Jr.

LOW	HIGH	NOTES		
SERIAL NUMBERS		**PRINTED**	**VF**	**CU**
BOSTON				
A00 023 154A	A00 052 039A	30,000	$1200.00	$1400.00
A-★			1500.00	2000.00
NEW YORK				
B00 336 581A	B00 400 600A	174,348	1150.00	1350.00
B-★			1400.00	1800.00
PHILADELPHIA				
C00 026 784A	C00 046 070A	78,000	1200.00	1400.00
C-★			1500.00	2000.00

CLEVELAND

D00 030 853A	D00 045 377A	28,000	1200.00	1400.00
D-★			1500.00	2000.00

RICHMOND

E00 022 873A	E00 028 252A	16,800	1250.00	1500.00
E-★			1500.00	2000.00

ATLANTA

F00 048 331A	F00 125 483A	80,964	1200.00	1400.00
F-★			1500.00	2000.00

CHICAGO

G00 228 961A	G00 268 666A	134,400	1150.00	1350.00
G00 003 800★	G00 004 094★		1400.00	1800.00

ST. LOUIS

H00 048 484A	H00 050 089A	39,600	1200.00	1400.00
H-★			1500.00	2000.00

MINNEAPOLIS

I00 012 384A	I00 012 547A	4,800	1300.00	1600.00
I-★			1600.00	2000.00

KANSAS CITY

J00 034 236A	J00 056 646A	21,600	1250.00	1500.00
J-★			1500.00	2000.00

SAN FRANCISCO

L00 071 330A	L00 097 535A	36,600	1200.00	1400.00
L-★			1500.00	2000.00

SERIES 1934C Mule

SERIAL NUMBERS: Continued sequence from previous series.

SIGNATURES: W.A. Julian, John W Snyder

LOW	HIGH	NOTES	VF	CU
SERIAL NUMBERS		PRINTED		
BOSTON				
A-A		1,200	$3250.00	$6000.00
NEW YORK				
B-A		168	3600.00	6000.00

FIVE THOUSAND DOLLAR NOTES

GOLD CERTIFICATE

Gold Seal

SERIES 1928

PLATE SERIALS: Face and back check. Begin with 1.

SIGNATURES: Walter O. Woods, A.W. Mellon

LOW SERIAL NUMBERS	HIGH	NOTES PRINTED	XF	CU
A00 000 001A	A00 024 000A	24,000	12,000.	15,000.

FEDERAL RESERVE NOTES

Green Seal

SERIES 1928

SERIAL NUMBERS Regular notes begin with 00 000 001. No stat notes printed.

PLATE SERIALS: Face and back begin with 1.

SIGNATURES: Walter O. Woods, A.W. Mellon

LOW SERIAL NUMBERS	HIGH	NOTES PRINTED	XF	CU
BOSTON				
A-A		1,320	$10,000.	$14,000.
NEW YORK				
B-A		2,640	10,000.	14,000.
CLEVELAND				
D-A		3,000	10,000.	14,000.
RICHMOND				
E-A		3,984	10,000.	14,000.
ATLANTA				
F-A		1,440	10,000.	14,000.
CHICAGO				
G-A		3,480	10,000.	14,000.
KANSAS CITY				
J-A		720	10,000.	14,000.
DALLAS				
K-A		360	10,000.	14,000.
SAN FRANCISCO				
L-A		1,300	10,000.	14,000.

SERIES **1934**

Light Green Seal

SERIAL NUMBERS: All serial numbers both regular and star notes began with 00 000 001.

PLATE SERIALS: Face and back check begin with 1.

SIGNATURES: W.A. Julian, Henry Morgenthau, Jr.

LOW SERIAL NUMBERS HIGH		NOTES PRINTED	XF	CU
BOSTON				
A-A		9,480	$9000.00	$12,500.
NEW YORK				
B00 000 691A	B00 002 403A	11,520	9000.00	12,500.
PHILADELPHIA				
C-A		3,000	9000.00	12,500.
CLEVELAND				
D-A		1,680	9000.00	12,500.
RICHMOND				
E-A		2,400	9000.00	12,500.
ATLANTA				
F-A		3,600	9000.00	12,500.
CHICAGO				
G00 000 362A	G00 001 272A	6,600	9000.00	12,500.
ST. LOUIS				
H00 000 340A	H00 000 429A	2,400	9000.00	12,500.
KANSAS CITY				
J00 000 073A		2,400	9000.00	12,500.

DALLAS

K00 000 042A K00 000 125A		2,400	9000.00	12,500.

SAN FRANCISCO

L-A		6,000	9000.00	12,500.

SERIES 1934A

SERIAL NUMBERS: Continued sequence from previous series.

SIGNATURES: W.A. Julian, Henry Morgenthau, Jr.

LOW	HIGH	NOTES		
SERIAL NUMBERS		PRINTED	XF	CU

ST. LOUIS

H-A		1,440	$10,000.	$14,000.

SERIES 1934B

SERIAL NUMBERS: Continued sequence from previous series.

SIGNATURES: W.A. Julian, Fred M. Vinson

LOW	HIGH	NOTES		
SERIAL NUMBERS		PRINTED	XF	CU

BOSTON

A-A		1,200	$10,000.	$14,000.

NEW YORK

B-A		12	12,000.	15,000.

TEN THOUSAND DOLLAR NOTES

GOLD CERTIFICATE
Gold Seal
SERIES 1928

PLATE SERIALS: Face and back check. Begin with 1.
SIGNATURES: Walter O. Woods, A.W. Mellon

LOW	HIGH	NOTES		
SERIAL NUMBERS		PRINTED	VF	CU
A00 000 001A	A00 048 000A	48,000	$18,000.	$24,000.

SERIES 1934

PLATE SERIALS: Begin with 1.
SIGNATURES: W.A. Julian, Henry Morganthau, Jr.

LOW	HIGH	NOTES
SERIAL NUMBERS		PRINTED
A00 000 001A	A00 036 000A	36,000

These 1934 notes had orange (not green) backs, and their text specified payment "in gold payable to the bearer on demand as authorized by law." The last four words have been added because these 1934 gold notes were for use only among banks and were not to be released into public circulation.
The Bureau occasionally exhibits its specimen sheet of these orange-back notes.

FEDERAL RESERVE NOTES
Green Seal
SERIES 1928

SERIAL NUMBERS: Regular notes begin with 00 000 001.
PLATE SERIALS: Face and back check numbers start with 1. No star notes printed.
SIGNATURES: Walter O. Woods, A.W. Mellon

LOW	HIGH	NOTES		
SERIAL NUMBERS		PRINTED	XF	CU
BOSTON				
A-A		1,320	$18,000.	$22,500.
A-★				
NEW YORK				
B-A		4,680	18,000.	22,500.
CLEVELAND				
D-A		960	18,000.	22,500.

RICHMOND			
E-A	3,024	18,000.	22,500.
ATLANTA			
F-A	1,440	18,000.	22,500.
CHICAGO			
G-A	1,800	18,000.	22,500.
ST. LOUIS			
H-A	480	18,000.	22,500.
MINNEAPOLIS			
I-A	480	18,000.	22,500.
KANSAS CITY			
J-A	480	18,000.	22,500.
DALLAS			
K-A	360	18,000.	22,500.
SAN FRANCISCO			
L-A	360	18,000.	22,500.

FEDERAL RESERVE NOTES
Light Green Seal
SERIES 1934

SERIAL NUMBERS: Both regular and star notes begin with 00 000 001.

PLATE SERIALS: Face and back check numbers start with 1.

SIGNATURES: W.A. Julian, Henry Morgenthau, Jr.

LOW HIGH			
SERIAL NUMBERS	**NOTES PRINTED**	**XF**	**CU**
BOSTON			
A-A	9,720	$18,000.	$22,500.
NEW YORK			
B-A	11,520	18,000.	22,500.
PHILADELPHIA			
C-A	6,000	18,000.	22,500.
CLEVELAND			
C-A	1,480	18,000.	22,500.
RICHMOND			
E-A	1,200	18,000.	22,500.
ATLANTA			
F-A	2,400	18,000.	22,500.

		NOTES PRINTED	XF	CU
	CHICAGO			
G-A	G00 000 772A	3,840	18,000.	22,500.
	ST. LOUIS			
H-A		2,040	18,000.	22,500.
	KANSAS CITY			
J-A		1,200	18,000.	22,500.
	DALLAS			
K-A		1,200	18,000.	22,500.
	SAN FRANCISCO			
L-A		3,600	18,000.	22,500.

SERIES 1934A

SIGNATURES: W.A. Julian, Henry Morgenthau, Jr.

LOW	HIGH	NOTES		
SERIAL NUMBERS		**PRINTED**	**XF**	**CU**
	CHICAGO			
G-A		1,560	$20,000.	$24,000.

SERIES 1934B

SERIAL NUMBERS: Continued sequence from previous series.
SIGNATURES: W.A. Julian, Fred M. Vinson

LOW	HIGH	NOTES		
SERIAL NUMBERS		**PRINTED**	**XF**	**CU**
	NEW YORK			
G-A		24	$20,000.	$24,000.

ONE HUNDRED THOUSAND DOLLAR NOTES

GOLD CERTIFICATE

Yellow Seal

SERIES 1934

PLATE SERIALS: Face & back check number. Begin with 1.

SIGNATURES: W.A. Julian, Henry Morgenthau, Jr.

LOW	HIGH	NOTES		
SERIAL NUMBERS		PRINTED	XF	CU
A00 000 001A	A00 042 000A	42,000		

Like the other 1934 Gold Certificates, this note also has an orange (not green) back and also specifies payment "in gold to the bearer on demand as authorized by law." Also like the other 1934 Gold Certificates (the $100, $1000, $10,000 notes) these notes were legal for use only among banks, but were not to be released into public circulation.

The Bureau occasionally exhibits its specimen sheet of these high-value orange-back notes.

APPENDIX I
UNCUT SHEETS

Perhaps the most prized and certainly a scarce item in any modern size paper money collection is an uncut sheet printed before 1976. Despite intensive research throughout the Treasury Department including the records of the Bureau of Engraving and Printing we find neither validity or completeness in the records that were examined. Information presented, which is the best available is contradicted many times by the census of known uncut sheets that follows the list of uncut sheets printed (?) or issued (?). We cannot learn for sure exactly HOW the uncut sheets reached the private collector. We do know that uncut sheets were available to collectors AT FACE value in the CASH DIVISION, Main Treasury Bldg. Washington, D.C. from the start of current size notes until Secretary Humphrey stopped the sale of uncut sheets during his tenure. Some scant records examined indicate the purchaser signed a "ledger" when making his purchase. Apparently there was no limit since some signatures appear several times on the same ledger sheet for purchase of separately serial number identified sheets of the same denomination and series. What we have not been able to learn is who requested (or ordered) the uncut sheets from the Bureau and how many were ordered. We have been unable to locate any delivery records of sheets from the Bureau to the Cash Division. We have fairly reliable HEARSAY evidence that IF the sheets remained in the Cash Division unsold, they were eventually cut up and passed over the teller counter as single notes.

Any information relative to either the printing, the issue, or the existence of uncut sheets is welcome.

Listed below is the best information available on the number of uncut sheets printed, followed by a census of uncut sheets known to exist and their value.

ONE DOLLAR

LEGAL TENDER
Red Seal

SERIES 1928
12 Subject Sheets – Est. Value $20,000.

SIGNATURES	SERIAL NUMBER RANGE	NUMBER OF SHEETS
W.O. Woods W.H. Woodin	A00 000 001A - A00 000 120A A01 872 001A - A01 872 012A	10 1

SILVER CERTIFICATE
Blue Seal

SERIES 1928
Est. Value $3000.00

H.T. Tate A.W. Mellon	A00 000 001A - A00 004 000A	No Record

SERIES 1928B

Walter O. Woods Ogden L. Mills	V51 000 001A - V51 000 012A	6

SERIES 1928C

Walter O. Woods W.H. Woodin	B29 448 001B - B29 448 120B D23 328 001B - D23 328 012B	10 1

SERIES 1928D

W.A. Julian W.H. Woodin	D82 596 001B - D82 595 720B	60

SERIES **1928E**

W.A. Julian
Henry Morgenthau, Jr.

F72 000 001**B** - F72 000 300**B**   25

SERIES **1934**

W.A. Julian
Henry Morgenthau, Jr.

A00 000 001**A** - A00 000 300**A**   25

SERIES **1935**

W.A. Julian
Henry Morgenthau, Jr.

A00 000 001**A** - A00 001 200**A**   100

SERIES **1935A**

W.A. Julian
Henry Morgenthau, Jr.

V43 128 001**A** - V43 129 200**A**   100
F41 952 001**C** - F41 954 148**C** N.Africa   25
F41 964 001**C** - F41 966 148**C** Hawaii   25

SERIES **1935B**

W.A. Julian
Fred M. Vinson

C93 348 01**D** - C93 385 200**D**   100

SERIES **1935C**

W.A. Julian
John W. Snyder

K99 996 001**D** - K99 997 200**D**   100

SERIES **1935D**

12 Subject Sheets

Georgia Neese Clark
John W. Snyder

R88 104 001**E** - R88 104 200**E**   100
Z33 324 001**E** - Z33 325 200**E**   100
B05 520 001**G** - B05 521 200**G**   100

SERIES **1935D**

18 Subject Sheets

G00 000 001**G** - G00 136 100**G**   100
N46 807 999**G** - N46 944 000**G**   2

SERIES **1935E**

Ivy Baker Priest
George M. Humphrey

N46 944 001**G** - N47 080 100**G**   100
R95 040 001**G** - R94 175 100**G**   100
U75 168 001**G** - U75 304 100**G**   100
X31 680 001**G** - X31 816 100**G**   100

TWO DOLLARS

LEGAL TENDER
Red Seal

SERIES **1928C**

12 Subject Sheets

SIGNATURES	SERIAL NUMBER RANGE	NUMBER OF SHEETS
W.A. Julian	B09 012 001**A** - B09 012 300**A**	25
Henry Morgenthau, Jr.	B83 988 001**A** - B83 988 500**A**	50

SERIES **1928D**

W.A. Julian, Henry Morgenthau, Jr.
Records indicate 50 sheets Serials **B**83 988 001**A** through **B**83 988 500**A** were printed for this series however sheets known with these serials are all Series 1928C. No sheets of this series are known.

SERIES **1928E**

W.A. Julian
Fred M. Vinson
D35 552 001**A** - D35 532 600**A**   50

SERIES **1928F**

W.A. Julian
John W. Snyder
D39 552 001**A** - D39 553 200**A**   100

SERIES **1928G**

Georgia Neese Clark
John W. Snyder
E07 074 001**A** - E07 705 200**A**   100

SERIES **1953**

18 Subject Sheets

Ivy Baker Priest
George M. Humphrey
A00 000 001**A** - A00 136 100**A**   100

FIVE DOLLARS

LEGAL TENDER
Red Seal

SERIES **1928E**

12 Subject Sheets

SIGNATURES	SERIAL NUMBER RANGE	NUMBER OF SHEETS
W.A. Julian	(One sheet offered as item 1111, in A. Kosoff sale of October 26, 1971.)	
Fred M. Vinson		

SERIES **1928E**

W.A. Julian
John W. Snyder
G68 352 001**A** - G68 353 200**A**   100

SERIES **1953**

18 Subject Sheets

Ivy Baker Priest
George M. Humphrey
A00 000 001**A** - A00 136 100**A**   100

SILVER CERTIFICATE
Blue Seal

SERIES **1934**

12 Subject Sheets

W.A. Julian
Henry Morgenthau, Jr.
A00 000 001**A** - A00 000 300**A**   25

SERIES **1934A**

None Known

SERIES **1934B**

12 Subject Sheets

SIGNATURES	SERIAL NUMBER RANGE	NUMBER OF SHEETS
W.A. Julian		
Fred M. Vinson		25*

* No record of any issues however sheets known to exist indicate an issue of 25 sheets.

SERIES **1934C**

W.A. Julian	L50 808 001**A** - L50 809 200**A**	100
John W. Snyder		

SERIES **1934D**

Georgia Neese Clark	Q71 628 001**A** - Q71 629 200**A**	100
John W. Snyder		

SERIES **1953**

18 Subject Sheets

Ivy Baker Priest	A00 000 001**A** - A00 136 100**A**	100
George M. Humphrey		

TEN DOLLARS

SILVER CERTIFICATE
Blue Seal

SERIES **1933**

12 Subject Sheets

SIGNATURES	SERIAL NUMBER RANGE	NUMBER OF SHEETS
W.A. Julian	A00 372 001**A** - A00 372 012**A**	1
W.H. Woodin		

SERIES **1933A**

W.A. Julian	A00 372 013**A** - A00 372 024**A**	1
Henry Morgenthau, Jr.		

SERIES **1934**

W.A. Julian	A00 000 001**A** - A00 000 120**A**	10
Henry Morgenthau, Jr.		

SERIES **1953**

18 Subject Sheets

Ivy Baker Priest	A00 000 001**A** - A00 136 100**A**	100
George M. Humphrey		

CENSUS OF UNCUT SHEETS
RECENTLY KNOWN TO EXIST
IN UNCUT CONDITION

We are deeply indebted to Mr. Aubrey E. Bebee for his assistance in supplying much of the sheet information and values. Thanks are also due Mr. John Morris and Mr. Robert H. Lloyd for their help in this area.

ONE DOLLAR

LEGAL TENDER
Red Seal

SERIES 1928
12 Subject Sheets
Value $20,000.

A00 000 013A	through	A00 000 024A
A00 000 025A	through	A00 000 036A
A00 000 037A	through	A00 000 048A
A00 000 049A	through	A00 000 060A
A00 000 061A	through	A00 000 072A
A00 000 073A	through	A00 000 096A
A00 000 097A	through	A00 000 108A
A00 000 109A	through	A00 000 120A

SILVER CERTIFICATE
Blue Seal

SERIES 1928
Value $3,000.

A00 000 061A	through	A00 000 072A
A00 000 121A	through	A00 000 132A
A00 000 193A	through	A00 000 204A
A00 000 205A	through	A00 000 216A
A00 000 277A	through	A00 000 288A
A00 000 433A	through	A00 000 444A
A00 000 589A	through	A00 000 600A
A00 000 601A	through	A00 000 612A
A00 000 637A	through	A00 000 648A
A00 000 661A	through	A00 000 672A
A00 000 673A	through	A00 000 684A
A00 000 697A	through	A00 000 708A
A00 000 709A	through	A00 000 720A
A00 000 733A	through	A00 000 744A

SERIES 1928A
None known

SERIES 1928B
None known

SERIES 1928C
Value $9,000.

B29 448 001B	through	B29 448 012B
B29 448 037B	through	B29 448 048B
B29 448 049B	through	B29 448 060B
B29 448 061B	through	B29 448 072B
B29 448 073B	through	B29 448 084B

SERIES 1928D
Value $3,000.

D00 000 025B	through	D00 000 036B
D82 596 037B	through	D82 596 048B
D82 596 049B	through	D82 596 060B
D82 596 061B	through	D82 596 072B
D82 596 085B	through	D82 596 096B
D82 596 109B	through	D82 596 120B
D82 596 121B	through	D82 596 132B
D82 596 133B	through	D82 596 144B
D82 596 205B	through	D82 596 216B
D82 596 217B	through	D82 596 228B
D82 596 265B	through	D82 596 276B
D82 596 277B	through	D82 596 288B
D82 596 313B	through	D82 596 324B
D82 596 337B	through	D82 596 348B
D82 596 349B	through	D82 596 360B
D82 596 361B	through	D82 596 372B
D82 596 433B	through	D82 596 444B
D82 596 445B	through	D82 596 456B
D82 596 481B	through	D82 596 492B
D82 596 517B	through	D82 596 528B
D82 596 529B	through	D82 596 540B
D82 596 577B	through	D82 596 588B
D82 596 637B	through	D82 596 648B
D82 596 661B	through	D82 596 672B
D82 596 673B	through	D82 596 684B

SERIES 1928E
Value $12,000.

F72 000 049B	through	F72 000 060B
F72 000 097B	through	F72 000 108B
F72 000 133B	through	F72 000 144B
F72 000 145B	through	F72 000 156B
F72 000 217B	through	F72 000 228B
F72 000 241B	through	F72 000 252B
F72 000 277B	through	F72 000 288B
F72 000 289B	through	F72 000 300B

SERIES 1934
Value $2,500.

A00 000 037A	through	A00 000 048A
A00 000 073A	through	A00 000 084A
A00 000 085A	through	A00 000 096A
A00 000 097A	through	A00 000 108A
A00 000 109A	through	A00 000 120A
A00 000 121A	through	A00 000 132A
A00 000 145A	through	A00 000 156A
A00 000 157A	through	A00 000 168A
A00 000 181A	through	A00 000 192A
A00 000 217A	through	A00 000 228A

SERIES 1935
Value $2,000.

A00 000 061A	through	A00 000 072A
A00 000 157A	through	A00 000 168A
A00 000 169A	through	A00 000 180A
A00 000 205A	through	A00 000 216A
A00 000 217A	through	A00 000 228A
A00 000 313A	through	A00 000 324A
A00 000 325A	through	A00 000 336A
A00 000 361A	through	A00 000 372A
A00 000 397A	through	A00 000 408A
A00 000 445A	through	A00 000 456A
A00 000 457A	through	A00 000 468A
A00 000 565A	through	A00 000 576A
A00 000 601A	through	A00 000 612A
A00 000 613A	through	A00 000 624A

A00 000 625A   through   A00 000 636A
A00 000 637A   through   A00 000 648A
A00 000 649A   through   A00 000 660A
A00 000 661A   through   A00 000 672A
A00 000 733A   through   A00 000 744A
A00 000 769A   through   A00 000 780A
A00 000 781A   through   A00 000 792A
A00 000 793A   through   A00 000 804A
A00 000 805A   through   A00 000 816A
A00 000 829A   through   A00 000 840A
A00 000 841A   through   A00 000 852A
A00 000 853A   through   A00 000 864A
A00 000 973A   through   A00 000 984A
A00 001 057A   through   A00 001 068A
A00 001 177A   through   A00 001 188A

SERIES 1935A
Value $1,750.

V43 128 025A   through   V43 128 036A
V43 129 045A   through   V43 129 056A
V43 129 069A   through   V43 129 080A
V43 129 081A   through   V43 129 092A
V43 129 093A   through   V43 129 104A
V43 128 205A   through   V43 128 216A
V43 128 109A   through   V43 128 120A
V43 128 313A   through   V43 128 324A
V43 128 325A   through   V43 128 336A
V43 128 373A   through   V43 128 384A
V43 128 505A   through   V43 128 516A
V43 128 529A   through   V43 128 540A
V43 128 656A   through   V43 128 576A
V43 128 589A   through   V43 128 600A
V43 128 601A   through   V43 128 612A
V43 128 613A   through   V43 128 624A
V43 128 661A   through   V43 128 672A
V43 128 817A   through   V43 128 828A
V43 128 901A   through   V43 128 912A
V43 129 153A   through   V43 128 164A

SERIES 1935A MULE

V43 128 037A   through   V43 128 048A

SERIES 1935A NORTH AFRICA
Yellow Seal
Value $4,500.

F41 952 007C through F41 952 012C left half
F41 954 005C through F41 954 010C right half
F41 952 019C through F41 952 024C left half
F41 954 017C through F41 954 022C right half
F41 952 031C through F41 952 036C left half
F41 954 029C through F41 954 034C right half
F41 952 049C through F41 952 054C left half
F41 954 047C through F41 954 052C right half
F41 952 067C through F41 952 072C left half
F41 954 065C through F41 954 070C right half
F41 952 085C through F41 952 090C left half
F41 954 083C through F41 954 088C right half
F41 952 091C through F41 952 096C left half
F41 954 089C through F41 954 094C right half
F41 952 211C through F41 952 216C left half
F41 954 209C through F41 954 215C right half
F41 952 217C through F41 952 222C left half

F41 954 215C through F41 954 220C right half
F41 952 223C through F41 952 228C left half
F41 954 221C through F41 954 226C right half
F41 952 229C through F41 952 234C left half
F41 954 227C through F41 954 232C right half
F41 952 253C through F41 952 258C left half
F41 954 251C through F41 954 256C right half
F41 952 265C through F41 952 270C left half
F41 954 263C through F41 954 268C right half
F41 952 271C through F41 952 276C left half
F41 954 269C through F41 954 274C right half

SILVER CERTIFICATE
Brown Seal

SERIES 1935A HAWAII
Value $4,000.

F41 964 077C through F41 964 012C left half
F41 966 005C through F41 966 010C right half
F41 964 013C through F41 964 018C left half
F41 966 011C through F41 966 016C right half
F41 964 019C through F41 964 024C left half
F41 966 017C through F41 966 022C right half
F41 964 025C through F41 964 030C left half
F41 966 023C through F41 966 028C right half
F41 964 037C through F41 964 042C left half
F41 966 035C through F41 966 040C right half
F41 964 043C through F41 964 048C left half
F41 966 041C through F41 966 046C right half
F41 964 055C through F41 964 060C left half
F41 966 053C through F41 966 058C right half
F41 964 061C through F41 964 066C left half
F41 966 059C through F41 966 064C right half
F41 964 067C through F41 964 072C left half
F41 966 065C through F41 966 070C right half
F41 964 079C through F41 964 084C left half
F41 966 077C through F41 966 082C right half
F41 964 103C through F41 964 108C left half
F41 966 101C through F41 966 106C right half
F41 964 127C through F41 964 132C left half
F41 966 125C through F41 966 130C right half
F41 964 151C through F41 964 156C left half
F41 966 149C through F41 966 154C right half
F41 964 211C through F41 964 216C left half
F41 966 209C through F41 966 214C right half
F41 964 229C through F41 964 234C left half
F41 966 227C through F41 966 232C right half
F41 964 235C through F41 964 240C left half
F41 966 233C through F41 966 238C right half
F41 964 283C through F41 964 288C left half
F41 966 201C through F41 966 286C right half
F41 964 301C through F41 964 306C left half
F41 966 399C through F41 966 304C right half
F41 964 313C through F41 964 318C left half
F41 966 311C through F41 966 316C right half
F41 964 325C through F41 964 330C left half
F41 966 323C through F41 966 328C right half

SILVER CERTIFICATE
Blue Seal

SERIES 1935B
Value $2,000.

C93 384 073D   through   C93 384 084D
C93 384 097D   through   C93 384 008D
C93 384 157D   through   C93 384 168D
C93 384 301D   through   C93 384 312D

C93 384 313D	through	C93 384 324D
C93 384 325D	through	C93 384 336D
C93 384 337D	through	C93 384 348D
C93 384 349D	through	C93 384 360D
C93 384 361D	through	C93 384 372D
C93 384 433D	through	C93 384 444D
C93 384 493D	through	C93 384 504D
C93 384 517D	through	C93 384 528D
C93 384 541D	through	C93 384 552D
C93 384 553D	through	C93 384 564D
C93 384 589D	through	C93 384 600D
C93 384 625D	through	C93 384 636D
C93 384 637D	through	C93 384 648D
C93 384 697D	through	C93 384 709D
C93 384 799D	through	C93 384 720D
C93 384 877D	through	C93 384 888D
C93 384 841D	through	C93 384 852D
C93 384 877D	through	C93 384 888D
C93 384 961D	through	C93 384 972D
C93 385 009D	through	C93 385 020D
C93 385 021D	through	C93 385 032D
C93 385 069D	through	C93 385 080D
C93 385 141D	through	C93 385 152D
C93 385 177D	through	C93 385 188D

SERIES 1935C
Value $1,500.

K99 996 265D	through	K99 996 276D
K99 996 289D	through	K99 996 300D
K99 996 313D	through	K99 996 324D
K99 996 326D	through	K99 996 336D
K99 996 349D	through	K99 996 360D
K99 996 361D	through	K99 996 372D
K99 996 373D	through	K99 996 384D
K99 996 385D	through	K99 996 396D
K99 996 409D	through	K99 996 420D
K99 996 433D	through	K99 996 444D
K99 996 457D	through	K99 996 468D
K99 996 529D	through	K99 996 540D
K99 996 541D	through	K99 996 552D
K99 996 565D	through	K99 996 576D
K99 996 577D	through	K99 996 588D
K99 996 589D	through	K99 996 600D
K99 996 613D	through	K99 996 624D
K99 996 637D	through	K99 996 648D
K99 996 661D	through	K99 996 672D
K99 996 685D	through	K99 996 696D
K99 996 757D	through	K99 996 768D
K99 996 781D	through	K99 996 792D
K99 996 817D	through	K99 996 828D
K99 996 853D	through	K99 996 864D
K99 996 865D	through	K99 996 876D
K99 996 889D	through	K99 996 900D
K99 996 925D	through	K99 996 936D
K99 996 973D	through	K99 996 984D

SERIES 1935D
12 Subject Sheet
Value $1,000.

R88 104 637E	through	R88 104 648E

R88 104 676E	through	R88 104 684E
R88 104 697E	through	R88 104 708E
R88 104 733E	through	R88 104 744E
R88 104 769E	through	R88 104 780E
R88 104 793E	through	R88 104 804E
R88 104 841E	through	R88 104 852E
R88 104 865E	through	R88 104 876E
R88 104 961E	through	R88 104 972E
R88 104 081E	through	R88 104 092E
R88 104 129E	through	R88 104 140E
R88 104 177E	through	R88 104 188E
R88 104 180E	through	R88 104 200E
Z33 324 073E	through	Z33 324 084E
Z33 324 085E	through	Z33 324 096E
Z33 324 325E	through	Z33 324 336E
Z33 324 373E	through	Z33 324 384E
Z33 324 493E	through	Z33 324 504E
Z33 324 505E	through	Z33 324 516E
Z33 324 697E	through	Z33 324 708E
Z33 324 769E	through	Z33 324 780E
Z33 324 781E	through	Z33 324 792E
Z33 324 829E	through	Z33 324 840E
Z33 324 985E	through	Z33 324 996E
Z33 324 853E	through	Z33 324 864E
Z33 324 021E	through	Z33 324 032E
Z33 324 045E	through	Z33 324 056E
Z33 324 153E	through	Z33 324 164E
Z33 324 325E	through	Z33 324 336E
B05 520 049G	through	B05 520 060G
B05 520 337G	through	B05 520 348G
B05 520 361G	through	B05 520 372G
B05 520 505G	through	B05 520 516G
B05 520 601G	through	B05 520 612G
B05 520 709G	through	B05 520 720G
B05 520 733G	through	B05 520 744G
B05 520 745G	through	B05 520 756G
B05 520 757G	through	B05 520 768G
B05 520 769G	through	B05 520 780G
B05 520 793G	through	B05 520 804G
B05 520 817G	through	B05 520 829G
B05 520 889G	through	B05 520 900G
B05 520 997G	through	B05 521 008G
B05 521 033G	through	B05 521 044G
B05 521 105G	through	B05 521 116G
B05 521 117G	through	B05 521 128G
B05 521 129G	through	B05 521 140G
B05 521 141G	through	B05 521 152G
B05 521 153G	through	B05 521 164G
B05 521 165G	through	B05 521 176G

SILVER CERTIFICATE
Blue Seal

SERIES 1935D
18 Subject Sheets
Value $1,750.

G00 000 011G	through	G00 136 011G
G00 000 012G	through	G00 136 012G
G00 000 013G	through	G00 136 013G
G00 000 014G	through	G00 136 014G

G00 000 015G	through	G00 136 015G	R95 040 035G	through	R95 176 035G
G00 000 016G	through	G00 136 016G	R95 040 036G	through	R95 176 036G
G00 000 017G	through	G00 136 017G	R95 040 037G	through	R95 176 037G
G00 000 018G	through	G00 136 018G	R95 040 048G	through	R95 176 048G
G00 000 019G	through	G00 136 019G	R95 040 063G	through	R95 176 063G
G00 000 020G	through	G00 136 020G	R95 040 072G	through	R95 176 072G
G00 000 021G	through	G00 136 021G	R95 040 076G	through	R95 176 076G
G00 000 025G	through	G00 136 025G	R95 040 083G	through	R95 176 083G
G00 000 053G	through	G00 136 053G	R95 040 093G	through	R95 176 093G
G00 000 055G	through	G00 136 055G	R95 040 095G	through	R95 176 095G
G00 000 056G	through	G00 136 056G	R95 040 096G	through	R95 176 096G
G00 000 057G	through	G00 136 057G	R95 040 097G	through	R95 176 097G
G00 000 058G	through	G00 136 058G	U75 168 010G	through	U75 304 010G
G00 000 059G	through	G00 136 059G	U75 168 012G	through	U75 304 012G
G00 000 060G	through	G00 136 060G	U75 168 018G	through	U75 304 018G
G00 000 070G	through	G00 136 070G	U75 168 029G	through	U75 304 029G
G00 000 072G	through	G00 136 072G	U75 168 030G	through	U75 304 030G
G00 000 073G	through	G00 136 073G	U75 168 043G	through	U75 304 043G
G00 000 078G	through	G00 136 078G	U75 168 055G	through	U75 304 055G
G00 000 080G	through	G00 136 080G	U75 168 056G	through	U75 304 056G
G00 000 085G	through	G00 136 085G	U75 168 062G	through	U75 304 062G
G00 000 086G	through	G00 136 086G	U75 168 067G	through	U75 304 067G
G00 000 087G	through	G00 136 087G	U75 168 069G	through	U75 304 069G
G00 000 088G	through	G00 136 088G	U75 168 089G	through	U75 304 089G
G00 000 089G	through	G00 136 089G	U75 168 090G	through	U75 304 090G
G00 000 090G	through	G00 136 090G	X31 680 002G	through	X31 816 001G
G00 000 092G	through	G00 136 092G	X31 680 013G	through	X31 816 013G
G00 000 097G	through	G00 136 097G	X31 680 038G	through	X31 816 038G
G00 000 099G	through	G00 136 099G			
G00 000 100G	through	G00 136 100G			

SERIES 1935E
18 Subject Sheet
Value $1,000.

FEDERAL RESERVE NOTE
Green Seal

SERIES 1981
32 Subject Sheets

N46 944 006G	through	N47 080 006G	A99 840 001A	through	A99 999 999A
N46 944 013G	through	N47 080 013G	A99 840 001B	through	A99 999 999B
N46 944 018G	through	N47 080 018G	A99 840 001C	through	A99 999 999C
N46 944 026G	through	N47 080 026G	A99 840 001D	through	A99 999 999D
N46 944 027G	through	N47 080 027G	A99 840 001E	through	A99 999 999E
N46 944 031G	through	N47 080 031G	A99 840 001F	through	A99 999 999F
N46 944 032G	through	N47 080 032G	A99 840 001G	through	A99 999 999G
N46 944 033G	through	N47 080 033G	A99 840 001H	through	A99 999 999H
N46 944 037G	through	N47 080 037G	B99 843 875I	through	B99 845 000I
N46 944 044G	through	N47 080 044G	C99 843 875A	through	C99 845 000A
N46 944 045G	through	N47 080 045G	D99 840 001A	through	D10 000 000A
N46 944 046G	through	N47 080 046G	D99 840 001B	through	D10 000 000B
N46 944 057G	through	N47 080 057G	D99 840 001C	through	D10 000 000C
N46 944 058G	through	N47 080 058G	D99 840 001D	through	D10 000 000D
N46 944 059G	through	N47 080 059G	D99 840 001E	through	D10 000 000E
N46 944 064G	through	N47 080 064G	D99 840 001F	through	D10 000 000F
N46 944 079G	through	N47 080 079G	D99 840 001G	through	D10 000 000G
R95 040 003G	through	R95 176 003G	D99 840 001H	through	D10 000 000H
R95 040 010G	through	R95 176 010G	E99 840 001A	through	E10 000 000A
R95 040 019G	through	R95 176 019G	E99 840 001B	through	E10 000 000B
R95 040 044G	through	R95 176 044G	E99 840 001C	through	E10 000 000C
R95 040 079G	through	R95 176 079G	E99 840 001D	through	E10 000 000D
N46 944 085G	through	N47 080 085G	E99 840 001E	through	E10 000 000E
N46 944 793G	through	N47 080 793G	E99 840 001F	through	E10 000 000F
R95 040 018G	through	R95 176 018G	E99 840 001G	through	E10 000 000G
R95 040 034G	through	R95 176 034G	F99 843 875A	through	F99 845 000A

G99 843 875A	through	G99 845 000A
H99 843 875E	through	H99 845 000E
I99 843 875A	through	I99 845 000A
J99 843 875A	through	J99 845 000A
K99 843 875A	through	K99 845 000A
L99 843 875A	through	L99 845 000A

SERIES 1981A

B99 840 001B	through	B10 000 000A
C99 840 001B	through	C10 000 000B
F99 840 001B	through	F10 000 000C
G99 840 001B	through	G10 000 000D
H99 840 001B	through	H10 000 000E
I99 840 001B	through	I10 000 000F
J99 840 001B	through	J10 000 000G
K99 840 001B	through	K10 000 000H
L99 840 001B	through	L10 000 000A

SERIES 1985

A99 840 001A	through	A99 999 999A
A99 776 001B	through	A99 999 999B
A99 904 001C	through	A99 999 999C
B99 840 001A	through	B99 999 999A
B99 776 001B	through	B99 999 999B
B99 904 001C	through	B99 999 999C
C99 840 001A	through	C10 000 000A
C99 776 001B	through	C99 999 999B
C99 904 001C	through	C99 999 999C
D99 840 001A	through	D99 999 999A
D99 776 001B	through	D99 999 999B
D99 904 001C	through	D99 999 999C
E99 840 001A	through	E99 999 999A
E99 776 001B	through	E99 999 999B
E99 904 001C	through	E99 999 999C
F99 840 001A	through	F99 999 999A
F99 776 001B	through	F99 999 999B
F99 904 001C	through	F99 999 999C
F99 904 001D	through	F99 999 999D
F99 840 001E	through	F99 999 999E
G99 840 001A	through	G99 999 999A
G99 776 001B	through	G99 999 999B
G99 904 001C	through	G99 999 999C
H99 840 001A	through	H99 999 999A
H99 776 001B	through	H99 999 999B
H99 904 001C	through	H99 999 999C
H99 776 001D	through	H99 999 999D
I99 840 001A	through	I99 999 999A
I99 776 001B	through	I99 999 999B
I99 904 001C	through	I99 999 999C
I99 776 001D	through	I99 999 999D
J99 840 001A	through	J99 999 999A
J99 776 001B	through	J99 999 999B

J99 904 001C	through	J99 999 999C
J99 904 001D	through	J99 999 999D
K99 840 001A	through	K99 999 999A
K99 776 001B	through	K99 999 999B
K99 904 001C	through	K99 999 999C
L99 840 001A	through	L99 999 999A
L99 776 001B	through	L99 999 999B
L99 904 001C	through	L99 999 999C

SERIES 1988

A99 904 001A	through	A99 999 999A
B99 904 001A	through	B99 999 999A
C99 904 001A	through	C99 999 999A
D99 904 001A	through	D99 999 999A
E99 904 001A	through	E99 999 999A
F99 904 001A	through	F99 999 999A
G99 904 001A	through	G99 999 999A
H99 904 001A	through	H99 999 999A
H99 904 001B	through	H99 999 999B
I99 904 001A	through	H99 999 999A
J99 904 001A	through	J99 999 999A
K99 904 001A	through	K99 999 999A
L99 904 001A	through	L99 999 999A

UNCUT HALF SHEETS

Green Seal

SERIES 1981

16 Subject Sheets

B99 840 001A	through	B99 999 999A
B99 840 001B	through	B99 999 999B
B99 840 001C	through	B99 999 999C
B99 840 001D	through	B99 999 999D
B99 840 001E	through	B10 000 000E
B99 840 001F	through	B10 000 000F
B99 840 001G	through	B10 000 000G
B99 840 001H	through	B10 000 000H
B99 842 750I	through	B99 843 875I
C99 842 750A	through	C99 843 875A
F99 842 750A	through	F99 843 875A
G99 842 750A	through	G99 843 875A
H99 840 001A	through	H10 000 000A
H99 840 001B	through	H10 000 000B
H99 840 001C	through	H10 000 000C
H99 840 001D	through	H10 000 000D
H99 842 750E	through	H99 843 875E
I99 842 750A	through	I99 843 875A
J99 842 750A	through	J99 843 875A
K99 842 750A	through	K99 843 875A
L99 842 750A	through	L99 843 875A

TWO DOLLARS

LEGAL TENDER
Red Seal

SERIES 1928
12 Subject Sheets
Value $5,000.

A00 000 037A	through	A00 000 048A
A00 000 049A	through	A00 000 060A

SERIES 1928A
None known

SERIES 1928B
None known

SERIES 1928C
Value $1,750.

B09 012 001A	through	B09 012 012A
B09 012 013A	through	B09 012 024A
B09 012 037A	through	B09 012 048A
B09 012 049A	through	B09 012 048A
B09 012 073A	through	B09 012 060A
B09 012 097A	through	B09 012 084A
B09 012 157A	through	B09 012 168A
B09 012 181A	through	B09 012 192A
B09 012 217A	through	B09 012 228A
B09 012 229A	through	B09 012 240A
B09 012 253A	through	B09 012 264A
B09 012 277A	through	B09 012 288A
B83 988 013A	through	B83 988 024A
B83 988 085A	through	B83 988 096A
B83 988 108A	through	B83 988 120A
B83 988 121A	through	B83 988 132A
B83 988 145A	through	B83 988 156A
B83 988 157A	through	B83 988 168A
B83 988 181A	through	B83 988 192A
B83 988 253A	through	B83 988 264A
B83 988 373A	through	B83 988 384A
B83 988 397A	through	B83 988 408A
B83 988 409A	through	B83 988 420A
B83 988 457A	through	B83 988 468A
B83 988 469A	through	B83 988 480A
B83 988 481A	through	B83 988 492A
B83 988 493A	through	B83 988 504A

SERIES 1928D
None known

SERIES 1928E
Value $1,200.

D35 532 001A	through	D35 532 012A
D35 532 013A	through	D35 532 024A
D35 532 037A	through	D35 532 048A
D35 532 061A	through	D35 532 072A
D35 532 073A	through	D35 532 084A
D35 532 085A	through	D35 532 096A
D35 532 133A	through	D35 532 144A
D35 532 145A	through	D35 532 156A
D35 532 157A	through	D35 532 168A
D35 532 169A	through	D35 532 180A
D35 532 193A	through	D35 532 204A
D35 532 205A	through	D35 532 216A
D35 532 229A	through	D35 532 240A
D35 532 241A	through	D35 532 252A
D35 532 289A	through	D35 532 300A
D35 532 301A	through	D35 532 312A
D35 532 349A	through	D35 532 360A
D35 532 361A	through	D35 532 372A
D35 532 385A	through	D35 532 396A
D35 532 397A	through	D35 532 408A
D35 532 409A	through	D35 532 420A
D35 532 433A	through	D35 532 444A
D35 532 445A	through	D35 532 456A
D35 532 469A	through	D35 532 480A
D35 532 481A	through	D35 532 492A
D35 532 493A	through	D35 532 504A
D35 532 541A	through	D35 532 552A

SERIES 1928F
Value $1,200.

D39 552 001A	through	D39 552 012A
D39 552 013A	through	D39 552 024A
D39 552 025A	through	D39 552 036A
D39 552 037A	through	D39 552 048A
D39 552 073A	through	D39 552 084A
D39 552 061A	through	D39 552 072A
D39 552 097A	through	D39 552 108A
D39 552 145A	through	D39 552 156A
D39 552 169A	through	D39 552 180A
D39 552 181A	through	D39 552 192A
D39 552 241A	through	D39 552 252A
D39 552 265A	through	D39 552 276A
D39 552 277A	through	D39 552 288A
D39 552 313A	through	D39 552 324A
D39 552 337A	through	D39 552 348A
D39 552 373A	through	D39 552 384A
D39 552 397A	through	D39 552 408A
D39 552 553A	through	D39 552 564A
D39 552 721A	through	D39 552 732A
D39 552 937A	through	D39 552 948A
D39 552 961A	through	D39 552 972A
D39 553 033A	through	D39 553 044A
D39 553 069A	through	D39 553 080A

SERIES 1928G
Value $1,000.

E07 704 037A	through	E07 704 048A
E07 704 073A	through	E07 704 084A
E07 704 097A	through	E07 704 108A
E07 704 145A	through	E07 704 156A
E07 704 169A	through	E07 704 180A
E07 704 181A	through	E07 704 192A
E07 704 193A	through	E07 704 204A
E07 704 229A	through	E07 704 240A
E07 704 325A	through	E07 704 336A
E07 704 481A	through	E07 704 492A

E07 704 493A	through	E07 704 504A
E07 704 541A	through	E07 704 552A
E07 704 649A	through	E07 704 660A
E07 704 661A	through	E07 704 672A
E07 704 709A	through	E07 704 720A
E07 704 781A	through	E07 704 792A
E07 704 829A	through	E07 704 840A
E07 704 841A	through	E07 704 852A
E07 704 853A	through	E07 704 864A
E07 704 877A	through	E07 704 888A
E07 704 961A	through	E07 704 972A
E07 704 973A	through	E07 704 984A
E07 704 985A	through	E07 704 996A
E07 705 021A	through	E07 705 032A
E07 705 057A	through	E07 705 068A
E07 705 117A	through	E07 705 128A
E07 705 177A	through	E07 705 188A
E07 705 189A	through	E07 705 200A

SERIES 1953
18 Subject Sheets
Value $1,750.

A00 000 028A	through	A00 136 028A
A00 000 032A	through	A00 136 032A
A00 000 034A	through	A00 136 034A
A00 000 039A	through	A00 136 039A
A00 000 040A	through	A00 136 040A
A00 000 041A	through	A00 136 041A
A00 000 043A	through	A00 136 043A
A00 000 045A	through	A00 136 045A
A00 000 048A	through	A00 136 048A
A00 000 051A	through	A00 136 051A
A00 000 052A	through	A00 136 052A
A00 000 053A	through	A00 136 053A
A00 000 055A	through	A00 136 055A
A00 000 058A	through	A00 136 058A
A00 000 062A	through	A00 136 062A
A00 000 063A	through	A00 136 063A
A00 000 067A	through	A00 136 067A

A00 000 071A	through	A00 136 071A
A00 000 073A	through	A00 136 073A
A00 000 074A	through	A00 136 074A
A00 000 078A	through	A00 136 078A
A00 000 079A	through	A00 136 079A
A00 000 080A	through	A00 136 080A
A00 000 084A	through	A00 136 084A
A00 000 087A	through	A00 136 087A

SERIES 1976
16 Subject Sheets

A00 015 001★	through	A00 640 000★

SERIES 1976
32 Subject Sheets

A00 640 001★	through	A00 960 000★
A00 960 001★	through	A01 273 400★
A01 273 401★	through	A01 280 000★
A00 015 001★	through	A00 640 000★
A00 960 001★	through	A01 273 400★
A00 960 001★	through	A01 273 400★
(16 note sheet)		
C00 002 001★	through	C01 280 000★
D00 064 001★	through	D00 960 000★
D00 963 001★	through	D01 264 000★
F00 648 001★	through	F01 280 000★
F01 140 001★	through	F02 280 000★
F00 972 897★	through	F01 277 600★
G00 040 046★	through	G00 948 494★
H00 640 001★	through	H01 280 000★
H00 645 001★	through	H00 750 000★
H00 750 001★	through	H01 280 000★
K00 644 001★	through	K01 266 600★
K00 652 001★	through	K01 278 500★
K00 646 601★	through	K01 262 452★
K00 652 001★	through	K01 278 500★
L01 280 001★	through	L01 920 000★

FIVE DOLLARS

SILVER CERTIFICATE
Blue Seal

SERIES 1934
Value $2,000.

A00 000 013A	through	A00 000 024A
A00 000 025A	through	A00 000 036A
A00 000 049A	through	A00 000 060A
A00 000 061A	through	A00 000 072A
A00 000 073A	through	A00 000 084A
A00 000 084A	through	A00 000 096A
A00 000 097A	through	A00 000 108A
A00 000 157A	through	A00 000 168A
A00 000 169A	through	A00 000 180A
A00 000 217A	through	A00 000 228A
A00 000 229A	through	A00 000 240A
A00 000 265A	through	A00 000 276A
A00 000 289A	through	A00 000 300A

SERIES 1934A
None known

SERIES 1934B
Value $3,500.

L27 456 001A	through	L27 456 012A
L27 456 013A	through	L27 456 024A
L27 456 049A	through	L27 456 060A
L27 456 097A	through	L27 456 108A
L27 456 121A	through	L27 456 132A
L27 456 157A	through	L27 456 168A
L27 456 169A	through	L27 456 180A
L27 456 193A	through	L27 456 204A
L27 456 217A	through	L27 456 228A
L27 456 229A	through	L27 456 240A

SERIES 1934C
Value $2,000.

L50 808 001A	through	L50 808 012A
L50 808 013A	through	L50 808 024A
L50 808 037A	through	L50 808 048A
L50 808 049A	through	L50 808 060A
L50 808 061A	through	L50 808 072A
L50 808 073A	through	L50 808 084A
L50 808 085A	through	L50 808 096A
L50 808 097A	through	L50 808 108A
L50 808 133A	through	L50 808 144A
L50 808 157A	through	L50 808 168A

SERIES 1934D
Value $1,750.

Q71 628 001A	through	Q71 628 012A
Q71 628 013A	through	Q71 628 024A
Q71 628 025A	through	Q71 628 036A
Q71 628 037A	through	Q71 628 048A
Q71 628 085A	through	Q71 628 096A
Q71 628 193A	through	Q71 628 204A
Q71 628 205A	through	Q71 628 216A
Q71 628 373A	through	Q71 628 384A
Q71 628 397A	through	Q71 628 408A
Q71 628 409A	through	Q71 628 420A
Q71 628 445A	through	Q71 628 456A
Q71 628 457A	through	Q71 628 468A
Q71 628 469A	through	Q71 628 480A
Q71 628 541A	through	Q71 628 552A
Q71 628 601A	through	Q71 628 612A
Q71 628 649A	through	Q71 628 660A
Q71 628 721A	through	Q71 628 732A
Q71 628 829A	through	Q71 628 840A
Q71 628 961A	through	Q71 628 972A
Q71 628 973A	through	Q71 628 984A
Q71 628 997A	through	Q71 629 008A
Q71 629 021A	through	Q71 629 032A
Q71 629 033A	through	Q71 629 044A
Q71 629 045A	through	Q71 629 056A
Q71 629 057A	through	Q71 629 068A
Q71 629 177A	through	Q71 629 188A

SERIES 1953
18 Subject Sheets
Value $2,000.

A00 000 027A	through	A00 136 027A
A00 000 029A	through	A00 136 029A
A00 000 030A	through	A00 136 030A
A00 000 031A	through	A00 136 031A
A00 000 032A	through	A00 136 032A
A00 000 036A	through	A00 136 036A
A00 000 037A	through	A00 136 037A
A00 000 039A	through	A00 136 039A
A00 000 050A	through	A00 136 050A
A00 000 052A	through	A00 136 052A
A00 000 055A	through	A00 136 055A
A00 000 057A	through	A00 136 057A
A00 000 058A	through	A00 136 058A
A00 000 059A	through	A00 136 059A
A00 000 060A	through	A00 136 060A
A00 000 063A	through	A00 136 063A
A00 000 067A	through	A00 136 067A
A00 000 069A	through	A00 136 069A
A00 000 070A	through	A00 136 070A
A00 000 075A	through	A00 136 075A
A00 000 079A	through	A00 136 079A

LEGAL TENDER
Red Seal
12 Subject Sheets

SERIES 1928
Value $7,500.

A00 000 049A	through	A00 000 060A

SERIES 1928A
None known

SERIES 1928B
None known

SERIES 1928C
None known

SERIES 1928D
Value $3,000.

G58 956 001A	through	G58 956 012A
G58 956 013A	through	G58 956 024A
G58 956 025A	through	G58 956 036A
G58 956 037A	through	G58 956 048A
G58 956 061A	through	G58 956 072A
G58 956 073A	through	G58 956 084A
G58 956 109A	through	G58 956 120A
G58 956 121A	through	G58 956 132A
G58 956 145A	through	G58 956 156A
G58 956 169A	through	G58 956 180A
G58 956 205A	through	G58 956 216A
G58 956 217A	through	G58 956 228A
G58 956 241A	through	G58 956 252A
G58 956 253A	through	G58 956 264A
G58 956 277A	through	G58 956 288A

SERIES 1928E
Value $1,500.

G68 352 001A	through	G68 352 012A
G68 352 013A	through	G68 352 024A
G68 352 037A	through	G68 352 048A
G68 352 061A	through	G68 352 072A
G68 352 073A	through	G68 352 084A
G68 352 109A	through	G68 352 120A
G68 352 121A	through	G68 352 132A
G68 352 145A	through	G68 352 156A
G68 352 169A	through	G68 352 180A
G68 352 205A	through	G68 352 216A
G68 352 217A	through	G68 352 228A
G68 352 241A	through	G68 352 252A
G68 352 253A	through	G68 352 264A
G68 352 277A	through	G68 352 288A
G68 352 337A	through	G68 352 348A

SERIES 1953
18 Subject Sheets
Value $2,200.

A00 000 031A	through	A00 136 031A
A00 000 032A	through	A00 136 032A
A00 000 033A	through	A00 136 033A
A00 000 035A	through	A00 136 035A
A00 000 040A	through	A00 136 040A
A00 000 044A	through	A00 136 044A
A00 000 046A	through	A00 136 046A
A00 000 053A	through	A00 136 053A
A00 000 055A	through	A00 136 055A
A00 000 056A	through	A00 136 056A
A00 000 057A	through	A00 136 057A
A00 000 058A	through	A00 136 058A
A00 000 059A	through	A00 136 059A
A00 000 060A	through	A00 136 060A

FEDERAL RESERVE NOTES
Green Seal
12 Subject Sheets

SERIES 1928
Value $7,500.

C00 000 025A	through	C00 000 036A
G00 000 037A	through	G00 000 048A
K00 000 013A	through	K00 000 024A
K00 000 025A	through	K00 000 036A

SERIES 1928B
Value $10,000.

I04 692 049A	through	I04 692 060A

SERIES 1928C
Value $10,000.

L50 808 133A	through	L50 808 144A

TEN DOLLARS

FEDERAL RESERVE NOTES
Brown Seal

SERIES 1929
Value $20,000.

B00 000 085A	through	B00 000 096A
B00 000 097A	through	B00 000 108A

SERIES 1928
Green Seal
Value $12,000.

B00 000 073A	through	B00 000 084A
C00 000 013A	through	C00 000 024A
C00 000 025A	through	C00 000 048A
G00 000 037A	through	G00 000 048A
I02 760 049A	through	I02 760 060A
K00 000 013A	through	K00 000 024A

SILVER CERTIFICATE
Blue Seal

SERIES 1934
Value $4,500.

A00 000 013A	through	A00 000 024A
A00 000 024A	through	A00 000 036A
A00 000 037A	through	A00 000 048A
A00 000 061A	through	A00 000 072A

A00 000 072A	through	A00 000 084A
A00 000 085A	through	A00 000 096A
A00 000 108A	through	A00 000 120A

SERIES 1953
Value $5,000.

A00 000 030A	through	A00 136 030A
A00 000 033A	through	A00 136 033A
A00 000 034A	through	A00 136 034A
A00 000 038A	through	A00 136 038A
A00 000 043A	through	A00 136 043A
A00 000 047A	through	A00 136 047A
A00 000 049A	through	A00 136 049A
A00 000 050A	through	A00 136 050A
A00 000 051A	through	A00 136 051A
A00 000 052A	through	A00 136 052A
A00 000 055A	through	A00 136 055A

TWENTY DOLLARS

FEDERAL RESERVE NOTES
Green Seal

SERIES 1928
12 Subject Sheet
Value $9,000.

C00 000 001A	through	C00 000 012A
C00 000 037A	through	C00 000 048A
G00 000 037A	through	G00 000 048A
I01 800 037A	through	I01 800 048A

ONE HUNDRED DOLLARS
LEGAL TENDER

Red Seal

SERIES 1966

★00 000 161A through ★00 002 161A

This sheet is on permanent loan to the American Numismatic Association and is on display at the Headquarters in Colorado Springs, Colorado.

CHANGEOVER PAIRS

Technically speaking, Changeover pairs, sometimes called hold-over or cross-over pairs should be the highest serial number of one series and the lowest serial number of the following series OF THE SAME DENOMINATION AND CLASS of note. Hence a $1.00 legal tender note Series 1928 could not be coupled with the next higher serial number of a 1928A $1.00 silver certificate and qualify as a changeover note. Also the $5 FRN could not be coupled with the $5 legal tender and fit the criteria of a changeover pair. Pairs of notes where the serial number is higher on the earlier series have been marginally accepted by collectors as so-called changeover pairs - but are referred to as REVERSE CHANGEOVERS.

During the early years (1928-1935) of printing the current size notes, because of the high cost of the engraved plates, and because the signatures were engraved IN the plates, it was customary for the Bureau of Engraving and Printing to use the plates long after the official whose signature appeared in the plate had left office. The result of this practice was that several series were being face printed simultaneously. When a stack of one series was placed on top of another series and sent to the third (serial number) printing, then consecutive numbered notes of different series were produced. An examination of the plate record card usage in BEP indicates quite a number of cases where several series were being printed on the same day. This is substantiated by the existence of known pairs of notes with consecutive serial numbers in various series combinations. For the $1.00 silver certificate for example, we know that both the 1928 and 1928A series were face printed on the same day. When these stacks were mixed and sent to the third printing, changeover pairs were - sometimes in proper sequence - sometimes in reverse sequence. We know also that 28A/28B, 28A/28C, 28A/28D, 28A/28E, 28B/28C, 28B/28D, 28B/28E, 28C/28D, 28C/28E and 28D/28E were run simultaneously, hence we know of or suspect changeover pairs in all of these combinations. For the $2.00 legal tender we know that Series 1928C/D/E/F were being printed simultaneously and again, we know of or suspect of all of those combinations. The $5.00 FRN Series 1934 through 1934D and the $5.00 silver certificate Series 1934 through 1934D were printed simultaneously, and finally we know that the $5.00 legal tender Series 1928D, E and F were face printed simultaneously. Higher denominations too numerous to mention were also printed as is confirmed by the existence of one or more changeover pairs presently known.

Because the wide and narrow backs of the $1.00 silver certificate Series 1935D are found intermingled in packs, changeover pairs of the variety are known in practically all blocks. Because of the relatively high number of changeover pairs in this series no census is attempted.

And finally, in the current $1.00 FRN (and higher denominations as well), while NOT being printed concurrently, some of the more astute collectors have managed to get the same serial number packs for consecutive series, and by matching the serial number of the earlier series with the next higher serial number of the later series, have created valid changeover pairs. This of course can be done with any series and any denomination if one worked hard enough at it - or was lucky enough to stumble up on the right combination of packs of notes.

While collectors have accepted as changeovers "skip" series, that is consecutive serial numbers on the 28A-28E or 28B-28D despite the fact other series were printed in between, we doubt that collectors would accept a skip in series for current FRN's EXCEPT where NO notes were printed in the intervening series. NO notes were printed for the $1.00 FRN Boston for Series 1969C-hence consecutive serial numbered notes for Boston Series 1969B/1969D would qualify as so-called changeover pairs.

Census of known changeover pairs follows, the author earnestly solicits your assistance in reporting any changeover pairs (except the 1935D) not listed.

ONE DOLLAR

SILVER CERTIFICATES

Changeover Pairs

1928	H15 982 026A	1928A	H15 982 027A	250.00
	H15 982 062A		H15 982 063A	250.00
	H24 067 110A		H24 067 111A	250.00
	H31 865 568A		H31 865 569A	250.00
	H98 173 747A		H98 173 748A	250.00
	H99 279 259A		H99 279 258A	250.00
1928A	F98 281 830A	1928	F98 281 831A	125.00
	H15 982 056A		H15 982 057A	150.00
	G36 363 637A		G36 363 945A	150.00
	G52 576 944A		G52 576 955A	150.00
	G87 380 634A		G87 380 635A	150.00
	G99 279 258A		G99 279 259A	150.00
	H98 173 746A		H98 173 747A	250.00
1928A	X62 614 692A	1928B	X62 614 693A	125.00
	Y22 437 608A		Y22 437 609A	125.00
	Y22 726 056A		Y22 726 057A	125.00
	Y32 068 044A		Y32 068 045A	125.00
	Y77 437 620A		Y77 437 621A	125.00
	Y77 437 710A		Y77 437 711A	125.00
	Y83 044 722A		Y83 044 723A	125.00
	Y83 044 758A		Y98 044 759A	125.00
	Y91 160 196A		Y91 160 197A	125.00
	Y91 160 436A		Y91 160 437A	125.00
	A11 118 390B		A11 118 391B	125.00
	A11 118 390B		A11 118 391B	125.00
	B40 140 366B		B40 149 367B	125.00
	D33 000 702B		D33 000 703B	125.00
	E14 561 478B		E14 561 479B	125.00
	F17 863 118B		F17 863 119B	125.00
	F17 863 506B		F17 863 507B	125.00
	F17 863 554B		F17 863 555B	125.00
	F18 533 022B		F18 533 023B	125.00
	F22 934 106B		F22 934 107B	125.00
	F22 934 118B		F22 934 119B	125.00
	F22 934 130B		F22 934 131B	125.00
	F22 934 142B		F22 934 143B	125.00
	F22 934 154B		F22 934 155B	125.00
	F86 995 693B		F86 995 692B	125.00
	F86 995 698B		F86 995 699B	125.00
	G03 965 052B		G03 965 053B	125.00
	G08 974 296B		G08 974 297B	125.00
	G09 087 486B		G09 087 487B	125.00
	G10 848 366B		G10 848 367B	125.00
	G29 341 914B		G29 341 915B	125.00
	G30 587 748B		G30 587 749B	125.00
	G52 576 944B		G52 576 945B	125.00
	G65 105 172B		G65 105 173B	125.00
	G72 518 850B		G72 518 851B	125.00
	G84 460 114B		G84 450 115B	125.00
	G90 273 552B		G90 273 553B	125.00
	H14 303 748B		H14 303 749B	150.00
	H23 495 970B		H23 495 971B	150.00
	H27 375 438B		H27 275 439B	150.00
	H38 698 602B		H38 698 603B	150.00
	H38 698 608B		H38 698 609B	150.00
	H55 163 196B		H55 163 197B	150.00

	H59 559 198B		H59 559 199B	150.00
	H66 614 687B		H66 614 688B	150.00
	I04 760 386B		I04 760 387B	250.00
	★35 790 882A		★35 790 883A	250.00
1928A	★35 168 274A	1928C	★35 168 275A	3750.00
1928B	Y88 301 814A	1928A	Y88 301 815A	175.00
	A10 358 598B		A10 358 599B	150.00
	A53 342 832B		A53 342 833B	150.00
	B55 757 382B		B55 757 383B	150.00
	C37 209 018B		C37 209 019B	150.00
	C85 181 274B		C85 181 275B	150.00
	F22 934 112B		F22 934 113B	150.00
	F22 934 124B		F22 934 125B	150.00
	F22 934 148B		F22 934 149B	150.00
	F86 995 680B		F86 995 681B	150.00
	F86 995 692B		F86 995 693B	150.00
	F87 881 970B		F87 881 971B	150.00
	G03 152 376B		G03 152 377B	150.00
	G30 587 742B		G30 587 743B	150.00
	G85 881 970B		G85 881 971B	150.00
	H27 375 480B		H27 375 481B	150.00
	H53 342 832B		H53 342 833B	150.00
	H66 205 332B		H66 205 333B	150.00
	H66 205 356B		H66 205 357B	150.00
	H66 205 476B		H66 205 477B	150.00
	★34 169 982A		★34 169 983A	200.00
1928B	F03 430 794B	1928C	F03 430 795B	400.00
	F41 758 236B		F41 758 237B	400.00
	H10 183 452B		H10 183 453B	400.00
	H10 183 902B		H10 183 903B	400.00
	H45 843 084B		H45 843 085B	400.00
	H45 843 270B		H45 843 271B	400.00
	H45 843 288B		H45 843 289B	400.00
1928B	F48 461 562B	1928D	F48 461 563B	300.00
	H23 667 810B		H23 667 811B	250.00
	H30 383 910B		H30 383 911B	250.00
	H30 383 958B		H30 383 959B	250.00
	H69 719 366B		H69 719 367B	250.00
	H98 188 212B		H98 188 213B	250.00
	I39 766 404B		I39 766 405B	250.00
	I40 504 050B		I40 504 051B	250.00
	I40 504 110B		I40 504 111B	250.00
	I40 504 170B		I40 504 171B	250.00
	I40 504 308B		I40 504 309B	250.00
	I40 504 326B		I40 504 327B	250.00
	I40 504 440B		I40 504 441B	250.00
	I40 504 452B		I40 504 453B	250.00
	I40 504 470B		I40 504 471B	250.00
	I40 504 494B		I40 504 495B	250.00
	I40 504 992B		I40 504 993B	250.00
1928B	I26 386 926B	1928E	I26 386 927B	250.00
	I92 908 290B	1928E	I92 908 291B	1,000.00
1928C	H99 610 002B	1928B	H99 610 003B	350.00
	H99 610 020B		H99 610 021B	350.00
	H99 610 068B		H99 610 069B	350.00
	H99 610 068B		H99 610 069B	350.00
1928D	H69 717 360B	1928B	H69 717 361B	275.00
	H69 717 372B		H69 717 373B	275.00
	I45 994 416B		I45 994 417B	275.00
	I64 933 206B		I64 933 207B	275.00
1928D	H90 945 102B	1928C	H90 945 103B	500.00

1928D	I52 499 060**B**	1928E	I52 499 061**B**	1,500.00
1928E	I92 908 296**B**	1928B	I92 908 297**B**	1,300.00
1928E	I52 488 054**B**	1928D	I52 488 055**B**	1,400.00
1935	(with 1935 back)	1935	(with 1935A back)	MULE

Pairs of this variety are known in several block combinations. Estimated price would be approximately the sum of the individual blocks doubled.

| 1935A | (with 1935A back) | 1935A | (with 1935 back) | MULE |

Same as above.

| 1935D | wide | 1935D | narrow | |
| 1935D | narrow | 1935D | wide | |

Same as above. Pairs are known in all block combinations except U-E, G-G and N-G.

TWO DOLLARS
UNITED STATES NOTES

1928B	B05 689 638**A**	1928A	B05 689 639**A**	750.00
1928D	D30 112 512**A**	1928E	D30 112 513**A**	50.00
	D30 112 536**A**		D30 112 537**A**	150.00
	D30 112 896**A**		D30 112 897**A**	150.00
	D31 420 986**A**		D31 420 987**A**	150.00
	D32 341 014**A**		D32 341 015**A**	150.00
	D32 341 062**A**		D32 341 063**A**	150.00
	D32 341 132**A**		D32 341 133**A**	150.00
	D32 341 574**A**		D32 341 575**A**	150.00
	D32 342 574**A**		D32 342 575**A**	150.00
	D32 342 610**A**		D32 342 611**A**	150.00
	D32 342 730**A**		D32 342 731**A**	150.00
	D32 343 096**A**		D32 343 097**A**	150.00
	D32 343 132**A**		D32 343 133**A**	150.00
	D32 343 168**A**		D32 343 169**A**	150.00
	D32 343 192**A**		D32 343 193**A**	150.00
	D32 343 354**A**		D32 343 355**A**	150.00
	D32 343 378**A**		D32 343 379**A**	150.00
	D32 343 468**A**		D32 343 469**A**	150.00
	D32 343 480**A**		D32 343 481**A**	150.00
	D32 885 508**A**		D32 885 509**A**	150.00
	D33 598 896**A**		D33 598 897**A**	150.00
1928E	D30 112 260**A**	1928D	D30 112 261**A**	150.00
	D30 112 464**A**		D30 112 465**A**	150.00
	D30 112 548**A**		D30 112 549**A**	150.00
	D32 341 020**A**		D32 341 021**A**	150.00
	D32 342 778**A**		D32 342 779**A**	150.00
	D32 343 114**A**		D32 343 115**A**	150.00
	D32 343 162**A**		D32 343 163**A**	150.00
	D32 343 198**A**		D32 343 199**A**	150.00
	D33 599 862**A**		D33 599 863**A**	150.00
1928E	D39 591 132**A**	1928F	D39 591 133**A**	250.00
	D39 591 186**A**		D39 591 187**A**	250.00
1928F	D80 445 094**A**	1928G	D80 445 095**A**	200.00

FIVE DOLLARS
UNITED STATES NOTES

1928A	D01 359 498**A**	1928	D01 359 499**A**	300.00
1928B	E56 022 618**A**	1928C mule	E56 022 619**A**	250.00
1928B mule	E58 751 094**A**	1928C	E58 751 095**A**	250.00
	E65 171 952**A**		E65 171 953**A**	250.00
1928C	E65 171 958**A**	1928B mule	E65 171 959**A**	250.00
1928C	E81 416 388**A**	1928C mule	E81 416 389**A**	350.00
1928C mule	E65 171 946**A**	1928B mule	E65 171 947**A**	350.00
1928C mule	E81 416 328**A**	1928C	E81 416 329**A**	350.00

	E81 416 358A		E81 416 359A	350.00
1928C	G54 848 322A	1928D	G54 848 323A	250.00
1928D	G55 758 072A	1928C	G55 758 073A	250.00
1928D	G56 058 504A	1928E	G56 058 505A	250.00
1928E		1928F		250.00

(Reportedly one pair known, serials not reported.)

FIVE DOLLARS
SILVER CERTIFICATES

1934	D95 883 696A	1934A	D95 883 697A	200.00
1934	D72 791 016A	1934A mule	D72 791 017A	250.00
	D82 075 890A		D82 075 891A	250.00
	D95 883 624A		D95 883 625A	250.00
1934		1934 mule		
1934A		1934A mule		

Pairs of these varieties are known. Estimated price would be double the sum of the individual blocks.

1934A	B83 602 825B	1934B	B83 602 824B	200.00
	L06 718 356A		L06 718 357A	200.00
	L11 507 076A		L11 507 077A	200.00
	L12 976 266A		L12 976 267A	200.00
1934A mule	F11 487 672A	1934A	F11 487 673A	150.00
1934B	L50 330 556A	1934C	L50 330 557A	150.00
	L50 330 568A		L50 330 569A	150.00
	L51 477 228A		L51 477 229A	150.00
	L74 667 702A		L74 667 703A	150.00
	L80 808 066A		L80 808 067A	150.00
1934C	L80 808 060A	1934B	L80 808 061A	200.00
	L86 524 098A		L86 524 099A	200.00
	M30 229 668A		M30 229 669A	500.00
	Q47 622 414A		Q47 622 415A	200.00
1934C	Q47 482 265A	1934D	Q47 482 266A	150.00
	Q48 088 626A		Q48 088 627A	150.00
	Q48 088 674A		Q48 088 675A	150.00
	Q55 331 346A		Q55 331 347A	150.00
	Q55 331 958A		Q55 331 959A	150.00
	Q56 907 930A		Q56 907 931A	150.00
	Q57 972 972A		Q57 972 973A	150.00
	Q60 674 436A		Q60 674 437A	150.00
	Q60 674 460A		Q60 647 461A	150.00
	★17 397 810A		★17 397 811A	200.00
	★17 459 160A		★17 459 161A	200.00
	★17 687 718A		★17 687 719A	200.00
	★17 700 966A		★17 700 967A	200.00
1934D	Q48 175 314A	1934C	Q48 175 315A	200.00
	Q55 331 940A		Q55 331 941A	200.00
	Q57 972 942A		Q57 972 943A	200.00
	Q57 972 966A		Q57 972 967A	200.00
	★17 448 270A		★17 448 271A	250.00
	★17 448 282A		★17 448 283A	250.00
	★17 459 178A		★17 459 179A	250.00
	★17 459 448A		★17 459 449A	250.00
	★17 459 514A		★17 459 515A	250.00
	★17 687 712A		★17 687 713A	250.00

FIVE DOLLARS
FEDERAL RESERVE NOTES

1928	J04 822 494A	1928A	J04 822 495A	500.00
1934	B33 072 168A	1934A	B33 072 169A	200.00
	G23 511 570A		G23 511 571A	200.00
	G24 527 156A		G24 527 157A	200.00

1934 mule	B29 015 562B	1934A	B29 015 563B	200.00
	B96 471 204A		B96 471 205A	200.00
	C52 611 672A		C52 611 673A	200.00
1934A	C30 365 118A	1934	C30 365 119A	175.00
	G24 437 150A		G24 437 151A	175.00
	L24 794 934A		L24 794 935A	175.00
1934A	C72 036 156A	1934B	C72 036 157A	200.00
	C72 036 185A		C72 036 186A	200.00
	C72 036 204A		C72 036 205A	200.00
	B76 314 420B		B76 314 421B	200.00
	B78 089 004B		B78 089 005B	200.00
	B78 604 392B		B78 604 393B	200.00
	B83 602 866B		B83 602 867B	200.00
	C72 036 120A		C72 036 121A	200.00
	C72 036 168A		C72 036 169A	200.00
	C72 036 372A		C72 036 373A	200.00
	C72 036 504A		C72 036 505A	200.00
	C72 036 552A		C72 036 553A	200.00
	D63 026 892A		D63 026 893A	200.00
1934B	B80 562 372B	1934A	B80 562 373B	150.00
	B81 038 868B		B81 038 869B	150.00
	B83 602 824B		B83 602 825B	150.00
	C72 036 126A		C72 036 127A	150.00
	C72 036 150A		C72 036 151A	150.00
	C72 036 186A		C72 036 187A	
	C72 036 462A		C72 036 463A	150.00
	D60 932 532A		D60 932 533A	150.00
	D62 128 722A		D62 128 723A	150.00
	G13 872 054B		G13 872 055B	150.00
	G13 872 066B		G13 872 067B	150.00
1934B	L74 667 702A	1934C	L74 667 703A	150.00
1934C	D69 301 788A	1934B	D69 301 789A	150.00
1934C	B64 863 882C	1934D	B64 863 883C	100.00
	B64 863 948C		B64 863 949C	100.00
	B64 863 966C		B64 863 967C	100.00
	B64 863 996C		B64 863 997C	100.00
1950 Wide	H29 999 028A	1950 Narrow	H29 999 029A	100.00

TEN DOLLARS

SILVER CERTIFICATE

1934	A44 023 045A	1934 mule	A44 023 046A	50.00
1934A	B18 525 576A	1934B	B18 525 577A	1,000.00
1934B	B18 432 102A	1934A	B18 432 103A	900.00

FEDERAL RESERVE NOTES

1928	F06 645 486A	1934 mule	F06 645 487A	350.00
1934	J20 907 474A	1934A	J20 907 475A	250.00
1934A	F33 075 792A	1934 mule	F33 075 793A	250.00
	G65 813 328A		G65 813 329A	250.00
	J00 623 940★		J00 623 941★	350.00
1934A mule	G66 224 412A	1934	G66 224 413A	250.00
1934A	B79 075 856D	1934B	B79 076 857D	200.00
	B80 851 308D		B80 851 309D	200.00
	B80 864 112D		B80 864 113D	200.00
	C23 630 226B		C23 630 227B	200.00
	C23 630 274B		C23 630 275B	200.00
	C26 942 310B		C26 942 311B	200.00
	C26 942 430B		C26 942 431B	200.00
	C26 942 526B		C26 942 527B	200.00
	C26 942 533B		C26 942 532B	200.00

	C26 942 580B		C26 942 581B	200.00
	L55 944 379B		L55 944 380B	200.00
1934B	B77 069 424D	1934A	B77 069 425D	175.00
	C23 630 220B		C23 630 221B	175.00
	C26 942 304B		C26 942 305B	175.00
	C26 942 376B		C26 942 377B	175.00
	C26 942 448B		C26 942 449B	175.00
	C26 942 520B		C26 942 521B	175.00
	C26 942 532B		C26 942 533B	175.00
	C26 942 586B		C26 942 587B	175.00
	C26 942 928B		C26 942 929B	175.00
	G37 051 704B		G37 051 705B	175.00
1934C	C02 424 468★	1934D	C02 424 421★	400.00
	C02 424 492★		C02 424 469★	400.00
	C02 424 720★		C02 424 493★	400.00
	C02 424 420★		C02 424 721★	400.00
1934D	C02 424 498★	1934C	C02 424 499★	350.00
	C02 424 648★		C02 424 649★	350.00
	C02 425 314★		C02 425 315★	350.00
	C02 425 368★		C02 425 369★	350.00
	C02 469 096★		C02 469 097★	350.00
	C02 469 972★		C02 469 973★	350.00
	C02 475 090★		C02 475 091★	350.00
	C02 475 102★		C02 475 103★	350.00

TWENTY DOLLARS

FEDERAL RESERVE NOTES

1934	D53 144 562A	1934A	D53 144 563A	350.00
1934	L19 857 588A	1934A mule	L19 857 589A	350.00
1934 mule	D53 144 562A	1934A	D53 144 563A	350.00
1934 mule	D59 844 186A	1934A	D59 844 187A	450.00
1934A	D52 931 742A	1934	D52 931 743A	300.00
	E48 966 960A		E48 966 961A	300.00
	H12 146 910A		H12 146 911A	300.00
1934A mule	B30 870 654A	1934	B30 870 655A	300.00
	D53 171 052A		D53 171 053A	300.00
1934A	C34 623 084A	1934 mule	C34 623 085A	300.00
1934A	B18 265 104B	1934B	B18 265 105B	350.00
	B18 265 134B		B18 265 135B	350.00
	B18 265 662B		B18 265 663B	350.00
	B18 265 674B		B18 265 675B	350.00
	B18 265 686B		B18 265 687B	350.00
	B18 265 698B		B18 265 699B	350.00
	B18 417 342B		B18 417 343B	350.00
	B34 669 086B		B34 669 097B	350.00
	B34 669 098B		B34 669 099B	350.00
	G06 978 396B		G06 978 397B	350.00
	G07 854 756B		G07 854 757B	350.00
	G07 854 780B		G07 854 781B	350.00
1934B	B18 265 128B	1934A	B18 265 129B	300.00
	B18 265 140B		B18 265 141B	300.00
	B18 265 656B		B18 265 657B	300.00
	B18 265 668B		B18 265 668B	300.00
	B18 265 680B		B18 265 681B	300.00
	B18 265 692B		B18 265 692B	300.00
	B24 785 304B		B24 785 305B	300.00
	B34 669 956B		B34 669 957B	300.00
	B34 669 080B		B34 669 081B	300.00
	B34 669 092B		B34 669 093B	300.00
	G07 854 744B		G07 854 745B	300.00

	G07 854 762**B**		G07 854 763**B**	300.00

FIFTY DOLLARS
FEDERAL RESERVE NOTES

1934	D06 698 418**A**	1934A	D06 698 419**A**	750.00
	J00 920 964**A**		J00 920 965**A**	750.00
	J00 920 983**A**		J00 920 982**A**	750.00
	J00 920 988**A**		J00 920 989**A**	750.00
1934A	B10 083 138**A**	1934	B10 083 139**A**	
1934	J00 920 976**A**	1934A	J00 920 977**A**	
1934B	C06 150 792**A**	1934C	C06 150 793**A**	500.00

ONE HUNDRED DOLLARS
FEDERAL RESERVE NOTES

1934	E02 612 556**A**	1934A	E02 312 557**A**	750.00
	K00 400 122**A**		K00 400 123**A**	750.00
	K00 400 129**A**		K00 400 128**A**	750.00
	K00 400 134**A**		K00 400 135**A**	750.00
	J01 636 848**A**		J01 636 849**A**	750.00
1934A	J01 636 842**A**	1934	J01 636 843**A**	750.00
1934B	H02 938 188**A**		H02 938 189**A**	750.00
1934C	G10 996 228**A**	1934B	G10 996 229**A**	750.00
	J02 520 786**A**		J02 520 787**A**	750.00
1934C	G11 364 348**A**	1934D	G11 364 349**A**	750.00

FIVE HUNDRED DOLLARS
FEDERAL RESERVE NOTES

1934	L00 153 444**A**	1934A	L00 153 445**A**	1,500.00

ONE THOUSAND DOLLARS
FEDERAL RESERVE NOTES

	J00 056 124**A**		J00 056 125**A**	2500.00

APPENDIX II

Multiple Endings
Novel Serial Numbers
Sequential Serial Numbers
Low Serial Numbers

MULTIPLE ENDINGS: (premium applies to $1.00 notes only)

Triple (Example 111, 222, 333, etc.).. 3.00
Quadruple (Example 3333, 4444, 5555, etc.) 5.00
Quintuple (Example 66666, 88888, etc.).. 10.00
Sextuple (Example 777777, 999999, etc.) 15.00
Septuple (Example 4444444, 6666666, etc.).. 25.00

MULTIPLE DIGITS MATCHED (so called poker notes) Other digits may be any number and similar digits may be arranged in any way.

Five digits the same 5.00
Six digits the same 7.50
Seven digits the same... 10.00

EVEN NOTES (zeros precede and end)

Even hundreds (Example 00 000 400)... 25.00
Even thousands (Example 00 002 000) 15.00
Even ten thousands (Example 00 010 000) 10.00
Even hundred thousands (Example 00 300 000) 10.00
Even millions (Example 21 000 000).. 15.00

MATCHED BEGINNING AND END (Example 43 000 043)

Two digit match 8.00
Three digit match 10.00
Four digit match 15.00

ODD NUMBER NOTES - Any note that has a catch serial number - far too many number arrangements to categorize - but some examples offered such as 00 45 45 00, 00 37 38 39, 00 454 545, 401 402 03 etc.

Price estimate $5.00 to $100.00 depending on appeal.

NOTE: Consideration must be given when novel serial number is on an otherwise scarce or rare note. Premium for novel number is in addition to any other premium.

PRICE ESTIMATES FOR NOVEL SERIAL NUMBERS

PALINDROMES (radars) are notes whose serial number reads the same backward as forward. Generally prefix and suffix letters are not important, however, when present such as AA, BB, CC etc. add slightly to value.

	$1.00	$2.00	$5.00 lt	$5.00 sc	$10.00	$20.00
ONE DIGIT	125.00	150.00	135.00	125.00	135.00	150.00
TWO DIGIT	25.00	35.00	35.00	25.00	32.50	40.00
THREE DIGIT	10.00	15.00	17.50	15.00	17.50	27.50
FOUR DIGIT	5.00	10.00	15.00	10.00	15.00	27.50

SEQUENCE NOTES

	$1.00	$2.00	$5.00 lt	$5.00 sc	$10.00	$20.00
SINGLE DIGIT (00000001)	125.00	200.00	150.00	150.00	135.00	145.00
TWO DIGIT (0000012)	90.00	135.00	115.00	115.00	115.00	125.00
23	40.00	85.00	50.00	50.00	60.00	60.00
34	25.00	60.00	30.00	30.00	35.00	40.00
45	25.00	60.00	30.00	30.00	35.00	40.00
56	17.50	35.00	20.00	20.00	25.00	35.00
67	17.50	35.00	20.00	20.00	25.00	35.00
78	17.50	27.50	22.50	22.50	30.00	35.00
89	17.50	27.50	22.50	22.50	27.50	35.00

THREE DIGIT
(00000123)

234,456, etc.	22.50	40.00	27.50	27.50	32.50	40.00
FOUR DIGIT	25.00	50.00	30.00	30.00	37.50	50.00
FIVE DIGIT	30.00	40.00	35.00	35.00	40.00	50.00
SIX DIGIT	50.00	75.00	50.00	50.00	50.00	60.00
SEVEN DIGIT	75.00	100.00	75.00	75.00	75.00	85.00
EIGHT DIGIT	126.00	200.00	125.00	125.00	130.00	145.00

REVERSE SEQUENCE (consecutive in descending order) 20% less than ascending sequence.

REPEATERS: (Premium generally limited to $1.00 notes.)

TWO DIGIT (Example 27 27 27 27) $25.00

FOUR DIGIT (Example 4345 4345) $15.00

PRICE ESTIMATES FOR LOW SERIAL NUMBER NOTES

As with any pioneering effort, we expect to be bombarded with disagreements of too "high" or too "low" — high disagreements of course will come from buyers, the lows from sellers. We welcome them all. The infrequency with which any appreciable quantity come on the market has created widespread differences in pricing by the various dealers throughout the country so that we are hopeful WITH YOUR comments future editions can provide price estimates that are fair to both buyer and seller. We do not mean that this effort is a casual one. Thousands of price lists, hundreds of examinations of notes and prices and countless hours correlating available data from the basis of prices shown. We believe we are close — but of course we hope for perfection — YOUR comments will help!

All price estimates are for CU notes, prices for circulated notes would be corresponding lower. PRICES are IN ADDITION to any other premiums that would apply — for example the 1963 $1.00 FRN Block D--B is currently selling for $75.00. Serial number 00 000 001 in this note would certainly sell for $200.00 or better.

DENOMINATION

SERIAL NUMBER	1.00	2.00	5.00	10.00	20.00	50.00	100.00
(0's precede)							
1	1750.	3000.	2000.	2000.	2000.	3000.	4000.
2	200.00	300.00	200.00	200.00	200.00	250.00	300.00
3 through 5	100.00	150.00	100.00	100.00	120.00	150.00	200.00
6 through 10	80.00	100.00	80.00	80.00	90.00	125.00	175.00
11 through 20	60.00	70.00	60.00	70.00	80.00	110.00	160.00
21 through 50	35.00	50.00	40.00	50.00	60.00	90.00	140.00
51 through 99	20.00	35.00	25.00	30.00	40.00	75.00	130.00
EVEN HUNDREDS							
100-900	25.00	35.00	30.00	35.00	42.50		
TRIPLES							
111-999	25.00	35.00	30.00	35.00	42.50		
SEQUENCE NOTES (includes reverse sequence)							
123, 456, 345, etc.	22.50	40.00	27.50	32.50	40.00		
ALL OTHER NUMBERS							
101-998	12.50	15.00	15.00	17.50	30.00		
EVEN THOUSANDS							
1000-9000	15.00	25.00	20.00	25.00	32.50		
QUADRUPLES							
1111-9999	15.00	25.00	20.00	25.00	32.50		
SEQUENCE NOTES (includes reverse sequence)							
3456, 4567, etc.	25.00	50.00	30.00	37.50	50.00		
ALL OTHER NUMBERS							
1001-9998	5.00	10.00	7.50	12.50	22.50		

FOOTNOTE: Because of the high face value the $50.00 and $100.00 notes command only a nominal premium.

APPENDIX III

Press Releases (By Date of Issue)

TREASURY DEPARTMENT
BUREAU OF ENGRAVING AND PRINTING

Washington, D.C.
March 14, 1933.

FOR IMMEDIATE RELEASE

The Bureau of Engraving and Printing issued the following statement today:

Late in the day of March 9, 1933, the day that marked the enactment of legislation to provide relief in the banking emergency that had developed, the Bureau of Engraving and Printing was directed to proceed with the physical production of new Federal Reserve Bank notes. These new bank notes were authorized to meet the need for currency resulting from the panic withdrawals from our banks. They are like our National bank notes in appearance, and they are secured by government bonds or by the obligations of member banks in turn secured by good assets.

The first shipment of the new notes, completed twenty-four hours after the order was received, was delivered in New York at the Federal Reserve Bank on the morning of March 11, 1933. The quick action on the part of the Bureau of Engraving and Printing is getting into production was made possible through the fact that much of the preliminary work was being accomplished at the same time that plans were being considered and the Bill being drafted.

There was not sufficient time to engrave new dies and make new plates for the printing of the Federal Reserve bank notes. The standard National bank currency, on which the Bureau of Engraving and Printing was already in production, was therefore pressed into service. First it was necessary to procure facsimile signatures of two officials of each of the twelve Federal Reserve Banks. These were taken from certificates in the files of the Department. Production of special logotype plates, bearing the signature of bank officials, was undertaken at the plant of the American Type Founders Company at Jersey City.

It was necessary to add employees to the staff of the Bureau of Engraving and Printing. On March 13, 1933, 475 persons were recruited in the service. Men who wives were not employed, women whose husbands were not employed, and veterans were given prefererence in the large number of former employees who applied for positions.

The initial order for Federal Rserve Bank notes amounts to 15,524,000 sheets, or 186,288,000 notes, with an approximate face value of $2,000,000,000.

The production at the Bureau of Engraving and Printing will reach its peak within the next week, if demands require it. At peak production over six million notes will leave the bureau every twenty-four hours. These notes will be shipped to the various Federal Reserve banks throughout the country.

The production program required by the Emergency Bank Act is unprecedented. To meet this program many quick changes had to be made in the methods of handling the currency as it passed from one operation to another. Vaults had to be expanded. The entire staff of the Bureau undertook the task in splendid spirit. Several of the important operations are continuing throughout twenty-four hours of the day.

March 26, 1935

The first sheets of $1 Silver Certificates of the small-size currency were delivered uncut by the Bureau of Engraving and Printing to the Treasury vaults. On July 10, 1929, when the new currency was put into circulation, the first sheet of these uncut sheets of 12 notes each was placed in the archives of the Treasury.

Certain other sheets were distributed to various officials of the Government, the President of the United States, Herbert Hoover, receiving the second sheet; the Secretary of the Treasury, Andrew W. Mellon, receiving the third; the Under-Secretary of the Treasury, Ogden L. Mills, receiving the fourth; the Assistant Secretary of the Treasury, Henry Herrick Bond, receiving the fifth. Other sheets were given to the heads of Treasury bureaus who aided materially in connection with the issue of the small-size currency, and the sheet to which this memorandum is attached is the fifty-first sheet.

A record is kept in the Office of the Treasurer of the United States showing the names of the holders of these sheets. There are only 80 of them in existence.

PLAN OF DISTRIBUTION
Uncut sheets and low-numbered notes of small-size currency series 1928.

$1 Silver Certificates

Recipient:	Sheet No.	Note No.
Archives of Office of Treasurer of the United States	1	1-12
Herbert Hoover, President of United States	2	13-24
A.W. Mellon, Secretary of the Treasury	3	25-36
Members of Cabinet (cut)	4	37-48
Goden L. Mills, Undersecretary of the Treasury	5	49-60
Henry Herrick Bond, Asst. Secretary of Treasury	6	61-72
A.W. Mellon, Secretary of the Treasury	7	73-84
Charles S. Dewey, Former Asst. Secretary of Treasury	8	85-96
Herbert Hoover, President of the United States	9	97-108
A.W. Mellon, Secretary of the Treasury	10	109-120
Henry Herrick Bond, Asst. Secretary of the Treasury	11	121-132
Henry Herrick Bond, Asst. Secretary of the Treasury	12	133-144
Lawrence Richey, Secretary to President Hoover	13	145-156
Ferry K. Heth, Asst. Secretary of the Treasury	14	157-168
A.W. Hall, Director, Bureau of Engraving & Printing	15	169-180
W. S. Broughton, Commissioner of Public Debt	16	181-192
W.O. Woods, Treasurer of the United States	17	193-204
Henry Herrick Bond, Asst. Secretary of the Treasury	18	205-216
Henry Herrick Bond, Asst. Secretary of the Treasury	19	217-228
Henry Herrick Bond, Asst. Secretary of the Treasury	20	229-240

APPENDIX IV

Signers of U. S. Paper Money

Secretary of the Treasury	Treasurer of the U.S.		
Andrew W. Mellon	H. T. Tate	4-30-1928	1-17-1929
Andrew W. Mellon	Walter O. Woods	1-18-1929	2-12-1932
Ogden L. Mills	Walter O. Woods	2-13-1932	3-3-1933
William H. Woodin	Walter O. Woods	3-4-1933	5-31-1933
William H. Woodin	W. A. Julian	6-1-1933	12-31-1933
Henry Morgenthau, Jr.	W. A. Julian	1-1-1934	7-22-1945
Fred M. Vinson	W. A. Julian	7-23-1945	7-23-1946
John W. Snyder	W. A. Julian	7-25-1946	5-29-1949
John W. Snyder	Georgia Neese Clark	6-21-1949	1-20-1953
George M. Humphrey	Ivy Baker Priest	1-28-1953	7-28-1957
Robert B. Anderson	Ivy Baker Priest	7-29-1957	1-20-1961
C. Douglas Dillon	Elizabeth Rudel Smith	1-30-1961	4-13-1962
C. Douglas Dillon	Kathryn O'Hay Granahan	1-3-1963	3-31-1965
Henry H. Fowler	Kathryn O'Hay Granahan	4-1-1965	10-13-1966
Joseph W. Barr	Kathryn O'Hay Granahan	12-21-1968	1-20-1969
David M. Kennedy	Dorothy Andrews Elston*	5-8-1969	9-16-1970
David M. Kennedy	Dorothy Andrews Kabis	9-17-1970	2-1-1971
John B. Connally	Dorothy Andrews Kabis	2-11-1971	7-3-1971
John B. Connally	Romana Banuelos	12-17-1971	5-16-1972
George B Shultz	Romana Banuelos	6-12-1972	5-8-1974
William E. Simon	Francine I. Neff	6-21-1974	1-19-1977
W. Michael Blumenthal	Azie Taylor Morton	9-12-1977	8-4-1979
G. William Miller	Azie Taylor Morton	8-6-1979	1-4-1981
Donald T. Regan	Angela M. Buchanan	3-7-1981	7-1-1983
Donald T. Regan	Katherine Davalos Ortega	9-23-1983	1-29-1985
James A. Baker III	Katherine Davalos Ortega	1-29-1985	8-17-1988
Nicholas F. Brady	Katherine Davalos Ortega	9-15-1988	6-30-1989
Nicholas F. Brady	Catalina Vasquez Villalpando	12-11-1989	1-20-1993
Lloyd Bentsen	Mary Ellen Withrow	3-1-1994	12-22-1994
Robert E. Rubin	Mary Ellen Withrow	1-10-1995	

*During her term of office, Mrs Elston married Walter L Kabis: the first time the signature of a United States Treasurer had been changed during the term of office.

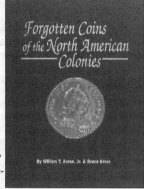
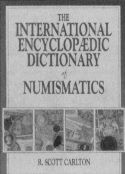

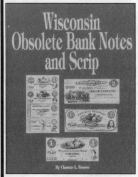

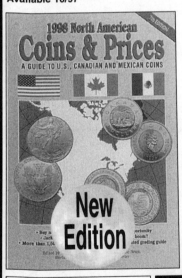